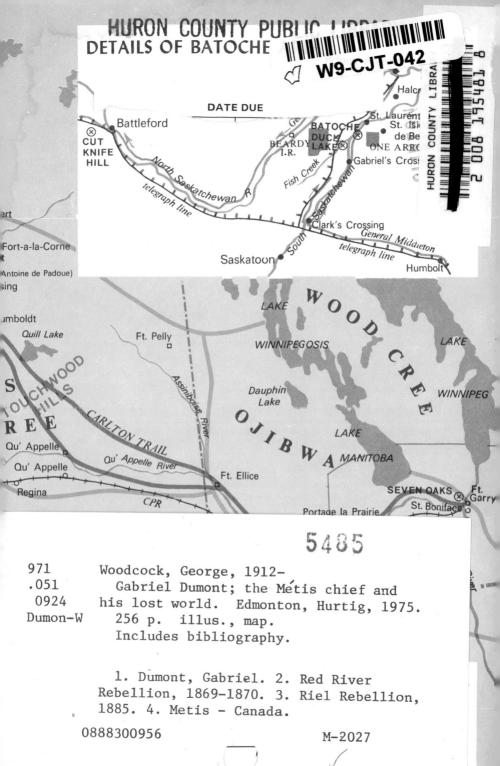

HURON COUNTY PUBLIC LIBRARY

DETAILS OF BATOCHE

W9-CJT-042

2 000 195481 8

HURON COUNTY LIBRA

DATE DUE

Battleford

CUT KNIFE HILL

North Saskatchewan R.

telegraph line

St. Laurent
St. Isi
de Be
BATOCHE
DUCK LAKE
BEARDY I.R.
ONE ARRO
Gabriel's Cross
Fish Creek
Saskatchewan

Halc

Clark's Crossing

General Middleton

telegraph line

Saskatoon South

Humbolt

Fort-a-la-Corne
Antoine de Padoue)
sing

umboldt

Quill Lake

Ft. Pelly

LAKE WINNIPEGOSIS

WOOD CREE

LAKE

LAKE WINNIPEG

Dauphin Lake

S
TOUCHWOOD HILLS
REE

Assiniboine River

CARLTON TRAIL

OJIBWA

LAKE MANITOBA

Qu' Appelle

Qu' Appelle River

Qu' Appelle

Regina

Ft. Ellice

CPR

SEVEN OAKS Ft. Garry
St. Boniface
Portage la Prairie

5485

971
.051
0924
Dumon-W

Woodcock, George, 1912-
    Gabriel Dumont; the Métis chief and
his lost world. Edmonton, Hurtig, 1975.
    256 p. illus., map.
    Includes bibliography.

    1. Dumont, Gabriel. 2. Red River
Rebellion, 1869-1870. 3. Riel Rebellion,
1885. 4. Metis - Canada.

0888300956   M-2027

_____ COUNTY PUBLIC LIBRARY

Gabriel Dumont

Gabriel Dumont

The Métis Chief and his Lost World

George Woodcock

5485

JUN 7 1976

Hurtig Publishers
Edmonton

Copyright © 1975 by George Woodcock

No part of this book may be reproduced or
transmitted in any form by any means,
electric or mechanical, including photocopying
and recording, or by any information
storage or retrieval system, without written
permission from the publisher, except
for brief passages quoted by a reviewer in a
newspaper or magazine.

Hurtig Publishers
10560 105 Street
Edmonton, Alberta

ISBN 0-88830-095-6

Printed and bound in Canada
by John Deyell Company

Contents

Introduction

There is one hour in the history of the Métis rebellions that has haunted me more than any other episode in Canadian history. It is not one of the more obviously dramatic hours: not the time of Riel's execution, or his condemnation, or of the illusory triumphs that punctuated both his existence and the history of the Métis people. It is the moment when fugitives gathered in a spring-green gully in northern Saskatchewan, and among the leafing willows Riel and Gabriel Dumont met and talked for the last time. There is only a fragmentary account of what they said, preserved in the brief narrative of the event which the illiterate Dumont dictated to his friends in Quebec in 1888, and that is unrevealingly laconic; neither Riel nor any of the witnesses — in flight themselves from the victorious Canadian expeditionary forces — left any further description of that final encounter before one man became a prisoner destined for the gallows and the other a fugitive. Yet it has always seemed to me that there must have been an extraordinary dramatic tension in that scene — which I shall later describe in what detail we have — when the prophet met the man of action who had allowed faith in his leader to overcome his practical judgment and who knew now, in defeat, that he himself had been right.

Not only has the relationship between Riel and Dumont had a peculiar resonance for me, as if it contained some special secret relating to the way our history has developed, but I have been fascinated by our attitude towards the two men, which I think

7

reveals a great deal about the view Canadians hold of themselves and their world. For ninety years now Riel has remained one of the perennially fascinating figures in Canadian history, and not only among French Canadians. He has been the subject of histories, biographies, poems, plays, and at least one opera: the object of execration, contempt, controversy, analysis, pity, and reverence. But Gabriel Dumont has gone almost uncelebrated, as a follower of Riel, as a kind of bluff, sturdy Sancho Panza to the Canadian Don Quixote, and this although he was in his own right a man of great interest and appeal. Significantly, the one book on Riel — and a very good book — in which something near justice is done to Dumont was written not by a Canadian but by an American; it is *Strange Empire*, by Joseph Kinsey Howard.

I am one of those who wrote a play on Riel. I wrote it as one of a series which the CBC commissioned from me in 1967, the year of the Centennial, and I included the story of Riel to counter in some way the kind of blind complacency that marked and marred the patriotic face we were expected to wear in that year. If others were celebrating Sir John A., I preferred to celebrate his most notable victim, and so to draw attention to the crimes against individuals and minorities that were part of the fabric from which the union of Canada, like almost every other major political achievement of its kind, was constructed. I gave Dumont — not Riel — the last words in the play; my own feeling spoke through them.

> They will hang him. They dare not let him live.
> But they will not escape his shadow
> darkening across their future.

It was a play called *The Defender of the Past*, and the title expressed the view I have always held of Riel. He belonged to a people against whose characteristic culture almost all the forces of the nineteenth century were aligned; even if he had survived, the way of life he defended could hardly have done so, and perhaps that was one of the reasons — one of the half-conscious ones at least — why he decided to die and even made sure of doing so by disputing his defence lawyers' pleas of insanity when he was tried at Regina. Yet in a negative way the

8

cause did live on, for Riel's death and the destruction of the
Métis culture represented something in our new world of Canada emerging into nationhood that, a century afterwards, we
cannot finally and wholly accept. In this way, while Riel's own
will was rooted in the past, his involuntary destiny belonged to
the future that in Canada today has become our present, the
present in which the disinherited whom Riel still symbolically
represents — the Métis, the Indians, the French Canadians, the
Doukhobors, the minorities in general — rise up against the very
world that defeated Riel and his past.

But why, in such a situation of revisionist views, is it Riel
who has become the symbol? Why not Dumont, who with such
spirit and such physical presence personified the Métis people
at their height of pride? While I was working on my play I was
disturbed by this curious fact, and in a book I wrote at the time
(it appeared in 1970 as *Canada and the Canadians*) I speculated
on the ambivalence of the Canadian attitude towards heroes
and on the kind of epic literature it had produced. I pointed
out that what epics we had — the stories of the fur traders' journeys, the building of the CPR, the sailing of the *Saint Roch*
through the Northwest Passage in a single season — were really
"epics of endurance, epics of imagination, not in any true sense
epics of heroism." (I would accept the further argument, which
Margaret Atwood later developed in *Survival*, that such heroism as does appear in our epics is also mainly *collective* heroism.)
I went on, in *Canada and the Canadians*, to discuss the broader
question of our attitude towards heroes, and reached the conclusion that the heroes we accept are like the epics we make;
they are endurers and survivers, like our explorers and railway
builders, like such politicians as Macdonald and Woodsworth,
like such discreet runaway rebels as Mackenzie and Papineau.
I concluded:

> Counting out Wolfe and Brock as born and bred outside the
> local tradition, there are probably only two men in Cana-
> dian history who might fit the pattern of the hero in the
> high romantic vein. One is Norman Bethune; but it is in
> China that Bethune is mainly venerated as a hero, not in
> Canada. The other is the Métis military leader in the North-

9

west Rebellion of 1885, Gabriel Dumont; but it is about Riel the martyr, not Dumont the hero, that plays have recently been proliferating on the stage, television and radio.*

The pattern is clear. Canadians distrust heroes, partly because heroism is always a kind of imposition; the hero is dominating us by his strength, by his brute courage, and we have become suspicious of such qualities, even when, as in the case of Dumont, they are mellowed by other attributes. We are suspicious because, as Canadians, we see ourselves generally imposed upon or, as Atwood put it, colonized. But more than that, we suspect the sheer gigantic irrationalism of the heroic, for we like to consider ourselves a reasonable people.

But why, rejecting the heroes, do we identify so easily with the martyrs who, though they may be imposed upon, impose on us in their turn as much as the heroes do, but in different ways: by their weakness rather than their strength, by a kind of resigned and destined obstinacy rather than by a wilful courage? Both heroes and martyrs succeed — even if they die in the achievement — through their power of *shaming* other men, of making them lose face with themselves, and that is an irrational appeal which can lead to totally negative ends, which can be and is exploited. "The blood of the martyrs is the seed of the Church" is a statement not only about faith, but also about power. And Riel's body was hardly cold off the gallows before his martyrdom was being used for the ends of power of Canadian politicians like Honoré Mercier.

An even more striking feature of the story of Riel is that, like modern Canadians in search of a symbol for their frustrations, a man so strong in character as Gabriel Dumont should

* Since I wrote those words a major series of television plays has been planned on Riel, and is being written for the CBC by the distinguished Canadian novelist, Rudy Wiebe. As against the flood of books and plays on Riel, the number of books or even pamphlets and dramatic productions on Dumont up to the publication of this book is startlingly small. Apart from newspaper features and a few magazine articles, he has been the subject of one 50-page "popular" booklet entitled *Gabriel Dumont: Indian Fighter*, of one long poem, *Gabriel Dumont at Batoche* by E. H. Carefoot (which had to be published by its author for lack of wider interest) and of one play, *Six Dry Cakes for the Fugitive*, which I wrote for CBC Radio.

be influenced by Riel to the extent that, seeing the rebellion of 1885 failing because of his leader's preoccupation with martyrdom, he still fought until everything was finished except his own life, and then departed in the hope of fighting on another day that never dawned. The extraordinary fact is that however much they might share his feelings towards Riel, modern Canadians have little understood or appreciated Gabriel Dumont.

Yet Dumont has all the qualities of the kind of folk or frontier hero who is a contemporary equivalent to the great braggart warriors of Homer and Shakespeare; in the United States he would have acquired a legendary status. As long as the buffalo lasted, he was the greatest of the Métis hunters, and few Indians of any nation knew more than he did of the lore of the wilderness. If he was virtually illiterate, he had the kind of intelligence and knowledge that knows little need of books.

For Dumont was the natural man par excellence, adapted perfectly to the life of the wilderness, and in this he was profoundly different from Riel, who was as alienated as any modern Canadian from that existence. Riel may have been a defender of the past, but like many such defenders he did not belong to what he defended, in his case the brief but intense traditions of the prairie hunters; his education had separated him from such a life. In 1885 on the South Saskatchewan he was trying to impose the theories and visions of a man trained in a classical college and maimed already by a long contest with the modern state, on the life of a people whose education was in the arts of a pre-agrarian and pre-political way of existence.

The fact — which historians have perhaps not sufficiently stressed and which it is one of my aims in this book to explore — is that there was a great difference between the Red River society of 1869 and the Métis settlements of hunters recently and unwillingly turned farmers that existed along the South Saskatchewan in 1885. On the Red River, Riel was involved not merely with the largely nomad Métis who formed the mass of his rebel militia, but with a miniature modern society. Fort Garry and the other settlements along the river may have appeared rustic in comparison with Montreal or the lakeside towns of Upper Canada, but the region had its structure of authority in the Council of Assiniboia, its law courts and newspapers, its steamers puffing upstream from the railhead south of

11

the border, its Scottish farmers descended from Selkirk's settlers, its aggressive Canadian immigrants, its American intriguers, its Fenian conspirators: the whole infrastructure, in other words, of the West as it was to become after Confederation swallowed it. Only the Mounties and the CPR were yet to come.

Riel spoke indeed for the grievances of the Métis, but what he tried to establish was not a traditional order — based on the precedents of the buffalo hunt — of the kind that Dumont and Father André were to create in 1873 when they established their local government among the hunters of St. Laurent; it was rather an establishment for Assiniboia (and he tended to attempt a repetition of the same pattern for Saskatchewan half a generation later) devised on the lines of the responsible governments which the Canadian provinces inherited from pre-Confederation days. There is no reason to suppose that, when the province of Manitoba was created, Riel was ever disappointed with the constitutional results of his efforts. The fact that the rights of the Métis had been insufficiently protected certainly did not immediately occur to him, and when it did he doubtless assumed that the right legislation would immediately rectify matters. He was a very modern man in his illusion that within a cage of political action one might preserve the vanishing splendours of a free and natural life.

Dumont, in contrast, was so much the free and natural man that even in 1869 the Red River seemed over-civilized for him. He preferred the farther prairies where the buffalo hunt had still half a generation to go. The people whose leader he became in the earlier 1860s were not refugees from the Canadian penetration into the Red River colony, though later on many of these came to the Saskatchewan. They were the free hunters who had avoided the settled life of the environs of Fort Garry and who had moved constantly farther into the West as the buffalo herds were hunted out of the eastern prairies, and who would continue to do so until they followed into history the great beasts they pursued.

Dumont was in full command of his world while it remained the world of the hunter. It was that world's sudden transformation at the end of the 1870s which destroyed the old prairie way of life and with it Dumont's authority and the security of his people. While, unconserved, the buffalo neared extinction, the

Métis who turned reluctantly to the soil for sustenance faced the settlers and speculators filtering into the prairies ahead of the railways, and against these, whatever rights they might feel were theirs, they had no legal titles to flourish. The Métis, in fact, were even worse off than the Indians, who at least had their reservations to live on.

It is understandable why Dumont, then the leading man among his people, agreed to call in Riel. An illiterate son of nature, however efficient in his own world, could not compete in an ambiance of legalities and petitions. Riel, who had shown himself politically adept in Manitoba (except for the disastrous error of executing Thomas Scott), presumably could. What Dumont and his comrades did not take into account was the veering in Riel's mind away from rationality during the years since he rode away from Fort Garry as Wolseley's troops appeared on the other shore of the Red River.* If the Métis expected a political leader, they received a prophet, an *exalté*, a prairie Gandhi without Gandhi's consistency, for Riel developed desperate policies that could succeed only by means of violence, and yet he shrank from violence when it came.

Dumont's solution to the problem was appropriately heroic. If the solution to Métis and Indian grievances had to be rebellion, then let it be total rebellion, with a guerilla war in which the Métis and their natural allies would paralyse the forces sent against them and fight the government to a stalemate that would make concessions inevitable. If later historical examples like that of Ireland between 1919 and 1921 are anything to go by, such a strategy stood at least a sporting chance of success. It was Riel's attempt to win by a show of violence instead of by its reality that doomed the 1885 rebellion from the start.

And this — which makes the amazing part of the story — Dumont understood throughout his association with Riel. From the beginning he urged action and, as we shall see, the plans he made — and which Riel consistently frustrated — show him to have been a very resourceful guerilla general. Yet, to the end, he deferred to Riel. He had the last of the classic hero's quali-

---

* Indeed, ninety years after Riel's death, the Métis have still not taken that veering of the mind into account, and to this day they loyally defend Riel's sanity, and so in effect defend their own willingness to accept his leadership.

ties: once he had given his fealty, he was totally loyal, and not with the mindless loyalty of the Light Brigade. He *did* reason why, and yet he was ready to do or die as need be until the moment when Riel abdicated the command to which Dumont and the other Métis had invited him.

Then Dumont fled, since there was no point in risking his life any further; he plotted Riel's rescue and failed; he returned to die in the place where he had fought, and today the only impressive thing left in the bleakness where Batoche once stood is the great rough boulder that lies on Dumont's grave, a curiously static monument to the dynamic nomad chieftain he was for the best years of his life.

And the question lingers: Why do we show our obvious preference for Riel? Why do we not make plays and poems and postage stamps about Dumont? Partly, I am sure, it is because we have ceased to live in a hero's black-and-white world; simple and direct people like Dumont embarrass us with the unspoken demand that we imitate their strengths or their virtues. Riel was more devious, with deeper ambiguities of intent; he belongs to a world like our own, more conscious of twilight than of dawn. He seems the personification of a besieged minority, and most Canadians see themselves as members of besieged minorities. He is a victim, and most modern men (not Canadians only, by any means) gain satisfaction from seeing themselves as victims. Even more important, Riel is the kind of victim who enables others to enjoy the role vicariously: the sacrificial victim who *really* dies and thus gives us time to slip over the border and return to die in our beds; most of us, however deeply we may feel we are empathizing with Riel in his moment of truth in the Regina courtroom, would still have made Dumont's choice if we had been at Batoche.

Yet if Dumont had stood beside Riel at the gallows in Regina, we would now remember him in the same thought as Riel, as we remember those very different men, Sacco and Vanzetti, with a single impulse. Dumont would have been the same man, with the same life, but the ending would have been different. And that seems to bring us to the crux of the issue. We see public figures not as men but as functions. It is not Riel himself we admire, for in many ways he was a man impossible to admire, and from all the accounts we have, Dumont was a far more likeable and estimable human being. It is Riel the symbol who catches our imagination, and what he symbolizes is our inner condition, our consciousness of deprivation and alienation from meaningful existence, our sense of rebellion without hope. And that, paradoxically, may be a good thing, for the end of hope is the beginning of resolution, and when resolution rises we may yet make a symbol of Dumont.

So I am still haunted by that last meeting in the gully at Batoche. Did Riel merely talk of his mission? Did Dumont merely say I told you so, and then try in vain to persuade Riel to escape with him? As they were men, that is probably all that did happen — that and a tense farewell. But we expect more of symbols than of men, and rightly so. It has always seemed to me that there has been much unanswered in the story of the 1885 rebellion; it seemed especially that, after all that has been written about Riel, there remained a book to be filled with the resonances of his encounter with Dumont, and as much as possible from Dumont's point of view. In the chapters that follow I have at last tried to write such a book.

1. The Nomad Patriarchs

For almost seventy years, or roughly a single human life, the Métis people lived in their pride as lords of the western prairies. One can mark the period by the dates of two incidents which the Métis have always referred to as battles. One was the ambivalent victory of Seven Oaks beside the Red River in 1816, when, newly conscious of their identity as a "nation", the half-breed hunters of the plains proved themselves by slaughtering Governor Semple — Lord Selkirk's lieutenant — and his followers. Sixty-nine years later, in the hard-fought defence of their hamlet of Batoche, the Métis under Gabriel Dumont were defeated after four days of fighting by the Canadian army (which incidentally was fighting its first independent campaign) and vanished as a power in the West.

The battles of Seven Oaks and Batoche were small affairs if one measures them by the normal criteria of military history: two or three dozen dead on the defeated side and many fewer on the other — "hardly more" — as R. E. Lamb once remarked — "than could be expected in serious rioting." The same applied to the other battles that were treasured in Métis memory not only as matters of pride but also because they served as peaks to vary the annual cycles of buffalo hunts and snowed-up winters which formed Métis history; to the defeat of the Sioux at Grand Coteau in 1851, to the illusory triumph of the Red River rising in 1869, to the defeats of the Canadians at Duck

Lake and Fish Creek in 1885 before the disaster of Batoche. A few policemen writhed to death in the snow under the bare poplar trees; a few Toronto and Winnipeg clerks in uniform dropped to the earth as the wounded horses screamed in a gulley where the purple heads of anemones were proclaiming the arrival of spring; a handful of ragged men were bayonetted in the rifle pits of Batoche after they had no more powder left to fire off nails and stones from their hunting guns. A month's count of homicides in New York during the 1970s would exceed the whole tally of men who died in the wars of the Métis.

But the important thing was not the smallness of the numbers of people who lived or died in the hope of sustaining their chosen way of existence, but rather the final shifting of power in the West from those who lived in and on and with the environment — whether they were Indians or Métis — and those who wished to live off it, to dominate and to exploit it. In the moral dimension, it was the destruction of the distinctive culture of a small number of people to serve the interests of vastly more numerous intruders. Such a fate involved in western Canada not only the Métis and their relatives the Indians; it was to engulf also other peculiar peoples, like the Doukhobors who went to the prairies hoping to live the religious life they had been denied in their native Russia and who eventually, beside the South Saskatchewan, became the neighbours of the Métis. In numbers the Métis of the Northwest Territory and the Doukhobors who came to Canada in the 1890s were roughly equal — never more than 10,000 of either group at the time of their acutest struggles with the newly created Dominion of Canada, and an even smaller number of activists; as general of the Métis in the 1885 rebellion, Gabriel Dumont never had, in any single battle, as many as 300 men under his command. If the majority of Canadians chose to suppress them, the defeat of such small groups was inevitable, and defeat was the lot of both Métis and Doukhobors, defeat and contemptuous assimilation.

Yet by merely happening, the defeats of such small peoples have called into question the success of the democratic system as it developed in Canada during the final decades of the nineteenth century. For the truest democracy is not that in which the majority imposes its will on all minorities. It is surely that in which minorities are allowed to flourish, even at some expense to the patience of the majority. It is, in other words, a pluralistic rather than a monolithic society, and only in recent years have we begun to understand that the federalism we prize in Canada can survive only in so far as it becomes pluralistic.

Gabriel Dumont and the Métis whom he led for a while and whom he so dramatically personified formed one of the Canadian minorities who asked only to be able to make their own adaptations, in their own way, to the changing patterns of history. That opportunity was not allowed them, any more than it was later allowed the Doukhobors, since the system that Sir John A. Macdonald and the early Canadian governments sought to impose on the prairies was an Ontario imperialism masquerading as federalism, aimed at making use of the land in ways most favourable to central Canadian interests. So the Métis — again like the Doukhobors, were challenged to fight in defence of their distinctive culture, and in defeat they were to be submerged.

If the Métis called themselves, during that seventy years when they still formed a power in the prairies, a distinctive "nation", they did not base the claim on population or on formal political arrangements. They made it because they felt themselves a distinct people who had a role to play in their world and who took a pride in that role, considering no life better than that of the adept hunter and guide and — when the necessity arose — prairie warrior. In the nineteenth century, when political entities were seen in terms of military viability, the notion that such a people could constitute a "nation" doubtless seemed absurd; today, in the late twentieth century age of nuclear truce when indefensible islands populated by a few thousand people can and do receive international recognition as members of the United Nations, the claims of the Métis would have gained much wider acceptance, and in the vastness of the West a Métis nation with a territory of its own would not have seemed impossible.

The times were against the Métis, and perhaps, as Auden said, in writing of Spain,

History to the defeated
May say Alas but cannot help or pardon.

19

Nevertheless, defeat is no excuse for forgetting, and it is not merely an intellectual balance that is adjusted when one revives the history of lost causes. Sometimes, in telling the story of a fight against an old injustice, we help to bring about something nearer to justice in the future. And so, in considering the Métis and their struggles, I suggest that we should not be unduly conscious of how small a people they were, for that does not diminish the special significance in Canadian history of their two rebellions within a single generation or the stature of the remarkable men their struggle projected into our memory, Louis Riel and Gabriel Dumont.

If 1816 was the year in which the Métis first brought themselves dramatically to the attention of people in British North America and of politicians in England through the somewhat gruesome circumstances of the "battle" of Seven Oaks, it was by no means their beginning as a distinct and recognized element in the population of the Northwest. They were already known to the French as *bois-brulés*, the people coloured like charred wood, and to the English as half-breeds; some even borrowed a word from India and referred to them somewhat contemptuously — as Sir John A. Macdonald did later on more than one occasion — as half-castes. They themselves preferred and still prefer the term *Métis*, which is related to the Mexican term *Mestizo* and derives directly from the French verb *métisser*, to cross breeds.

The mingling of breeds began as soon as French *coureurs de bois* in the seventeenth century entered into marriages according to the custom of the wilderness with the Indian women of the tribes with whom they traded for furs. *Métissage* took on the character of an institution after 1696, the year when the government of New France, scared by a glut of furs in the warehouses of Montreal and Quebec, sought to end the trading for furs in the *pays d'en haut* by revoking licences and recalling the *coureurs de bois*. Some of the *coureurs* were already operating without licences and others had become so accustomed to the wild, free life of the forests that they had no desire to return to the authoritarian little France of the St. Lawrence, ruled by governor and intendant and bishop, by seigneur and priest. These stayed on in the *pays d'en haut,* fathering *Métis* descendants who inherited their names and their European techniques and religion, which they combined with the wilderness knowledge of their mothers' peoples. As they moved on to the prairies, they began to intermarry with the Cree women and adopted Cree, the lingua franca of the fur trade west of the Red River, as a second tongue to the peculiar French patois which they developed in the Northwest. By the time an amnesty was granted to the truant *coureurs de bois* in the early eighteenth century, the Métis lines were established, and when the French fur trade began again, many of its voyageurs were of mixed blood. The tiny settlements that emerged on the rivers and lakes west of Lachine were inhabited largely by Métis hunters and voyageurs, whose numbers were increased as French explorer-traders with their servants began to travel into and eventually to winter in the Saskatchewan valley. By the time the Scots, after the Conquest, took over the fur trade of Montreal from the French, and formed the various partnerships that culminated in the North West Company, most of the northmen who manned the brigades of canoes going inland from Grand Portage and later Fort William at the head of the Great Lakes into the Athapaska country were Métis who lived in the Northwest and rarely left it.

In the 1770s the Hudson's Bay Company began to react to the competition of the "pedlars", as it contemptuously called the traders from Montreal, and to abandon its old practice of waiting in its forts on the Bay for the Indians to bring in their furs. As it established posts in the Saskatchewan country, and created canoe and boat routes for its brigades to bring the furs to York Factory on the Bay, it was forced to supplement the Orkneymen who had been its original servants with voyageurs who knew the country and were more adept at canoe transport, so that during the great conflict between the rival companies that culminated in their union in 1821, both were employing French and Métis voyageurs, though the Northwesters did so to a much greater extent than their rivals.

One of the voyageurs who took up employment with the Hudson's Bay Company was a Montreal Frenchman named Jean-Baptiste Dumont. Dumont came west to the Saskatchewan in the 1790s and probably first entered the Company's service at Edmonton House, which was established in 1795. Later he appears to have served at Fort Carlton and afterwards at Fort Pitt; his descendants were to be associated with both of these trading posts. Round about 1800 he married a pure-blooded woman of the Sarcee tribe according to the custom of the country; since missionaries did not become active in the Saskatchewan country until long afterwards, it is unlikely that they were ever married by a priest. By his Sarcee wife, Jean-Baptiste had three sons, Gabriel, Jean, and Isidore, and at least one daughter. It was Isidore who would become the father of the second and more famous Gabriel Dumont. Their maternal ancestry differentiated the Dumonts from most of the other Métis families, whose Indian ancestors were mainly Crees of the forest bands, the people whose canoe culture had formed the basis of the fur traders' transport systems. The Sarcee, though they were related by ancestry and language to the Athapaskan tribes of the boreal forest regions, had long before moved south into open country and been absorbed into the horse culture of the plains. By the time Jean-Baptiste chose his wife from among them they were living on the upper reaches of the Athapaska River not far from Edmonton House, and they had been accepted into the Blackfoot Confederacy, though they were a more artistic and perhaps a less arrogant people than the tribes who sponsored them in this formidable alliance. Undoubtedly, the links between this notable tribe of buffalo hunters and the Dumont family contributed to the mastery of prairie lore for which the Dumonts were later celebrated even among Métis hunters and to the influence they enjoyed among the tribes of the plains.

Jean-Baptiste Dumont lived out his life in the Saskatchewan valley and died there, and, however much his sons and grandsons might wander, the region remained the focus of their lives, so that they were always distinguished by habitat as well as ancestry from the Red River Métis. Of Jean-Baptiste's wife we get a fleeting last glimpse in a statement which Roger Goulet of the Winnipeg Lands Office, himself a Métis, made in support of her grandson Gabriel's claims to land in 1893. "The old woman who I remember well came to die in St. Boniface with her daughter Mrs. Lafournaise more than forty-five years ago. I was young then, but I remember her." This Indian grandmother of the Dumonts, who in her last days in the 1840s so impressed herself on the memory of a Red River boy, has gone unnamed; the burial records of St. Boniface were destroyed when the Cathedral burned in 1860, and the oral tradition remembers her only as Jean-Baptiste's widow.

Jean-Baptiste's sons grew up to be physical giants, illiterate and untrained in any formal sense, but from childhood in perpetual contact with the necessities of a wilderness life, in which they were expected to play the part appropriate to their age, so that by an unlettered process of education, by example and practice, they became great hunters and guides, and also great fighters. John Kerr, who hunted with the Saskatchewan Métis in the early 1870s, remembered Isidore and Jean, then already men in their sixties, as being "over six feet in height . . . and heavily built." By the time the brothers were able to live by their own efforts as hunters and trappers, the union of the two great fur-trading companies had greatly reduced the number of servants who could be employed, and so the three young Dumonts lived as free hunters. They spent their summers hunting the buffalo for the pemmican and hides which they sold and their winters hunting for food and trapping, as well as carrying on some minor trading with the Indians they encountered on their wanderings. Each autumn they would come to the nearest Hudson's Bay post to buy their supplies for the winter. They soon acquired the repute among the Company's officers of being "very good fur and animal hunters", and Gabriel became known and feared for his prodigious drinking and his violent temper. This in fact made him the first Dumont to achieve official recognition, for the records of Fort Edmonton note that in October 1823 he, Joseph Laframboise, and Baptiste Primeau "kept drinking and singing like Indians over their cups for the best part of the night." Ten years afterwards, again with Baptiste Primeau, this elder Gabriel Dumont figured in an uglier scene. Because of the lack of hunters to accompany the Bow River expedition, the Hudson's Bay officers found themselves obliged during the summer of 1833 to break rules and offer the encouragement of rum to the Métis. The result was a great drinking party in which Gabriel Dumont and Primeau killed the stepson of the hunter Miegan, and when Miegan pursued them they "assaulted him and bruised and cut him with their guns and dags in such a manner that they left him for dead."

It was the same Gabriel Dumont who in later years performed great services to the Oblate missionaries by guiding them to suitable places for the establishment of parishes among the Indians and the Métis. In 1842 he led into the Saskatchewan country the pioneer Abbé Thibault. Thibault founded the mission and the Métis settlement at Lac Ste. Anne in the Edmonton region and it was he who in the same year sanctified the elder Gabriel Dumont's marriage which had been made according to the custom of the country. Dumont became the leader of the Lac Ste. Anne band, and still held this position in 1858 when, at the time of the Palliser expedition into the western prairies, Palliser's assistant, Dr. Hector, came upon the band's winter hunting camp. Hector was trying to recruit men to guide and otherwise assist him in crossing the Rockies, but though there were two hundred Métis in the camp — men, women, and children living in tents of sewn buffalo hides — none of them would go without Dumont's consent. Hector found that the old leader had crossed the Rockies many times, and that he could speak the languages of the Blackfoot and of other tribes who inhabited the plains bordering the great mountain chain. But when it came to crossing the southerly passes into the Oregon country, Dumont knew nothing, and the only person who did was an old hunter, also from a family that emerged in the Saskatchewan country, named Paul Cayen. The elder Gabriel Dumont remained all his life a man of the Rocky Mountain foothills between the Tête Jaune and Crowsnest Passes. His centres of activity were Lac Ste. Anne and Fort Edmonton, and after the early years he appears to have maintained very little direct contact with the rest of the Dumont clan.

His younger brothers, Isidore and Jean, drifted eastward along the Saskatchewan valley. In 1833 Isidore Dumont, then a young man of twenty-three, married Louise, the sister of Joseph Laframboise. Early the next year Louise gave birth to their first son, Isidore, and in 1835 to their first daughter, Pélagie.

Less flamboyantly violent than their brother Gabriel, Isidore and Jean Dumont were equally good hunters and courageous fighters, well-versed in the techniques of survival on the prairies, and much respected by the Indians of the plains, who conferred on Isidore the Cree name of Ai-caw-pow (a name — meaning The Stander — once conferred in honour of Isidore on a creek that runs into the Qu'Appelle River in what is now southern Saskatchewan) and on Jean that of Ska-ka-ta-ow.

About this time, during the early 1830s, there was an inclination among the scattered Métis in the Saskatchewan region to find their way back towards the Red River valley, which in recent decades had become the centre of a developing consciousness of collective identity among the Métis.

Historians may have tended to ascribe to the North West Company and its officers more responsibility than is in fact their due in developing the myth of a Métis nation which emerged along the Red River during the early years of the nineteenth century. The actual events around which that notion arose were indeed dramatic. External influences had tended at that time to turn the valley into a vital crossroads of the Northwest. Theoretically, like the whole region whose rivers drained into Hudson's Bay, it was part of Rupert's Land and therefore of the domain granted to the Hudson's Bay Company by Charles II in 1670. But in fact, up to the conquest of Quebec in 1760, the French fur traders and explorers had maintained a free thoroughfare across the Red River into the Saskatchewan country. After the conquest, the Scottish traders from Montreal extended their routes — always linked to the St. Lawrence waterway — into the Athapaska country and later across the Rockies to the Pacific coast and down the Mackenzie to the Arctic Sea.

The right of way that crossed the Red River and continued along the Assiniboine into the far west had thus become vital to the Northwesters. So also had the supply of pemmican they needed for wintering in the Athapaska region, a supply that could only be sustained if they had access to the products of the buffalo hunts carried out by Indians from the Red River valley and increasingly by Métis hunters, some of whom were directly employed by the Northwesters while others were already freemen, selling their pemmican and hides — almost as the Indians did — in return for trade goods.

A complicating factor was introduced after 1778 by the

presence of another country in the upper reaches of the Red River. As American fur trading interests developed and began to penetrate the mid-west in advance of the agricultural pioneers, a strong south-north movement emerged at right angles to the Northwest Company's east-west route from Montreal to the Rockies, with the Hudson's Bay Company probing southward from the mouth of the Red River, and American interests thrusting northward out of the Ohio region and through what later became the Minnesota and Dakota Territories towards Rupert's Land. Three different versions of Manifest Destiny were thus on the march in this crucial region of Rupert's Land: a genuine Canadian westward movement represented — as Donald Creighton has so elaborately argued — by the establishment of strongly defended trade routes out of Montreal to the far west; a British colonization movement thrusting down from Hudson's Bay and given formal validity by the Hudson's Bay Company's grant to the Earl of Selkirk in 1812 of the right to establish a settlement and populate it with displaced Scottish crofters; and the more familiar American version which was too weak to manifest itself during the War of 1812 and in fact did not begin to gain impetus until the middle of the century at the time of the Oregon Boundary Dispute of 1846.

In this situation of the early years of the century, when the two main conflicting interests were actively at work in the same area almost like two rival states disputing a vital buffer territory, it was inevitable that the Northwesters and the Hudson's Bay people with Selkirk at their head should seek to win to their side whatever local forces with military potentialities existed in the region. The Indians of the Red River were militarily unimpressive and the Sioux of the farther prairies were too deeply feared to be considered as possible allies by either side. The Métis, on the other hand, were not only expert marksmen but practiced in prairie warfare through their encounters with the Indians of the western plains.

They were also in the peculiar intermediary situation between imperial invaders and exploited natives that has so often given peoples of mixed breed a special historical role and the sense of internal solidarity that accompanies it. Such peoples are rarely willing to identify themselves completely with the native races from which their mothers came, and yet are equally

26

rarely willingly accepted (the Portuguese territories are perhaps the only clear exception outside the Moslem world) by the ruling race to which their fathers belonged. The consequence is that they become a third people, desperately intent on developing a sense of identity and a special role in which to root their pride. This happened with the Eurasians or Anglo-Indians in India, and also with the Spanish-Quechua halfbreeds of the Andes, the Cholos, who during the eighteenth century ceased to intermarry with the pure Indians and became a virtually separate people, devoted mainly to trading in the mountain towns and villages but willing also to serve the white rulers as minor officials, policemen, or non-commissioned officers in the army. The peculiar role of the Métis in what later became western Canada was to form the mass of servants — and where necessary the body of defensive militia — for the fur-traders in the *pays d'en haut* west of Fort William. Eventually, by natural increase, the Métis became too numerous for all of them to be employed in the Northwesters' posts, and the remainder became free hunters, allying themselves according to the inclinations of the moment with whichever of the rival fur-trading interests presented the most attractive terms. As the struggle between the Companies intensified, particularly from 1790 onwards, the Métis found themselves involved as irregular forces in small-scale para-military operations (skirmishes and ambushes rather than battles), and this gave them a sense of their own importance as distinct from the Indians to whom they were related. This sense of distinctness was increased when the missionaries from Quebec, led by Joseph Provencher who arrived in 1818 to take up his duties at St. Boniface and was named bishop of Juliopolis *in partibus* in 1820, began a deliberate effort to keep them within the Catholic faith, so that their simple and rather superstitious piety became a further sign of their distinctness, both from the unconverted Indians and from the Protestant majority among the English and Scottish fur traders.

Thus, even before the nebulous notion of a Métis "nation" began to circulate, the French-speaking halfbreeds had already begun to think of themselves as a separate people (separate because of their religion even from the English-speaking halfbreeds), taking a pride in their accomplishments as voyageurs,

27

hunters, and amateur soldiers, and possessing not only a special function in the world of the West but also certain rights which at first were vaguely conceived and expressed, but which eventually, under the urgings of Northwest traders pursuing their company's interests, began to centre around the idea of land. They were the sons of Indians, it began to be argued, and so they had a share in the first-comers' rights to the wide lands on which men from outside, and in particular Lord Selkirk's settlers, were beginning to encroach.

In the early days of the century the small pieces of farming land that were settled by Selkirk's followers were not in themselves important, since the buffalo were still numerous and the Métis were disinclined to become tillers of the soil when they could live a much more exciting and congenial life as hunters. It was when the intruders, personified in Selkirk's lieutenant Miles Macdonell, began to interfere with the hunt, its products and profits, that the Northwesters were able to rouse the Métis. Without the force to sustain his edicts, Miles Macdonell rashly attempted early in 1814 to stop the export of pemmican west from Assiniboia without his permission. His regulations may have been desirable to ensure adequate reserves of food for the Red River settlement in its crucial formative seasons, but they were interpreted by the Northwesters as a threat to the supply of provisions needed by the traders and servants who wintered in Athapaska, and by the Métis as an interference in the freedom of hunting which they so much treasured. The Northwesters deliberately fomented resentment among the Métis, since, though they recognized that the Hudson's Bay charter gave them as traders no rights at all in Rupert's Land, they might plausibly support Métis demands for a share in the aboriginal right. They combined arguments along these lines with flatteries of the pride of the Métis, and they induced educated half-breeds whom they employed as clerks, such as Cuthbert Grant and Nicholas Montour, to set themselves up as leaders of the new "nation". After two years of propaganda, the Northwesters arranged a gathering at Qu'Appelle of Métis company servants and free hunters, and appointed Cuthbert Grant to the resounding office of "Captain-General of all the Half-Breeds". A Métis flag was devised, and the Northwester Alexander Macdonell declared that: "The new nation under their leaders are coming forward to clear their native soil of intruders and assassins," by which were meant Selkirk, his settlers and the employees of the Hudson's Bay Company. It was thus in 1816 that the talk of a Métis nation, which resounded in the Northwest for the next two generations, first began.

In 1816 the "new nation" acted as a little more than the private army of the Northwesters. They ambushed a Hudson's Bay Company brigade on the Assiniboine River, seized the Company's post at Brandon House, and then set off to the Red River and fought the skirmish of Seven Oaks which they called a Battle and their opponents called a Massacre, and in which Governor Semple and twenty-one of his men were killed for the cost of one Métis death. The pros and cons of Seven Oaks have been sufficiently discussed by other authors (and especially by Margaret MacLeod and W.L. Morton in *Cuthbert Grant of Grantown*), and no more than a brief comment is necessary here. The event reflected no credit on the North West Company whose officers provoked it, and little on the Métis who acted with a savagery they were not to repeat in their later battles, and in the end, though the illiterate Métis bard Pierre Falcon made a fine rousing song out of it, nothing was gained by either of these temporarily victorious parties. For the final result of the prolonged controversy over the fur trade in Canada which Seven Oaks set echoing as far away as Westminster was the union of the two companies in 1821, in which Northwest interests were subordinated and the Métis faced a rigorous consolidation of services carried out by George Simpson as Governor of the united company, in which many of them were thrown out of work in a land where the fur traders were the only employers.

The settling of the Métis and English half-breeds discharged from Company employment was in fact one of the first problems Simpson faced when he entered on his duties, and in 1822 he warned the Company's officers in London that if the unemployed half-breeds were "allowed to remain in their present condition, they will become dangerous to the Peace of the Country and the safety of the Trading Posts." He went on to suggest that "these people ought to be removed to Red River where the Catholics will naturally fall under the Roman

Catholic Mission which is established there, and the Protestants and such orphan children as fall to be maintained and clothed by the Company, may be placed under the Protestant Establishment and Schools."

By now Bishop Provencher had established missions in the Red River valley, notably at St. Boniface and, as we have seen, at Pembina just south of the international border, where a small Métis settlement had already begun in 1780. Many of the Métis settled on land south of the Hudson's Bay Company's new post of Fort Garry, in narrow river-front lots which continued almost to the frontier through what eventually became the parishes of St. Vital, St. Norbert, and Ste. Agathe. A more cohesive group was established under Cuthbert Grant at Grantown on the White Horse Plains which bordered the Assiniboine River about fifteen miles west of Fort Garry. Grant, who claimed seigneurial authority, continued to regard himself as the leader of the half-breeds, and while the English-speaking members of that group were inclined to ignore his pretensions, the Métis tended to follow his lead largely because he flattered them by keeping alive the myth of their nationhood.

White Horse Plains, the haunt of a ghostly steed in a prairie legend of Indian lovers killed in a tribal vendetta, was a particularly fertile stretch of black-soiled prairie, but most of the Métis who lived there were merely squatters who maintained a habitation and some grazing for their horses but were mainly interested in hunting, freighting, and trading. Their presence was tolerated by the Company, even at the expense of agriculture, because they not only provided a steady supply of the indispensible pemmican but also formed a westerly bulwark to protect Fort Garry and the Red River villages from attack by the dreaded Sioux. Grant was given the grandiose title of Warden of the Plains, and appointed to represent the Métis on the Council of Assiniboia which was established to govern the Red River country. Until late in the 1830s, Grant also led the buffalo hunts with their elaborate quasi-military organization.

Recognition as a vital part of the Red River community and establishment of Fort Garry as a kind of physical centre for their activities combined to increase the Métis sense of being a "nation" of their own within the life of the Northwest, and though they remained relatively calm until the middle of the century, they were inclined to show signs of rebellion whenever they sensed a threat to their rights and liberties. In 1830, when Simpson tried to clear some Métis squatters from land he needed for other purposes, they complained that "this was their country and the soil was theirs," and in January 1835 the Governor remarked that "The Brulés are becoming clamorous about their rights and privileges as Natives of the Soil and it required all our most skilful management to maintain the peace of the Colony during the holidays while Rum was in circulation." It was not merely a matter of land; the "rights and privileges" which the Métis were much more inclined to stress at this period were those relating to hunting and trading, for the Company's monopoly was already becoming irksome at a time when American traders were operating south of the border and were offering attractive prices to the free hunters in exchange for the furs they trapped or collected from the Indians.

It was about this time that Isidore Dumont arrived from the Saskatchewan to settle beside the Red River, and here — at St. Boniface — his second son was born in December 1837* and named after his formidable uncle Gabriel. For a short period during young Gabriel's early childhood, Isidore tried the life of the settled man, with a long narrow farm holding beside the river and extending back to the grazing land of the prairies. By the time of the Red River census of 1838 he had broken and ploughed three acres of land to grow potatoes and barley, but he raised no other animals than horses, of which he had five, for no Métis worth his name would think of eating anything other than wild meat, preferably hunted and killed by himself, and the raising of cattle for milk was as yet unknown west of Upper Canada. Isidore built himself a small mud-plastered house and barn, and possessed a canoe to fish on the Red River and Lake Winnipeg, and owned four Red River carts, all their parts made of wood, which he and Louise and their children

* Various dates between 1836 and 1838 have been given in the past, but this is the date which Dumont himself gave in a statement he made in validating his claim to land at Batoche in 1893.

31

would drive out to the prairies on the annual buffalo hunts and which at other times he hired out for freighting on the trail that ran south into American territory beside the Red River. He was, by local standards, well-off.

Though it was still inhabited by only a few hundred families, life in the Red River settlement had its own bucolic excitements. In winter the Métis loved to display themselves in their best blue capotes, with fine *ceintures flechés* bound around their waists, riding about in carioles drawn by their finest horses. Métis parties, and especially the *noces* or wedding parties, were occasions of relentless gaiety, with drink flowing freely and the fiddles playing the night through to accompany the energetic monotony of dancing the Red River jigs. But Gabriel was too young — as he remarked long afterwards — to remember any of this, and Isidore soon lost his taste for the settled life and monotonous flatness of the Red River Valley and began to long for the unconstrained life of the wilderness and the rolling wooded countryside of his native Saskatchewan. Not long after his third son, Joseph, was born in 1839, he gave up his land and went to live with his father-in-law Laframboise, who had also moved to St. Boniface. And in the late summer of 1840 Isidore Dumont loaded his Red River carts with his family and his few possessions and set out on the long trek over the Carlton Trail back to the Saskatchewan country.

But before he departed, Isidore Dumont took part in the great buffalo hunt of 1840, the largest expedition yet to leave the Red River, which Alexander Ross accompanied and described many years afterwards when he wrote *The Red River Settlement*. The buffalo hunters were always accompanied by their families, since the women and even quite young children took part in the work of drying the buffalo meat or turning it into pemmican, and so there is no doubt that Gabriel Dumont, as a child of less than three, was there, perched under the awning of one of his father's creaking carts, when the hunters of St. Boniface began their slow way along the upriver trail to the rendezvous at Pembina. In all, some 1,630 people gathered for the hunt, of whom almost four hundred were children. There were 1,210 carts in the procession, some drawn by horses and others by oxen, and the creaking of their ungreased wooden axles must have been deafening; in addition to the draft beasts there were more than four hundred picked horses to be used by the hunters as buffalo runners. Finally, more than five hundred dogs accompanied the cavalcade as it stretched for five miles over the prairie, to which would be added, once the herds were reached, many hundreds of wolves and coyotes who followed to feast off the discarded remnants of the slaughtered beasts.

Once the hunters had assembled at Pembina, they gathered to elect their officers and lay down the rules by which the expedition should be conducted. Since these procedures had already acquired the weight of tradition and were to form the basis of the attempt at Métis self-government in which Gabriel Dumont became active thirty years later, Ross's account has a special interest. First — he tells us — the ten captains of the hunt were chosen, and one of them was named "the great war chief or head of the camp; and on all public occasions he occupied the place of president." In the hunt of 1840 the president was not a Métis, but a Scottish half-breed named Jean-Baptiste Wilkie (sometimes known as Welkey) who had been brought up as a child among the Métis. He was, as Ross remembers, "a man of good sound sense and long experience, and withal a fine bold-looking and discreet fellow; a second Nimrod in his way." Long afterwards, when his days of leading the hunt were over, this "second Nimrod" was to become Gabriel Dumont's father-in-law, and it is possible that the first time Gabriel set eyes on his future wife Madeleine was on this great hunt of 1840, for she was born in that year at Pembina to Jean-Baptiste and his wife, Isabella Azure.

Each of the captains under Wilkie had, Ross tells us,

ten soldiers under his orders; in much the same way that policemen are subject to the magistrate. Ten guides are likewise appointed. . . . Their duties were to guide the camp, each in his turn — that is day about — during the expedition. The camp flag belongs to the guide of the day; he is therefore standard-bearer by virtue of his office.

The hoisting of the flag every morning is the signal for raising camp. Half an hour is the full time allowed to pre-

33

pare for the march; but if any one is sick, or their animals have strayed, notice is sent to the guide, who halts till all is made right. From the time the flag is hoisted, however, till the hour of camping arrives, it is never taken down. The flag taken down is the signal for encamping. While it is up, the guide is chief of the expedition. Captains are subject to him, and the soldiers of the day are his messengers: he commands all. The moment the flag is lowered, his functions cease, and the captains' and soldiers' duties commence. They point out the order of the camp, and every cart, as it arrives, moves to its appointed place. This business usually occupies about the same time as raising camp in the morning; for everything moves with the regularity of clock-work.

Before leaving Pembina, Jean-Baptiste Wilkie with the nine other captains and the hunters of distinction, including Isidore Dumont, gathered to vote on the rules of the expedition. They were in fact doing little more than validate once again for a new year the by-laws already established on previous hunts, and very similar rules continued to be observed until the last years of the buffalo hunts forty years afterwards.

1. No buffalo to be run on the Sabbath-day.
2. No party to fork off, lag behind, or go before.
3. No person or party to run buffalo before the general order.
4. Every captain with his men, in turn, to patrol the camp, and keep guard.
5. For the first trespass against these laws, the offender to have his saddle and bridle cut up.
6. For the second offence, the coat to be taken off the offender's back, and be cut up.
7. For the third offence, the offender to be flogged.
8. Any person convicted of theft, even to the value of a sinew, to be brought to the middle of the camp, and the crier to call out his or her name three times, adding the word "Thief!" at each time.

What one immediately notices about the punishments decreed in the rules of the hunt is their relative mildness. Physical sanctions seem to have been regarded as the last resort, to be used only against the habitual offender and against the worst crime of a hunter, which was to break order and risk scaring the buffalo herd prematurely. For the most part, reliance seems to have been placed on the moral effect of public ridicule among a proud people who found losing face more difficult to endure than losing possessions. The same sense of a community ruled by opinion embodied in a few simple and generally accepted moral rules emerges from Ross's descriptions of the gatherings of captains and elders at the end of each day's travelling or hunting, when they would sit tailor-fashion on the ground to hold council, "each having his gun, his smoking-bag in his hand, and his pipe in his mouth." Ross found these meetings both interesting and agreeable, as the past day's happenings were discussed and plans for the morrow were decided. "I must say, I found less selfishness and more liberality among those ordinary men than I had been accustomed to find in higher circles. Their conversation was free, practical and interesting; and the time passed more agreeably than could be expected among such people, till we touched on politics."

The touching on politics, which caused some distress to Ross as a mid-nineteenth century upholder of the hierarchical order which Hudson's Bay factors were inclined to favour, reveals the Métis as members of an egalitarian community influenced deeply by the kind of primitive and direct democracy which existed among the great Indian tribes of the plains, where the authority of the chief depended always on the revocable consent of his braves. Long before they were goaded into rebellion in 1869 and 1885, the Métis appear to have nurtured a sense of individual liberty as strong as any Indian warrior, or, for that matter, as any rebellious mediaeval Swiss peasant or citizen of Pericles' Athens. Reading Ross's remarks, indeed, I could not help being reminded of Gerald Brenan's moving descriptions of the illiterate anarchist prophets who roved the remote hill villages of Andalusia in the days before the Spanish Civil War.

"Like the American peasantry," Ross tells,

these people are all politicians, but of a peculiar creed, favouring a barbarous state of society and self-will; for they cordially detest all the laws and restraints of civilized life,

35

believing all men were born to be free. In their own estimation they are all great men, and wonderfully wise; and so long as they wander about on these wild and lawless expeditions, they will never become a thoroughly civilized people, nor orderly subjects in a civilized community. Feeling their own strength, from being constantly armed, and free from control, they despise all others; but above all, they are marvellously tenacious of their own original habits. They cherish freedom as they cherish life. . . . They are all republicans in principle, and a licentious freedom is their besetting sin.

Such were the Métis at the height of their pride and their good fortune, when the buffalo herds still seemed inexhaustible and the only existing government was virtually inoperative beyond the stockades of the Hudson's Bay Company's fort. Lawless perhaps they were in the technical sense of possessing no authoritarian structure of government, no immutable code of laws, and yet the descriptions by Ross himself and by many other observers agree on the splendid organization of the buffalo hunt, which was achieved by voluntarily agreeing on a series of rules and restraints which everybody accepted and observed. Nor should the degree of mutual aid which was shown during the hunt be overlooked, for most of the best hunters would give away much of the meat they killed to the poor or incapacitated people who accompanied every expedition. Perhaps the Métis attitude can best be defined as one of anarchic egoism, tempered by mutual respect among the strong and by generosity towards the weak. Bakunin, who stressed the virtues to be found in people not entirely absorbed into modern industrial society, would have loved, if he had known them, these free hunters who were his contemporaries. Such were the men Gabriel Dumont saw constantly around him when as a child he travelled in the great hunts: the men he admired and imitated, and of whom he himself became in the end one of the best as well as one of the last examples.

Like all the great hunting expeditions, that of 1840 was accompanied by its priest, who celebrated mass before the flag was unfurled on the morning of departure. That first day the cavalcade marched some twenty miles, starting at six in the morning, and continuing, with a short break to rest the animals, until six in the evening; later days' journeys varied according to the terrain, but they averaged about fifteen miles. Each evening the captains and the soldiers would arrange the camp, moving the Red River carts into a defensive circle and posting sentries to watch out for lurking Sioux, since the hunts often took place over terrain hunted also by that formidable tribe. In 1840, the buffalo still wandered comparatively near to the Red River, and after nineteen days of travel the hunters saw their first herds, in American territory, somewhere between the Sheyenne and the Missouri.

Since the method used was for the buffalo hunters to ride simultaneously through the herd, shooting the beasts from almost pointblank range, the greatest co-ordination in starting the hunt was necessary.

No less than 400 huntsmen, all mounted, and anxiously waiting for the word "Start!" took up their position in a line at one end of the camp, while Captain Wilkie, with his spyglass at his eye, surveyed the buffalo, examined the ground, and issued his orders. At 8 o'clock the whole cavalcade broke ground, and made for the buffalo; first at a slow trot, then at a gallop, and lastly at full speed. . . . When the horsemen started, the cattle might have been a mile and a half ahead; but they had approached to within four or five hundred yards before the bulls curved their tails or pawed the ground. In a moment more the herd took flight, and horse and rider are presently seen bursting in among them; shots are heard, and all is smoke, dust and hurry.

In that day's run no less than 1,375 buffalo were killed. The best hunters, on the best horses, firing from the hip and loading at the gallop from mouths filled with ball, killed ten or twelve beasts each; those with inferior horses had to be content with two or three. The carts set off after the hunters, who were already skinning their beasts when the carters arrived. As soon as the loaded carts reached the camp the work was taken over by the women, who prepared the pemmican, dried the jerked meat, and cleaned the hides. For them, once the hunting grounds were reached, the expeditions were all work, whereas each day the men had the renewed excitement of the ride into

37

the herd, with all its exhilaration and all its perils, for horses and men were often gored by the bulls, or injured from falling on the uneven ground or sometimes from the bursting of their own antiquated guns which they had overstuffed with powder.

After two months and two days, on 17 August, the expedition returned to the Red River. One man had been surprised and killed by a band of Sioux of whom eight were killed in turn by a pursuing party of Métis. (The affair was compounded by the raising of a small collection to be given to the Sioux chief in compensation for eight lives having been taken in payment for one.) The diplomacy of Jean-Baptiste Wilkie had saved the expedition becoming involved in skirmishing between the Sioux and their rivals the Saulteaux. Five people had been killed by lightning in a prairie storm, and several children had narrowly escaped drowning in the flooded tents. These were unexceptional misfortunes in terms of prairie existence, and the expedition was regarded as a great success when it returned with about 500 tons of dried meat and pemmican, though, as Ross remarked, the wastage had been enormous, and at least as much usable meat was left to be eaten by predators or to rot among the white bones that already strewed the prairie like a crop of strangely shaped fungi. The Dumonts' share, counting by Isidore's four carts, was probably about 3,500 pounds, apart from what they had consumed during the hunt in such immediately cooked delicacies as tongues and humps. Some of this, as a recognized hunter, Isidore could sell to the Hudson's Bay Company, and some was bought by private individuals. With the cash he received he paid off his debts to the Company for the ammunition needed on the hunt just terminated, and bought the supplies for his trip to Fort Pitt and for the trading he intended to carry on there. The remaining pemmican and dried meat would serve on the long trip northwest up the Carlton Trail. It had been, for all concerned, a more successful hunt than most that followed.

2. Journeys of Childhood, Battles of Youth

The country into which the Dumonts journeyed at the end of summer in 1840, in company with other hunters returning to the Saskatchewan Valley, was not only the region where Isidore was born; it became also the source and centre of Gabriel's first memories. In the hot September days they travelled at cart pace over the flat lands along the Assiniboine to Portage la Prairie, keeping alert as soon as they had left the White Horse Plains for the sign of raiding Sioux, and at night, when they slept within their teepee-like skin tents inside the tight little circle of carts, always placing their sentries.

After Portage la Prairie they turned onto an old buffalo hunt trail that led them down towards Fort Brandon, whence they struck across country to Fort Ellice. The ground rose slowly, and often they were delayed by the need to descend into the deep valleys which creeks and rivers had cut into the surface of the prairie; the abrupt slopes were difficult to negotiate with loaded carts, but fortunately it was the dry season, the streams were low, and most of them could be forded. When they could not, the carts were dismantled, and after their great wheels, unweighted by metal, had been strapped beneath them as floats, they were drifted across like rafts, with the horses swimming behind them. There were some particularly difficult coulées near Fort Ellice, where the travellers had to descend some 250 feet to cross the Assiniboine near its junction to the Qu'Appelle, and then climb the same distance once again. After Fort Ellice

the trail — it was not yet the well worn and travelled thoroughfare of later decades — struck over the grasslands in the direction
of the Touchwood Hills, where the travellers first began to see
the characteristic rolling hills, often furred over by heavy woods,
of the northern savannah country which the mid-century
prairie fires had not yet ravaged. In the Touchwood Hills there
was much game, and here they lingered to supply themselves
with fresh meat and with wildfowl from the sloughs and marshes
around the Quill Lakes and in the Great Salt Plain. By now
the mosquitoes which plagued that region in summer had vanished, and the swampy trail had dried out, so that they were
able to travel quickly, and when they ascended to the higher
spots on the route they could enjoy wide vistas of rich parkland,
broken by copses already turning colour with the first brisk
nights of autumn, and by ponds glittering blue in the sunlight
within the golden rings of the late summer reedbeds.

Eventually they came to the crossing of the South Saskatchewan. Here, in the days of the great rivalry between the
Northwesters and the men from the Hudson's Bay Company,
rival posts had been established, both of which were attacked
in 1793 by Gros Ventre Indians and abandoned; later they were
rebuilt, and it was in the North West Company's South Branch
House that the furtrader diarist Daniel Harmon met in 1805
the Métis girl whom he first took to live with him in the country
fashion and later married; she was to be his lifelong companion
and to accompany him when he left the Northwest and retired
to end his days in Vermont. All traces of Harmon's post had
vanished by 1840, and as yet there was no beginning of the
Métis settlement of Batoche that would later arise on this spot
and provide a setting for the climactic drama of Gabriel's life.
There was not even a ferry to cross the wide river, but a kind of
rough scow belonging to the Hudson's Bay post at Fort Carlton
was moored under the bank; Isidore and his companions had to
track it upstream and then row diagonally across as the force
of the current swept them downstream. There was room only
for their goods and their dismembered carts, and the horses had
to swim for it; fortunately the river was low and the ice that
sometimes made crossing dangerous in the late autumn had not
yet begun to form.

Beyond the river, the trail crossed an undulating parkland

to Fort Carlton, which lay within its wooden stockade on a low bench beside the North Branch of the Saskatchewan. It was one of the oldest surviving posts in the area, having been re-erected on its present site in the year of Isidore's birth, and it was fortified, as Paul Kane noted not long afterwards, "with blunderbusses on swivels mounted in the bastion." But the site was peculiarly indefensible, being closely overlooked by open hillsides, and its inhabitants lived in perpetual fear of the Blackfoot, on the edge of whose country it lay. As was the custom among travellers, the Dumonts changed into their best clothes to present themselves at the Fort, and they camped there for several days to rest their animals and feast and dance with the local Métis before crossing the North Branch and continuing through the sharpening October days on the remaining hundred and fifty miles of their trip, which lay across country, north of the river.

Fort Pitt was one of the newer trading posts in the Saskatchewan region. It was built between 1829 and 1831 by a party of Métis from Edmonton employed by the Company; one of whom, François Laframboise, was related by marriage to Isidore Dumont. As Paul Kane described it, on first arriving in 1847, Pitt was "a neat and compact little fort", of whitewashed buildings enclosed within a stockade dominated by two turrets, from each of which projected a two-pounder gun. Like Fort Carlton, it was overlooked by hills, a weakness — like that of Carlton — which was rather surprising in view of the fur traders' long experience of the perils of badly defended sites.

In other ways, Fort Pitt was excellently situated, located between the territories of the Blackfoot and the Cree, so that both these tribes of hereditary enemies went to trade there. The land was fertile, and potatoes and other roots grew to a great size, and were much relished by visitors. It was also one of the best regions in all the prairies for hunting the buffalo. Kane's accounts of his visits to Fort Pitt at this period, only a few years after Isidore Dumont's arrival, testify to the extraordinary size of the herds which gathered there in the autumn and winter. In September 1847, travelling westward from the fort in the direction of Edmonton, he and his companions "had not proceeded more than ten miles, when we fell in with immense numbers of buffaloes" and for three days travelling up-

41

river to Edmonton House "we saw nothing else but these animals covering the plains as far as the eye could reach, that at times they impeded our progress, filling the air with dust almost to suffocation." A few months later, in January 1848, on approaching Fort Pitt from Edmonton, Kane noted that "the animals had, we were told, never appeared in such vast numbers, nor shown themselves so near the Company's establishments; some have even been shot within the gates of the fort. They killed with their horns twenty or thirty horses in their attempt to drive them off from the patches of grass which the horses had pawed the snow from with their hoofs for the purpose of getting at the grass, and severely gored many others, which eventually recovered."

Kane goes on to say that his remarks "convey but a faint idea of the astonishing number of these animals" which he encountered passing through the Saskatchewan country, and then adds (writing in the hindsight of 1858): "They were probably migrating northwards, to escape from the human migrations which are so rapidly filling up the southern and western regions, which were formerly their pasture grounds."

There is of course no doubt that the establishment of the Red River settlement as both an agricultural centre and a base for hunting expeditions like that of 1840 inevitably drove the buffalo farther away and had the effect of producing in the remoter regions the impression that, far from diminishing, the buffalo were not only a durable but even a growing resource. It was at this time that the Métis hunters began to think in terms of two great herds, one to be found mainly in the Missouri region and towards Montana, and the other in the Saskatchewan region: the southern herd and the northern herd. But it seems likely that the division among the buffalo may in fact have been created by the annual thrust, each year farther westward, of the great hunt riding out from the Red River.

Certainly there can have been little thought among the hunters of Fort Pitt — such related clans as the Dumonts and the Fishers and the Laframboises, the Cayens and the Beauchamps and the La Vallées — that the abundance they saw about them in the 1840s would ever come to an end. To realize in a concrete way what that abundance meant, and how well one could live merely off the land in the Saskatchewan Valley in the 1840s, let us take a farewell glance at Paul Kane, enjoying at Edmonton House on Christmas Day, 1847, a dinner of characteristic Northwest fare:

At the head, before Mr. Harriett, was a large dish of boiled buffalo hump; at the foot smoked a boiled buffalo calf. Start not, gentle reader, the calf is very small, and is taken from the cow by the Caesarian operation long before it attains its full growth. This, boiled whole, is one of the most esteemed dishes among the epicures of the interior. My pleasing duty was to help a dish of mouffle, or dried moose nose; the gentleman on my left distributed, with graceful impartiality, the white fish, delicately browned in buffalo marrow. The worthy priest helped the buffalo tongue, while Mr. Rundell cut up the beavers' tails. Nor was the other gentleman left unemployed, as all his spare time was occupied in dissecting a roast wild goose. The centre of the table was graced with piles of potatoes, turnips, and bread conveniently placed, so that each could help himself without interrupting the labours of his companions.

Such, in the seasons when buffalo gathered abundantly in the Saskatchewan country and when the fishing was good in the lakes, was the fare of the simple hunters as well as the Company's officers, except that instead of bread the hunters would eat the unleavened wheatcakes known as galettes, which were in fact a kind of bannock. It was the surplus that was dried for preservation or made into pemmican, but so great was that surplus that Fort Pitt operated more as a provisioning depot than as a fur trading post. Its main function was to collect supplies that would enable traders in regions that were rich in furs but poor in edible game to survive the winters, and so the main items of trade were dried meat and pemmican, buffalo fat and buffalo robes. The Indians to the north brought in a few fine furs, but apart from buffalo hides, the main skins traded were those of wolves, and the wolves, of course, were part of the ecosystem that centred around the great herds.

It was in this trade that Isidore Dumont and his fellow Métis, except for the few who were actually working around the fort, mainly occupied themselves. During the winter they stayed near Fort Pitt, in rough log cabins which they built to weather the cold months. Game was then close at hand, but in other seasons they had to go farther afield, and then they travelled as nomads, with all their goods loaded into their Red River carts, following the buffalo, visiting the lakes at the appropriate seasons for netting whitefish, and trading on a small scale with the outlying groups of Indians who did not come to the fort. It was rather like the life of the plains Indians at that period before the breakdown of the aboriginal culture, one in which an abundance of natural things was combined with a scarcity of civilized amenities, in which austerity was combined with ostentation. Men and women alike, the Métis loved bright clothes — neatly beaded mocassins and kneebands and bright sashes for the men, gaudy frocks and kerchiefs for the women — and the men prided themselves on their horses and their guns, with a preference in later years for Winchesters. At the same time, their homes were as comfortless as those of the Indians, and even more drab, since their tents lacked the heraldic paintings that made the lodges of the plains Indians so colourful, and their huts, when they occupied them, were almost totally unfurnished. Usually, a wooden chest in which their best clothes were kept would be the main piece of furniture. Meals were eaten on the floor, with the diners seated on buffalo robes and the food set out in tin plates; the same robes, spread on the floor, served in hut and tent alike as beds and coverings. Accumulated possessions were not important in the Métis culture. The prosperous man was the hunter who could always kill more game than he needed, and so have a surplus for trading in order to fulfill his whims. Isidore was one of these, and so were all the Dumonts. The poor man was the inadequate hunter who at times had to rely on the generosity of his more adept neighbours. The accounts of Victorian travellers and of Hudson's Bay men brought up in a thrifty tradition are almost unanimous in condemning the improvidence of the Métis, yet that improvidence was of a kind that went with the virtues the Métis shared with other rootless peoples like the Bedouin and the Gauchos, the virtues of generosity and unstinting hospitality which were the other side of the medal to their love of gambling and drinking and revelry and their general disrespect for money. The idea of a bank account was as alien to the Métis culture as the idea of a clock. They lived off the land in the same

44

way as they lived according to the sun and the seasons. Perhaps the most negative aspect of their free and extravagant way of life was that they had lost the arts of their French ancestors, the folk arts of Quebec, without having retained the arts of the Indians, and this particular deprivation reflected their historical position, as a transitional and traditionless people, poised between the old Indian order on the prairies and the new order of the farmer and the rancher that would displace the peoples who lived by the hunt.

It was in this semi-nomadic world that Gabriel Dumont passed his boyhood, with Fort Pitt as the centre of his world, Edmonton House and Fort Carlton as its extremities, and a mixture of Scottish fur traders, Métis voyageurs and hunters, and Indians of many tribes as its inhabitants. Away from the Red River, where the various groups tended to segregate themselves from each other, there was much more mingling between the Company's officers and their Métis hunters and voyageurs on the one hand, and between the Métis and the Indians on the other. The Métis were treated as at least distant relatives by the tribes from which their mothers came, and they would often join the native hunters in their buffalo drives, though they were not always entirely welcome, since they were better horsemen and shots than the Indians and therefore always killed more buffalo. Though the Cree and the Métis had lived in amity for many years and even regarded themselves as allies against the Sioux and the Blackfoot, the Cree chiefs complained in 1858 to the geographer Henry Youle Hind about "the half-breeds' hunting buffalo during the winter in the Plain Cree country." But there was at least no overt hostility, and as a boy Gabriel Dumont made as many friends among young Cree of his own age as he did among the children of the Métis. He was also taken, on his father's trading trips, to visit his grandmother's people, the Sarcee, and he came to know the Blackfoot and the Gros Ventres, the Assiniboines and the Sioux. He had the facility for languages which most Métis — who were always at least bilingual — developed, and in the end he spoke six Indian languages as well as French, though he never learnt more than a few words of English.

Yet he remained an illiterate to the end, only on rare occasions in later years substituting a laboriously drawn signature for the mark he normally used. Very few of the Métis in their early days received any degree of formal education — men like Louis Riel and Louis Schmidt were exceptions — and this was due to the nomadic condition of their childhood. Father Joseph Goiffon complained that when he was priest at Pembina in the 1850s the only time he had any chance to teach the children of the nomadic Métis even as much as the catechism was during the two months when he went out with them as chaplain to the hunt, and he remarked that often young Métis as much as twenty-two years old had not yet made their first communion and "did not know anything". As late as 1872 George Grant found that even in the settled Métis communities with resident priests, like St. Albert and Lac Ste. Anne, "The children are sent to school only when they have no buffalo to hunt, no pemmican to make, or no work of greater importance than education to set them at." Yet in certain vital ways every Métis, in order even to survive in the wilderness, had to learn a great deal and learn it well, and the apprenticeship of daily life in which he acquired that knowledge was its own kind of education. Certainly, when one considers the accomplishments Gabriel Dumont acquired in childhood, the absurdity of equating literacy and education is revealed in all its extremity. For Gabriel Dumont learnt much more than seven languages, and grew up, in terms of his culture, to be a highly educated boy.

The accounts of Gabriel's youth are scanty. We know little in sharp and concrete detail of what happened to him and his family between the day they reached Fort Pitt and the day Isidore Dumont decided to join a caravan of his fellow hunters returning to Red River in the spring of 1848. This means that life probably followed a fairly regular routine determined by the seasons, a pattern of vigorous hunting when the opportunity arose, of friendly trading with the Indians, and of feasting and leisure when the hunting and trading had been successful. Other children were born to complete the family produced from Isidore's marriage with Louise Laframboise: Judith and Isabelle, Edouard and Elie the youngest, who was born in 1847. Two of the children, Joseph and Judith, were to die young, but no less than six of the eight would survive, Isidore, Edouard and Elie to fight beside Gabriel in his battles, Pélagie and Isabelle to marry his friends. Their survival to adulthood is a tribute not

46

only to the vitality of the Dumonts at a time of high childhood mortality, but also to the efficiency with which Isidore provided and Louise cared for them and to the good fortune that saved them from the smallpox that in their youth became endemic — and at times epidemic — throughout the prairies.

Gabriel Dumont did a great deal more than survive. He grew up to be a strong, stocky boy, thickset and heavy-chested; he would never attain the height of his father and his uncles, and as an adult he was so squarely built that he seemed shorter than his 5'8". He developed the kind of strong, well-moulded face that delights portrait sculptors, with high Indian cheeks, dark eyes that often had the stern fixity of expression of those who have lived in wide open vistas, and a wide, rather coarse-lipped mouth that somewhat detracted from the general effect. No portraits have survived of Gabriel in his childhood or even in his young manhood, but those that exist of him in middle and old age project a sense of physical vitality like that of a wild animal in its prime, so that at times one senses a haunting relationship to the great bull bison which he killed so often and helped to hunt to their doom.

The education of Gabriel Dumont, apart from encouraging his natural linguistic talents, made him a fine hunter and a good trapper. By the age of ten he could not only ride a pony but break one in. Long before he handled a rifle, he learned to shoot with deadly accuracy the bow used by his grandmother's people, the Sarcee. He was a good fisherman, he could handle a canoe in the turbulent northern waters — and, rare among the Métis, he became an excellent swimmer. He accompanied his father, and sometimes his Indian kinsmen, on their buffalo hunts, and in the process he learnt the topography of the prairies so well that he became an excellent guide; as a white hunter who knew him long afterwards remarked, "Gabriel . . . knows the prairies as a sheep knows its heath, and could go anywhere blind-folded."

He was certainly present, during those childhood years, on some of the occasions when the Indians of the North Saskatchewan, long after it had been abandoned in the rest of the prairies, used the old pre-equestrian method of driving the buffalo into pounds or large traps where they could be killed at leisure. Paul Kane saw such a hunt in 1847, and Henry Youle

47

Hind was present at what must have been one of the last of
them in 1858. Hind's description is particularly interesting,
since it suggests at least one of the sources of the tactical con-
ceptions on which in later years Gabriel Dumont based his
method of guerilla warfare.

He tells how, one pound having become offensive even to
the Indians because of the stench rising from the remnants of
hundreds of carcasses, it was decided to make a new pound.

This was formed in a pretty dell between sand hills,
about half a mile from the first, and leading from it in two
diverging rows, the bushes they designate "dead men", and
which serve to guide the buffalo when at full speed, were
arranged. The "dead men" extended a distance of four miles
from the prairie, west of and beyond the Sand Hills. They
were placed about 50 feet apart, and between the extremity
of the rows might be a distance of from one and a half to
two miles.

When the skilled hunters are about to bring in a herd of
buffalo from the prairie, they direct the course of the gallop
of the alarmed animals by confederates stationed in hollows
or small depressions, who, when the buffalo appear inclined
to take a direction leading from the space marked out by
the "dead man", show themselves for a moment and wave
their robes, immediately hiding again. This serves to turn
the buffalo slightly in another direction, and when the animals, having arrived between the rows of "dead men", endeavour to pass through them, Indians here and there stationed behind a "dead man", go through the same operation, and so keep the animals within the narrowing limits
of the converging lines. At the entrance to the pound there
is a strong trunk of a tree placed about one foot from the
ground, and on the inner side an excavation is made sufficiently deep to prevent the buffalo from leaping back when
once in the pound. As soon as the animals have taken the
fatal spring they begin to gallop round and round the ring
fence looking for a chance of escape, but with the utmost
silence women and children on the outside hold their robes
before every orifice until the whole herd is brought in; they
then climb to the top of the fence, and, with the hunters who

48

have followed closely in the rear of the buffalo, spear or shoot with bows and arrows or fire-arms at the bewildered animals, rapidly becoming frantic with rage and terror, within the narrow limits of the pound. A dreadful scene of confusion and slaughter then begins, the oldest and strongest animals crush and toss the weaker; the shouts and screams of the excited Indians rise above the roaring of the bulls, the bellowing of the cows, and the piteous moaning of the calves. The dying struggles of so many huge and powerful animals crowded together, create a revolting and terrible scene, dreadful from the excess of its cruelty and waste of life, but with occasional displays of wonderful brute strength and rage; while man in his savage, untutored, and heathen state shows both in deed and expression how little he is superior to the noble beasts he so wantonly and cruelly destroys.

Gabriel Dumont and his brothers may at first have looked on such scenes with a mixture of astonishment and fear, which Dumont always recognized as present even in the most courageous man, but it is unlikely that, brought up as they were to the life of the hunt and the daily presence of bloody and dismembered carcasses, they would have regarded it with the same repugnance as Hind, the Victorian scientist. Certainly they would have been near enough in feeling to the Indians to realize that, despite appearances, the hunters sustained a deep sense of empathy towards the beasts they slaughtered with such apparent abandon, and at least ceremonially paid debts of gratitude and expiation to these fellow children of Manitou who gave their flesh for the Indians to survive and towards whom, given their totemic beliefs, they felt none of the superiority which western man sees as implicit in his relationship with the animals. Gabriel, especially, must have been near enough to the Indians to understand such matters, for at this time he learnt from his Sarcee relatives the already rare art of calling the buffalo — as other men called the moose — to a blind where the hunters waited in hiding. More than twenty years later, when the art was forgotten even by the Indians, the Canadian hunter John Kerr saw Dumont perform his calling and lure towards him a dozen or so animals which the hunters killed.

49

Why Isidore Dumont decided in 1848 to leave the good hunting of Fort Pitt and its surroundings we do not know. Perhaps it was merely the restlessness that at this time seems to have been a characteristic of the nomadically-inclined Métis, as distinct from the English half-breeds, who more willingly accepted the settled life of the farmer. Perhaps it was the news that the situation on Red River was becoming more troubled as factions began to divide the colony and Métis discontent with the Hudson's Bay Company increased. In 1845 the Métis, anxious for their share of the trade in the colony, had petitioned locally for the abolition of goods coming in from the United States. In 1846 almost a thousand persons, mainly French and English half-breeds, signed or put their marks to a much more extensive petition of grievance, addressed to the Queen and complaining about the lack of civil rights under Company rule, about the absence of schools, about the Company's monopoly of trade, and about the high prices charged for imported goods.

The situation was complicated by the fact that the Red River colony was no longer the isolated enclave it had been earlier in the century. Catholic missionaries and Oblate priests from France rather than from Quebec were beginning to appear in greater numbers, and so were the first Canadians from the colonies along the St. Lawrence, with their ideas of responsible government and their ambitions of westward expansion. The onward thrust of settlement south of the border was finally making the United States a factor of importance in Red River affairs. In 1845, for the first time, Métis from the settlement had been stopped by American cavalry and told that they must elect either to live south of the border or to abandon the customary hunting grounds there. The prohibition was not yet rigidly enforced, and a more regular source of discontent among the Métis was the presence of American fur traders along the border who were willing to pay good prices for furs to hunters or free traders from Rupert's Land and were only prevented from doing so by the Company's monopoly of trade, guaranteed by a charter issued nearly 180 years before and inappropriate to the circumstances that were emerging at the end of the 1840s.

News — old though it sometimes became during the process of transmission — travelled west with the fur brigades and the occasional individual travellers, so that a kind of primitive oral system of communication linked Fort Victoria in the far west with the Red River and ultimately with the settlements of Upper and Lower Canada. Incapable though they were of reading newspapers even if such had been available, there is little doubt that Isidore Dumont and the fellow hunters who travelled with him, Alexis Fisher and Petit Cayen, had a fair idea of what they could expect when they reached the Red River, and that they looked forward to the promise of excitement. But for Gabriel Dumont, still little over ten, and for the companions of his own age in the cavalcade wandering laboriously over the hills and parklands of the Carlton Trail, it was the immediate experiences of the road that were exciting, especially the adventure that set Gabriel on the way to becoming a legendary marksman among the Métis.

The party had crossed — with some difficulty because of the high spring waters — the two branches of the Saskatchewan and had made their way through the Touchwood Hills without any unusual incident. They were now traversing the descending prairie towards Fort Ellice, and one night they camped near a slough where the mosquitos were numerous and troublesome. Young Isidore and Gabriel were sent to make smudge fires on the windward side of the camp, and were gathering dry branches in a nearby copse when Gabriel heard the sound of many hooves. It was country the Sioux often raided, and he thought his family and their companions were about to be attacked by these traditional enemies of the Métis.

Gabriel ran to warn his father. He wanted to help in defending the encampment, and asked for one of the flintlock muskets the hunters carried with them. His father and the other hunters quickly put out the camp fires and went towards the copse. Isidore Dumont knelt and put his ear to the ground. He rose with a relieved look. His practiced ear had assessed the sounds in a way his son was not yet capable of doing. "They are no horsemen!" he said. "They are buffalo!" And a short while afterwards the great herd came surging out of the darkness; fortunately the copse divided them so that they ran on each side of the camp, which otherwise might have been trampled into the ground by the thousands of beating hooves. Gabriel was ashamed of his mistake, but afterwards, when the hunters and their families gathered around the relit camp-fire, his uncle

Alexis Fisher warded off the jests that were directed against the boy by pointing out that even if his power of distinguishing between sounds made by the hooves of buffaloes and sounds made by those of horses was not yet perfectly developed, his courage had been amply displayed, since when he thought the Sioux were coming he had not tried to hide in his mother's lap but had asked for a gun to fight them. He should have his gun, Fisher declared, and he picked a stubby trading musket that seemed fitted to the boy's stature and gave it to him. Gabriel treasured it and called it Le Petit — the Little One — and this name he transferred to his other guns to the end of his life, much as a lover of horses or dogs will record his joy in the company of the animals who have died by conferring their names on those who succeed them. Very soon, by dint of diligent practice, Gabriel Dumont had become as fine a marksman with the gun as he was already with the Indian bow.

Isidore Dumont did not return to the Métis villages that had developed beside the Red River in his absence. He had not forgotten the claustrophobia he had felt even among such unenthusiastic agriculturists as those of St. Boniface and St. Vital, and he preferred to settle at White Horse Plains, which was not only the westerly outpost of the settlement, but was inhabited mostly by hunters after his own heart, who did not even make a pretense of becoming farmers, and who a few years later were to arouse the disapproval of Henry Youle Hind because they grew no orchards (though wild plums and cherries grew freely in the prairie copses) nor even any gardens in the rich black soil of the Plains. In fact, by 1848 White Horse Plains had become little more than a camp of nomads living in rough shacks near the Assiniboine and spending the greater part of their years wandering in search of pemmican, hides, and furs, as Isidore Dumont proceeded to do.

Not many months after his family's return to the Red River region, Gabriel Dumont — a boy not yet twelve — had his first sight of rebellion. Over the winter from 1848 to 1849 the tension between the Métis and the Hudson's Bay authorities had been building up. The Company was trying desperately to sustain a trading monopoly which circumstances had already superseded, and the Métis were incited by the American merchants in Pembina and St. Paul, who now had annexation as well as trade in

52

their minds. Moreover, the literate minority among the Métis — more numerous on Red River than by the Saskatchewan — had undoubtedly learnt of the rebellions that in 1848 had swept Europe and, when the great Chartist demonstrations assembled in London, had set fear even in the hearts of British rulers.

The conflict became open in the spring of 1849, when the Governor of the Hudson's Bay Company prosecuted Pierre Guillaume Sayer and three other Métis for trading illegally in furs. There was no doubt that the defendants had been trading; they tried to evade the charges by maintaining that they had received the furs as presents from their Indian relatives and had given whiskey in return, but this was the form trading with the Indians customarily took, and there was no convincing denial on the part of the Métis of the charge that they had in fact broken the Company's monopoly by trading the furs south of the border instead of taking them to Fort Garry.

But, as the Governor found, there was a vast difference between proving technical guilt and imposing any kind of sanction that would reinforce the Company's monopoly. James Sinclair, a leading Scottish half-breed, organized the defence and, in the absence of any lawyers except for Adam Thom who presided over the trial as Recorder of Rupert's Land, acted as advocate for the defendants. Perhaps more potent than Sinclair's defence was the fact that — as the trial took place on 17 May just before the departure of the summer buffalo hunts — the Métis hunters, the wild nomads of the prairies, were gathered either in the Red River villages or at White Horse Plains, and on the day of the trial rode in their hundreds to assemble clamorously outside the court house at Fort Garry. In so far as their presence was part of a planned agitation rather than a spontaneous outburst of mingled resentment and high spirits, it appears to have been the work of a miller named Louis Riel, whose son and namesake would later become the leader of the Métis nation in two much more serious rebellions. Though we have no record of his presence, it is unlikely that Isidore Dumont would have been absent from such an exciting occasion in the normally dull life of the Red River settlement, and we can imagine him among the crowd of armed and shouting hunters, and Gabriel among the boys who watched and cheered from the middle distance.

The jury's conclusion was a technical victory, but an actual defeat, for the Hudson's Bay Company. The verdict was that Sayer had indeed been guilty of trading in furs, but the jury recommended mercy "as it appeared he thought he had a right to trade, and as he and others were under the impression that there was a free trade." The excited Métis, perhaps because of their not very fluent knowledge of English, took this to mean that there was indeed a free trade, and immediately the crowd outside the courthouse began to shout, "Le commerce est libre! Vive la liberté!" and to fire off a *feu de joie* with the loaded guns they had brought with other possibilities in mind. It was obvious now even to the Company's officers that another such confrontation might end much less happily, and from this point trade was indeed free in so far as Métis hunters could wander without hindrance as pedlars among the Indians of the prairies and the fringes of the boreal forest. In fact, it made less difference to the Company than might have been expected, for, as Arthur S. Morton remarked in his monumental *History of the Canadian West,* the Métis "had neither the capital nor the organization to penetrate into the wooded North whence the Company derived its wealth of furs. Bands could wander with their Red River carts up the valley of the Assiniboine, and even to and beyond the Saskatchewan. . . . Even so, not all their furs went to the United States, for they often found themselves in need of supplies and forced to trade their furs for such at the nearest post of the Company." Nevertheless, from this point, the traditional link between the Métis and the fur-trading companies grew steadily looser.

The following month Isidore set off with his family on the annual hunt, which made rendezvous at Pembina and then proceeded west as before to the hunting grounds in Dakota, where the Métis were fortunate and encountered neither American cavalry nor hostile Sioux. By this time Gabriel was old enough to play almost a man's role, looking after the carts, swimming the horses across rivers, shooting small game, helping to skin the buffalo his father shot, and assisting in every duty of the hunt except for the actual killing of the buffalo, which was an arduous feat even for grown-up men. After returning from this hunt with pemmican and robes to be sold at Fort Garry, Isidore travelled west again with a load of trade goods and settled for the winter in the neighbourhood of Fort Qu'-Appelle, where he built one of the rough square Métis cabins of logs laid horizontally, and carried on a trade with the local Indians, exchanging such goods as knives, hatchets, blankets, powder, and ball for buffalo robes, wolf and coyote pelts, and even a few fox and beaver skins. In the spring he returned to Fort Garry, and again in the summer of 1850 went on the buffalo hunt into the Missouri region. The hunt was still led by Jean-Baptiste Wilkie, whose active life as a hunter was drawing to an end, and it was accompanied by Father Lacombe, the newly arrived priest who would later become celebrated for his work among the Blackfoot as chaplain. Again it was a peaceful and successful hunt, and again the Dumont family spent a winter trapping and trading along the Qu'Appelle River.

The year 1851 began with the same pattern as other years: the springtime trek back to White Horse Plains and Fort Garry; the departure in mid-summer for the hunting grounds that straddled the international border. But this was to be the most dramatic of all the great buffalo hunts, climaxed by the battle of Grand Coteau. The White Horse Plains contingent, consisting of about three hundred persons, of whom sixty-seven were hunters, with two hundred carts, assembled on 15 June outside the church of St. François-Xavier that had recently been built in Grantown. It has been said that Isidore Dumont was the leader, but in fact he appears to have been merely one of the captains, and the actual leader was Baptiste Falcon, one of the sons of the Métis bard Pierre Falcon. The hunters were accompanied by Father Laflèche, Grand Vicar to the Bishop of St. Boniface, and later to achieve celebrity as the ultramontane Bishop of Three Rivers, one of the dedicated enemies of liberalism in Quebec.

Four or five days after they had set out, the White Horse Plains party met the hunters from the Red River villages at Pembina; in all, the Red River contingent consisted of about a thousand people, of whom two hundred and fifty were hunters, with about nine hundred carts. Altogether there were fewer people and fewer carts than had taken part in the great hunt of 1840, and this was one of the many signs that the buffalo were beginning to withdraw too far into the western prairies for the Red River to remain much longer a viable hunting centre. The rendezvous itself was in fact no more than the prelude to a parting, for during the past months a disagreement had arisen between the Red River hunters and those from White Horse Plains. The reason for it is not known, though it has been conjectured that it arose over arguments about the way the Sayer case was conducted in 1849. Be that as it may, all that happened in the meeting at Pembina was a discussion of mutual defence against the Sioux, who were said to have lost patience with Métis incursions into their territory and to be planning an attack.

Once the leaders of the two groups and their captains had worked out a plan of moving southwestward on parallel routes, far enough apart not to interfere with each other's hunt (which meant an interval of between twenty and thirty miles), and had made arrangements to maintain communications in case either group needed help, they proceeded on separate ways. The White Horse Plains party, in which Gabriel Dumont (now thirteen) and his seventeen-year-old brother Isidore were both carrying guns, appears to have travelled in the direction of Devil's Lake in Dakota. On about 28 June, the larger party, which had taken a more southerly route, encountered a group of Sioux, but — in accordance with an agreement they had reached with the other Métis — they kept the Indians out of their camp and sent a warning to the White Horse Plains hunters. Soon afterwards both Métis groups approached, at different spots, the outlying ridges of the Grand Coteau, the great break in the land — partly in the United States but running northwesterly into Saskatchewan and dividing the basins of the Missouri and the Assiniboine — that forms the step between the two levels of the great plains of North America. It is not merely an escarpment created by the action of prairie rivers; it is also the remnant of a great moraine left over by the Ice Age. Edward McCourt, in his *Saskatchewan*, describes it thus:

> The Missouri Coteau is . . . a band, in the border country about fifty miles wide, of grotesquely tumbled earth, eroded clay hills, odd isolated buttes, dried-out lake bottoms hedged about by high clay banks. This is wild, desolate, brooding land — beautiful for a fleeting moment in spring when the grass and wild flowers pattern with colour the slopes of the

grey old hills; hot and dusty in summer (the dust fanned by furnace blasts that seem to have come hot from hell itself); melancholy in autumn, for there are few trees or shrubs to mask with glowing colours the coming hulk of death; and in winter a vast, snow-shrouded moon-surface from which all traces of life have been wiped clear away.

The Grand Coteau, like other nodes of rough hilly country in the prairies, was a great haunt of game, particularly as hunting became more intensive towards the mid-nineteenth century; it was also ideal country for ambushes and in general for the kind of guerilla fighting to which both Indians and Métis were addicted. The Métis advanced with scouts moving before them; on ascending the first high point of the Coteau, the scouts saw a great encampment of the Teton Sioux, which they estimated at four to five hundred lodges, or approximately twenty-five hundred warriors. It was an unusually large gathering for the plains Indians unless they were on the war path, and it actually signified a deliberate and concerted attempt to expel the Métis from what the Sioux regarded as their traditional hunting grounds. The scouts signalled a warning and the Métis immediately halted and proceeded to make camp in their characteristic defensive fashion, similar to the laager used by the Boers in fighting against the Bantu. They drew the two hundred carts into a circle, great wheel to wheel, with the shafts in the air. They thrust poles through the wheels from cart to cart so as to prevent any of the carts being pulled away from outside to make an opening. They stuffed their possessions and the bundles of meat and pemmican they had gathered under the carts to strengthen the barricade. Ponies and oxen were kept within the laager, and the women and children sheltered in shallow trenches dug behind the carts. Everyone took part in these preparations, men, women, and children, and the hunters themselves dug rifle-pits in open land, forming a ring about sixty yards outside the laager. Their fire from the ring of rifle pits would prevent the Indians getting near enough to the carts to do much damage to the animals gathered inside, for without their draft animals it would be hard, especially for the many women and children, to survive the journey back to the Red River.

While these defensive preparations were being made there had already been an encounter with the Sioux. Five of the hunters had been sent forward to reconnoitre, and they seem to have behaved with a singular foolhardiness, climbing to the top of a bluff to look at the Indian camp below them and then riding boldly towards the camp itself. A group of Indian braves under the war chief White Horse rode out to meet them and immediately, before parley, surrounded them. It was obvious that the Métis scouts were being taken prisoner, and two of them broke away and galloped back under fire to the carts; the three others, Jérome Magdalis, Baptiste Malaterre, and James Whiteford, were held by the Sioux.

The Métis immediately prepared to fight. Sixty-four hunters remained, and there were also thirteen boys who could handle a gun, Gabriel Dumont among them. Isidore Dumont appears to have hesitated about putting his young son into one of the rifle pits, but Gabriel insisted and stayed at his post throughout the fight, though it is not certain that — as his legend asserts — he killed his first man on this day; he himself does not appear to have made that claim, and Gabriel Dumont could never be accused of an excess of modesty. Father Laflèche did not take a gun, and remained within the laager to comfort the women and children, though with some of them this was quite evidently unnecessary, since Isabelle Falcon and other women took guns and at crucial moments fired on the Indians from between the carts. The good abbé kept an axe beside him, and intended to go down fighting if the circle of carts were breached.

And indeed, there were moments during the following hours when such a disaster seemed an imminent possibility. The Sioux had approached the laager after they took their hostages. They claimed that, because strangers were hunting over their territories, they were in great need. They promised to return next day to give back the prisoners, and hoped they would then receive some gifts. Neither Falcon nor Laflèche trusted them, and when another group of three Indians rode near later in the day, ten of the hunters rode out to prevent their approaching near enough to see the camp's defence system. Asked what they wanted, the Indians were evasive and rode away. The Métis settled down to guard their improvised fort. As soon as darkness fell they sent two men to alert the Red River party and bring help, and then they watched as the moon rose and soon afterwards was blacked out by the shadow of the earth in an eclipse that enables us to date the battle of the next day as having taken place on 13 June 1851.

At dawn Father Laflèche heard the confessions of the defenders and celebrated Mass under the open sky. Shortly afterwards the Indians appeared, the hundreds of warriors from the great camp, numberless in appearance to the watching Métis, gaudy in their war panoply, with the early sunlight flashing on their guns and the tips of their lances, with their warsongs rising on the cold morning air. The Sioux halted some distance away from the camp, and thirty Métis hunters rode out to meet them. At the head of the Indian advance guard rode White Horse, unarmed out of contempt for his opponents, and carrying a kind of rattle made of a hide bag filled with lead shot, which he shook as he rode forward singing. As the parties approached each other, the Métis saw that their three captured comrades were among the Indians. All at once Jérome Magdalis made a bid for escape and, as his horse was a good one, succeeded in reaching his friends before the Indians could overtake him. He was obviously terrified by what he had seen and heard among the Sioux, and he warned the Métis not to let the Indians near the camp, since they intended to destroy it and everyone within it.

The Métis now offered presents to White Horse and his fellow chiefs, and asked them to turn back. White Horse ignored both presents and petitions. If the Métis did not give him what he wanted, he said, he could take their whole camp with ease. And with that he signalled his braves who began to ride forward while the Métis wheeled and galloped back to their camp. The Indians tried to intercept them, but their ponies were not so fast as those of the half-breeds, who were able to ride into the laager, close the barricade of carts, and then creep out to their places in the rifle pits.

The Indian cavalry charged, headed by one of their best young chiefs, who was felled in the Métis volley. Baptiste Falcon claimed that he fired the first shot; there are other accounts that attribute the act to young Isidore Dumont and one of his Laframboise cousins, firing simultaneously. The Indians wheeled away, leaving several men and horses dead on the ground. It was in the confusion caused by this charge and its repulse that the two other prisoners tried to escape. Whiteford, who had a good horse, succeeded; Malaterre, whose horse was inferior, could not keep ahead of his pursuers, and fell to the ground under their fire. After the battle, it was found that his body had three bullet wounds and was pierced with sixty-seven arrows. It was also mutilated, for the Indians lopped off various extremities and organs and waved them on lances to terrify the Métis.

In all this, Father Laflèche, wearing his vestments, paraded within the camp with his crucifix held high, exhorting the defenders, a sight Gabriel Dumont and some of his companions must have remembered when it seemed to repeat itself more than thirty years later as they lay in the rifle pits of Batoche and Louis Riel carried his cross as he encouraged them in their fight against another and a more numerous enemy.

But Batoche, fought in the same way as Grand Coteau, would end in defeat for the Métis, since the enemy would be better equipped as well as more numerous. At Grand Coteau it was the Métis who were better equipped and who, using their wagons as mobile forts, had evolved — in an unknown number of skirmishes forgotten to history — a kind of warfare in advance of any yet seen on the great plains. And so Grand Coteau became their great victory. After the failure of their first charge, the Sioux spent many hours skirmishing around the defences, but achieved no more than to expose themselves to the fire of the Métis, well hidden in their pits. The Sioux surrounded the camp so completely that none of the Métis could get out; on the other hand, none of the Indians ever got near enough for an arrow to fall inside the laager, though occasionally one of their gun shots found its target in some unfortunate pony or ox. Through the day the fighting continued desultorily, and the Métis sweated as they lay at the alert under the hot mid-day sun without water and only occasionally with food; Gabriel Dumont was fortunate, since some sacks of dried meat served the function of sandbags at his rifle pit and so, as he afterwards jested, he was able to "eat the ramparts". During the afternoon the Sioux attempted a second assault, which turned out as costly and unsuccessful as the first, and then, dispirited by their loss of men, they retreated in the Indian manner, a few at a time, until finally the prairie around the camp was empty of them. One chief, it is said, cried out: "The Wagon-men have a Manitou with them. That is why we cannot kill them." And indeed it is possible that in the Indian mind the presence and the strange ritualistic gestures of the robed Father Laflèche may have seemed connected with the disconcerting fact that they were being killed and the Métis were not, and with the sudden thunderstorm that made them finally retreat towards their lodges.

Once the Indians had gone, the Métis went out, accompanied by Father Laflèche, to find and bury Malaterre's body. Then they held council and decided to retreat in the direction of the Red River party. They had to take into account the possibility of being attacked as they marched away at the pace of their pack animals, and so, the next morning, they threw out a screen of scouts and formed the carts into four columns so arranged that they could quickly be swung around to form a square. They had travelled little more than an hour when the scouts signalled that the Sioux were in pursuit and the defence plan had to be put into operation. Once again the Sioux charged, with a great clamour of warcries and firing muskets, and once again they were thrown back. Then, as before, the skirmishing tactics were resumed, and they lasted for five hours, with the defences holding until the weather of the Coteau again favoured the Métis as another thunderstorm built up over its slopes. The Sioux made one last galloping, shouting, volleying circle around the laager, and then rode away. It was the end of the battle of Grand Coteau, for shortly afterwards the Red River hunters arrived, accompanied by three hundred Saulteaux Indians, traditional enemies of the Sioux, and the combined column of almost seven hundred fighting men was too large for the Sioux to consider attacking after they had failed to defeat a party a tenth its size.

In terms of the world's battles, Grand Coteau was minute. Métis traditions asserted that eighty Indians were killed; Father Lacombe, who accompanied the rescue party but was not present for the battle, maintained that the number was only eighteen. It was probably somewhere in between the two. As for the Métis, Malaterre was the only one of them killed in the two days of fighting. Three were wounded, including the elder Isidore Dumont, but the wounds were slight, and more important as casualties were the twelve cart-ponies and the four oxen that were killed because there was really no way of adequately protecting them.

Altogether, it was no mean achievement to have repelled such a large party of the most formidable warriors of the plains, the people who twenty-five years later would destroy Custer and his American cavalry column so effectively that only one riderless horse escaped. Certainly the fighting of the Dumonts and the Laframboises, the Falcons and the McGinnises and the other clans of White Horse Plains who took part in the battle led to a respect for the Métis on the part of the Sioux that created an uneasy truce over the next decade and even, later on, a kind of alliance. Never, with any of the Indians of the plains, did the Métis have to fight again a battle on the scale of the engagement of Grand Coteau.

Gabriel emerged unscathed and elated from his first battle; while still less than fourteen, he had gone through one of the testing experiences that in his world led to the recognition of manhood. During the ensuing years he became the expert hunter, translating his horsemanship and marksmanship (as John Kerr remembered, he could shoot a duck through the head at a hundred paces) into that union of movement and accuracy, that perfect combination of timing and aiming, which was achieved only by the best of the buffalo hunters when they galloped at full speed into the herd, firing as they rode with such precision that every beast they aimed at fell beside the path of their run.

During these years as adolescence passed rapidly into manhood, Gabriel's life was shaped by the changing pattern of the western buffalo hunt. The division between the Red River hunters and the White Horse Plains hunters was not resolved, and in 1852 there was not even the formality of a meeting at Pembina. The White Horse Plains hunters went out on their own along the Assiniboine and across the Souris River, led by the prematurely aged Cuthbert Grant. It was Grant's last hunt; two years later he would be dead, and other hunters, Pierre Gariepy and later Isidore Dumont, would take over the leadership of the band of hunters, for whom White Horse Plains became each year a less attractive wintering place. A division within the Métis nation had appeared that was not resolved until the early 1880s, and not even completely then: the division between the people of the Red River Valley, whose inclination was increasingly to accept the settled life, agriculture, and consequent assimilation, and the people of the western prairies, who sought to prolong as long as they could the old free life they inherited from their predecessors, the *coureurs de bois*. The hunters of the Red River were mostly men who traditionally had hunted into regions now incorporated into the United States; the hunters from White Horse Plains were those who, from old association with the North West Company, had some knowledge and often a long experience, as in the case of the sons of Jean-Baptiste Dumont, of the Saskatchewan River territory and the Athapaska country beyond it. Circumstances in the 1850s, and particularly the spread of American power in the mid-west below the 49th parallel and the northwestward drift of the buffalo herds, made the hunters of White Horse Plains turn increasingly towards these remote and northerly regions. Not only did they begin to seek hunting grounds that were farther away, towards Blackfoot and Cree rather than Sioux territory, but they began also to winter increasingly often in such regions. In the years after Grand Coteau, the Dumont family wintered at least as frequently around Fort Ellice as at White Horse Plains, though the Red River remained for a long time their principal trading centre.

When the White Horse Plains hunt turned back towards the ancestral haunts of the Dumont family in the Saskatchewan Valley beyond Fort Ellice, Gabriel Dumont and his brothers were immersed, as their father and uncle had been, in that dynamic mingling of various Indian peoples and the Métis that characterized the western plains of Rupert's Land in the mid-nineteenth century. A general feeling of cousinship made the presence of the Métis acceptable — if not always joyfully welcomed — wherever the Plains Cree were dominant, as they were in the northern parklands as far west as Edmonton. The special ancestry of the Dumonts, however, gave them access not only to the Cree but also to their relatives, the Sarcee, and, indirectly through the Sarcee, to the other tribes of the Blackfoot confederacy, with whom, in later years, they eventually became great treaty makers. It was during this period of riding the western prairies when they were still inhabited by so many notable peoples at the height of their cultures and their well-being — by the Blackfoot and the Blood, by the Gros Ventres and the Sarcee, by the Assiniboine and the Plains Cree — that Gabriel Dumont perfected not only his unexampled skills in prairie ways of hunting and fighting, but also his knowledge of the languages spoken by almost every tribe north of the international boundary, as well as by the Sioux who lived to the south.

The legends of Gabriel Dumont in this period when boyhood so quickly gave way to manhood are manifold and romantic. He developed almost unconsciously the reckless style admired in the whole frontier culture that stretched from the Saskatchewan down into Mexico; he was, as the Mexicans would say, *muy hombre.* John Kerr remembered both his first meeting with Gabriel in 1872 and his last in 1876 as having been celebrated over the opened heads of kegs of brandy. Kerr also claimed to have seen Gabriel spending three whole days and nights at cards, though one is inclined to wonder where in that virtually cashless economy of the pre-settlement Northwest the means for such prolonged gambling sessions could have existed. And, indeed, many of the exploits of the youthful Gabriel Dumont as they have passed down through oral and literary tradition, with little confirmatory documentation, have a flavour that reminds one of the early cinema of the Wild West and the printed romances that preceded it.

When I first read some of the exploits attributed to this young Gabriel Dumont in the 1850s by a popular biography sold on prairie newstands, I felt it impossible to restrain a sense of *déjà vu,* bound up with the recollections of the four-penny Buffalo Bill romances of my childhood.

There was, for example, the romance which told how, at the age of eighteen, Gabriel was in a Cree camp when one of the braves staggered in with his scalp almost torn off, having been ambushed by the Blackfoot, who had carried off his wife. Gabriel was bound to the man through some past link of brotherhood and so, with Cree companions, he crept at night

64

into a camp of twenty-five Blackfoot warriors, slit the side of the teepee where the woman was imprisoned, slaughtered a few Blackfoot sentries, scattered the band's horses, and then rode tandem into the dawn with the liberated lady, a Cree Pearl White.

Another story tells how, with a notable Métis firebrand named Louis Marion who was one of his hunting companions as long as the buffalo lasted, Gabriel Dumont crept to the edge of another Blackfoot camp where the braves were dancing around a fire on which a pot of meat was boiling. As they capered grotesquely, each brave in turn speared a lump of meat and spoke the name of a Cree warrior he had killed. After the two Métis had watched for a while this gruesome ritual, Gabriel leapt into the circle. Instead of seizing their weapons to deal with the intruder, the Blackfoot apparently gaped in astonishment as the Métis danced forward to spear his morsel and shout: "I am Gabriel Dumont! I have killed eight Blackfoot! What do you say to that?" Even now, according to the legend, these men who had the repute of being the proudest and fiercest warriors of the plains sat silent in their amazement, until the highest chief who was present admiringly offered his hand and congratulated Gabriel Dumont on his courage. Afterwards, continues the legend, the Dumonts led the other Métis to a meeting with the Blackfoot where a treaty was pledged between the two peoples.

I have been unable to find any reliable evidence to support either of these two stories, though encounters with the Blackfoot certainly took place, since as the Métis began to hunt farther west they could not avoid encroaching on territory where the Blackfoot also hunted. To my mind the crucial fact is that Gabriel Dumont, who was never modest in talking of his own feats and even gained the reputation of being a braggart among Canadians in the Northwest, never seems to have claimed either to have killed eight Blackfoot or to have perilously defied the Blackfoot by boasting of it.

However, when he was an old man of sixty-five, Dumont did talk to an anonymous admirer whose notes in French were preserved in the archives of the Union Métisse de Saint-Joseph and eventually found their way into the Manitoba Provincial Archives. On this occasion he told three tales of adventure during his youth which have a pristine credibility lacking in the two narratives I have just paraphrased; they project quite a different personality, a personality nearer to Homer than to Hollywood and undoubtedly nearer to the true spirit of life in the far prairies when the buffalo still seemed as inexhaustible as the proud ways of hunters seemed immortal.

Each story tells of a simple encounter; only one tells of a killing, and that with little boasting. In the first tale, Dumont is riding on the prairie and sees a horseman approaching. He recognizes him as a Blood and therefore an enemy of the Cree with whom the Métis are in alliance. The machismo of the prairies comes into operation, and like knight errants in the old romances the two men rush at each other as fast as their horses will carry them, each hoping the other will lose courage and turn tail. Neither does, and everything happens so quickly that before the Indian, who is carrying a bow, can get an arrow out of his quiver, their horses collide shoulder to shoulder. The Indian cannot stop his horse quickly enough, but Gabriel pulls his pony back on its haunches, turns sharply, and overtakes the Blood, grabbing him so fiercely by the arm and round the waist that the Indian does not attempt to defend himself. He lets Gabriel lead him back to his camp, where he is given a pipe which he smokes sitting on his horse, and then, being told he can leave, flees as fast as he can ride. Two decades later, when Gabriel was making peace between the Cree and other Indian tribes, he recognized in a high chief named Bull's Hide his former prisoner, and they greeted each other as brothers.

The touch of the rough but generous jester that appears in this story is intensified in its successor. This time Gabriel is acting as scout for the buffalo hunt; it must have been in his early manhood, the days before he became a hunt leader. To look out over the plains for herds or foes, he hobbles his horse at the foot of a butte, which he climbs, but instead of exposing himself to view on the summit he crawls belly-flat among the hillside boulders. On the opposite hill he sees an upright shape which he knows must be a living being, though he cannot tell whether it is kneeling man or seated wolf. If it moves off horizontally, he thinks, lengthening as it moves, it will be a wolf. If it lowers itself to the ground, it will be a man on the same scouting mission as himself. The shape in fact lowers itself to the

66

ground, so Gabriel returns to the foot of his bluff, mounts his horse, rides circumspectly to the back of the hill where he saw the shape, hobbles his horse again, and climbs cautiously upward. What he sees is a Gros Ventre Indian, a potential enemy, sleeping on the ground, with his gun beside him. Gabriel creeps forward, inch by inch, without waking the Indian, until he can lift the gun out of the man's reach. But how shall he wake the man? Reasoning that with a member of a hostile tribe there is no need for the niceties of introduction, he decides to do it with the big whip of plaited hide he carries with him. He stands over the man and lashes out with all his strength. The Indian starts awake with an expression of uncomprehending terror, and then kneels at Gabriel's feet with his head bowed and covered with his arms. Gabriel bursts into laughter, and the Gros Ventre, looking up at him, realizes that no harm is intended, and also begins to laugh, yet he is so shaken that when he sits down beside his assailant to smoke with him, he trembles so much that he can hardly hold the pipe. Finally Dumont stands up and gives the Indian his gun. Together they walk back towards Gabriel's horse, but when he is about to bend down and unhobble the animal, he feels a twinge of apprehension. Might not the Gros Ventre shoot him when his back is turned? So Gabriel signs to the Indian to go to his own horse, which is standing nearby, and he does this and flees "at full speed as if the devil were after him", while Gabriel rides back to report to his companions of the hunt.

The third story is a darker one, lacking the sardonic humour of those I have just related and illustrating how the honour code of the prairies could sometimes force a man half-willingly into an act that troubled his memory. It is the one story of an actual killing we have from Dumont's mouth before the rebellion of 1885, though the suggestion runs through the tale that this was not the first time he had been responsible for a man's death.

On this occasion he is leading a small group of Métis hunters who have put up their six or seven tents on the edge of a friendly Cree encampment. One day when he is away hunting, a Cree chief comes and commandeers a horse tethered outside Dumont's tent. Gabriel is annoyed, less for the sake of the horse as a piece of property than because of the disrespect im-

67

plied, and that evening, as the Crees hold a war dance to warm
them up for an expected encounter with the Blackfoot, he goes
to the ceremonial lodge, enters it, and sits down among the
women. When the dance has ended, he goes among the braves
and begins to deliver the kind of harangue he knows they will
appreciate, telling how he is feared by his enemies, and respected
by his friends for his horsemanship and marksmanship, the two
qualities most admired by the peoples of the prairies. Now, by
taking his horse, they have offended him, and he does not mean
to accept the offence.

The Crees declare that they have no desire to offend him,
but that it is their custom on the eve of a battle to require that
not only the members of the band, but also their friends and
allies, give their best horses to fight against the enemy. Gabriel
declares his indifference to their laws. But he promises to fight
beside them in order to show what he can do. If any of their
warriors can overtake him in rushing on the enemy, then they
can have his horse; but if he is foremost in battle, then they will
have no right to touch his property without his consent. They
agree, and the next day, when the Crees encounter the Blackfoot, he goes with them. As the two bands approach each other,
one Blackfoot, braver than the rest, rides forward alone, singing
his warsong. Gabriel dashes at him, and the Blackfoot turns and
flees, but the Métis catches up with him, "as if he were a
buffalo," and when he is almost beside him fires from the hip.
The Indian falls forward under the nose of Gabriel's horse,
which rears with such violence that he is almost thrown, but he
rights himself and seizes the Blackfoot's pony. As he rides back,
he sees that the Indian is dead.

"And that made me sad," Dumont exclaimed when he told
the tale long afterwards, "for he had never done me any harm."
It was the code of the prairie that made him kill the man. "I
killed him," he summed up the tale, "to show the Cree that I
was better than they were, so that they should respect me." Such
respect was not merely demanded by Dumont's pride as a Métis.
It was also an element in survival, for in that world of anarchic
egoists which was prairie society before the law moved in with
the North West Mounted Police, to prove one's ability in war
was indeed a way to be left in peace.

It was this tough, resourceful, and rather ruthless young

68

man who at the beginning of his twenties accepted the responsibilities of manhood, marriage, and eventually leadership. He was not — existing photographs confirm the accounts of those who knew him — an example of the dark handsomeness that sometimes resulted from the mingling of French and Indian stocks. His features were rough-hewn, often clouded with a scowl. His black mane of hair derided his straggly beard, and though he was light on his feet and swift in movement, his great chest and shoulders gave him a bulky, top-heavy look. Yet with his courage and fury, with the slight regard for life that went with the hunter's trade, he combined loyalty and good sense, generosity, a surprising gentleness towards the young and the unfortunate. There would be times when Gabriel Dumont acted brutally: never times when he acted meanly.

3. Returning West

The year 1858 was in many ways unfortunate. It was the time of one of the great smallpox epidemics, when men shunned each other, even in the vast expanses of the prairie, for fear of catching the dread sickness. The buffalo was hunted, for life must go on, though there was little trading, and even those who avoided the pestilence lived on short commons.

It was also the year when Gabriel's mother died, as the clan was wandering in the Saskatchewan valley; the smallpox did not kill her, but it is possible that she died of consumption, already a dark scourge among the Métis. Five years later, Isidore would be married again, to a French widow named Angèle Landry from the Red River, and by her he would have the last three of his eleven children, Marguerite, Azilda, and a second Joseph. These late-borne siblings were to play no significant role in Gabriel Dumont's life, though the bond between the sons of Louise Laframboise remained strong to the end of their lives.

It was also during 1858 that Gabriel Dumont married Madeleine Wilkie. Jean-Baptiste Wilkie had ceased to hunt, and now he was a trader at Fort Ellice, where in recent years Gabriel had spent several winters. However, the marriage was celebrated by a French missionary priest, Father Joseph Goiffon, in the little Métis village of St. Joseph, south of the border in Dakota. St. Joseph, which the Métis called St. Joe, had recently replaced Pembina as a Métis centre in the United States, and in the late 1850s it had become the point of rendezvous for the dwindling remnant of the buffalo hunt from the Red River.

Madeleine Dumont, from the scanty accounts of her that have survived, appears as a typically hardworking and resourceful Métis woman, reared in the tough prairie childhood of hunting and camp life. If any photograph was taken of her, which is unlikely, it has not survived, and she lived too much in Gabriel's massive shadow for anyone who knew him to have thought of saying what she looked like. Like most of the Métis women, she was pious, without Gabriel's streak of anti-clericalism, was hospitable to missionaries, and had the repute of being compassionate and helpful to people less fortunate than she. She could endure long journeys, on horseback in summer and in winter on snowshoes, and she thought nothing, while Gabriel remained to hunt on the Saskatchewan, of travelling down the Carlton Trail to Winnipeg in the company of other Métis to sell the skins and hides her husband had obtained by trapping or trading. She had an advantage in such small commercial matters because, unlike Gabriel, she spoke English.

Madeleine and Gabriel were intensely loyal to each other, and there seems to have been a special touch of companionship in their marriage; once when an Indian had behaved offensively to her, Gabriel remarked: "We are always together, and what is done to her is as if it were done to me." Madeleine's greatest regret was that she had no children by Gabriel, and it was his regret too, for he was fond of children and good with them, as a few old men in Batoche who were young during his old age can still remember. But he never seems to have thought of the situation as anything more than a shared misfortune, which they tried to alleviate by adopting a child named Annie, born of unknown parentage on the Red River in 1863 and possibly a Scottish half-breed related to Madeleine. Annie remains a shadowy figure in Dumont's life, and she faded out of it completely after Madeleine's death, leaving the Métis world and eventually marrying an American named William Allen Hamilton and dying in Calgary. The affection Gabriel might have given a son seems to have been directed mainly towards young Alexis Dumont, whom he called his nephew; in fact, the boy was the son of his cousin Jean, and grandson of old Isidore's brother of the same name.

Like his brother Isidore, Gabriel left the family group as soon as he was married, and now hunted on his own, except for the great communal hunting expeditions. Until the autumn of

1860, he returned at least once in the year to the Red River region and did business with the Hudson's Bay trader William Flett, in charge of Lower Fort Garry. Like his father and brother, Gabriel regarded rather lightly his indebtedness to the Company, for on 5 June 1862 the magistrate Robert McBeath handed in to the General Court a series of accounts sworn before him by Flett, which showed the elder Isidore in debt since August 1861, his son and namesake in debt for purchases in 1860 and 1861, and Gabriel in debt for 1859 and 1860.

Gabriel's list of purchases tells a great deal about his way of life, and the list of his sales to the Company leaves one with a better understanding of the way the hunters were exploited by the trading monopoly. In both years Gabriel appeared in September, at the end of the summer hunt from White Horse Plains.

In 1859 the hunt had set out in mid-June, and Lord Southesk passed through the village of White Horse Plains on the day before its departure. "The whole place was swarming with half-breed hunters and their families, who, with innumerable carts and horses, were gathering there preparatory to their start for the prairies on their great annual summer buffalo hunt. I was glad to escape from this scene of noise and confusion, when we were at length enabled to resume our march." Before resuming his march, Southesk bought a lean but hardy cart pony from one of Gabriel's Laframboise cousins, and may well have encountered Gabriel himself. On returning that year Gabriel stayed in the Red River region for at least two weeks, for he made his first purchases on 1 September, and his last on 14 September, when he bought ten shillingsworth of sundries and persuaded Flett to advance him £2 in cash. Clearly Flett regarded him as a reliable hunter and expected that he would be returning regularly to the Red River region. However, it was not until September 1860 that Gabriel came back with goods to offset his debt at least in part. He brought 343 pounds of pemmican, for which he received threepence a pound, one buffalo hide which he sold for five shillings, and a quantity of pounded meat and soft fat which he sold for 7/7, for a total of £4.18.4. He did not appear at all in 1861.

Against this credit, Gabriel bought goods to the value of £9.13.2 in 1859 and £1.4.0 in 1860. In the 1859 purchases Mad-

72

eleine's inspiration is obvious. There were four yards of green flannel and three of red, thirteen yards of print and eight of braid, five shillingsworth of ribbon, three steel thimbles, and a shillingsworth of needles; against that modest pile of material for feminine garments, Gabriel acquired a capote and a pair of cord trousers, a black cloth vest, a silk handkerchief, and three cotton handkerchiefs, the standard items that made the costume of Métis men at this period seem to outsiders as monotonously unvaried as a uniform. The scanty items of groceries suggest how self-sufficient, in terms of living almost entirely off the land, was the Dumont family economy; it consisted of one long bar of soap that cost four shillings, and ten pounds of tea; as Alexander Ross once remarked, the Métis "surpass everything yet heard of in the article of tea-drinking." Some halter rings and a couple of clasp knives completed the purchases with which Gabriel Dumont and Madeleine set off to winter in the prairies in 1859. When Gabriel came back in the same month of 1860 to sell his pemmican, he bought merely a counterpane and a hundredweight of flour for making galettes.

Such slight purchases in 1860, and the scanty amount of pemmican offered by so notable a hunter, suggest that Gabriel Dumont was already shifting the scene of his activities westward and trading with other Hudson's Bay posts, probably Fort Ellice and Fort Carlton, as well as, perhaps, with the American traders who filtered north over the border in the days before the North West Mounted Police began to patrol the Canadian plains. The American presence was evident in other ways. There is no doubt, for example, that the thrust of Yankee power into the prairies, soon to provoke the uprising of the Minnesota Sioux in 1862 followed by years of intermittent warfare in the old hunting grounds of the Red River Métis, turned the attention of the hunters of Rupert's Land more than ever towards the northern parklands and those hilly regions farther south in British territory, like the Touchwood Hills, Cypress Hills, and Wood Mountain, where the buffalo at certain seasons tended to gather in large numbers. Many of the hunters who had once wintered regularly at White Horse Plains now settled in cold-weather shacks near Fort Ellice or around the lakes on the Qu'-Appelle River near Fort Qu'Appelle; others, including the Dumonts and the Laframboises, moved in a northwesterly direction, and already in 1860 there were winter camps in the Touchwood Hills and around Duck Lake. One effect of this permanent occupation of the land by Métis hunters, following the buffalo in summer and autumn, and turning to the lakes in winter for supplies of fish which they preserved by freezing, was a rapid diminution in the abundance of wildlife Paul Kane had observed in the 1840s. If buffalo had then been shot outside and even inside the stockades of the Saskatchewan forts, in 1862 Milton and Cheadle were to report: "The buffalo have receded so far from the forts, and the quantity of whitefish from the lakes, one of the principal sources of supply, has decreased so greatly, that now a winter rarely passes without serious suffering from want of food. . . . The days when it was possible to live in plenty by the gun and net alone, have already gone by on the North Saskatchewan."

It was at this time in the Red River region, even more affected by the decline in hunting, that the land question became more insistent than ever before, as the local Métis — reluctantly facing the possibility of having to live by farming and stock-raising — began to reproach the Hudson's Bay Company for not having followed a just land policy. The Métis asserted their claims as heirs to the Indians, now a declining remnant in the Red River valley, and at a meeting in the village of Winnipeg in March 1860, they and the English half-breeds united in describing themselves as "natives" and in declaring that they were not merely "present occupants", but also "representatives of the first owners of the soil, with whom no satisfactory arrangement ever has been made."

In the Saskatchewan country there as yet appeared no need to make such assertions of aboriginal title, for the Indians were the only people likely to dispute the right of the Métis to camp and hunt, and the ties of actual relationship and of adoptive brotherhood between the two groups were strong enough to make serious disputes, at least between the Métis and the Cree, extremely rare. Even with the other tribes, as the threat from the common white enemy became more pressing, the incidence of overt hostility between them and the Métis declined notably, and during the later 1860s the Métis began to assume in the prairies the special role of go-betweens and peacemakers, which

74

gave them a status rather like that of the taboo-men in ancient Polynesia, who passed between warring tribes, often mediating their differences.

One can indeed almost date the shift in the relationship between the Métis and the Indians, which preluded a gradual cessation of warfare among the Indians themselves in the face of the common threat that spread its shadow over the prairies, whether that shadow was cast by American Longknives or Canadian Redcoats.

In 1861 there was still a great deal of fighting between the Métis and the Blackfoot over the theft of half-breed horses, while in August 1862, when they arrived at Fort Ellice, Milton and Cheadle found that "The half-breed hunters had just been driven in by the Sioux, who had killed four of their party, having surprised them while cutting wood away from the camp. The remainder of the half-breeds came up, however, and drove them off, killing one, whose bow and arrow they showed us."

It is possible that these "half-breed hunters" may have been the band with whom Gabriel Dumont was at this time associated, for it is certain that later in 1862 the leading members of the Dumont clan, Gabriel and old Isidore and Jean, took a leading role in a meeting south of the border at Devil's Lake between the Métis and the Dakota Sioux, apprehensive of American aggression and therefore anxious to make peace with other enemies. Some writers have claimed that Gabriel Dumont led the negotiations from the Métis side, but John Kerr, who knew the Dumonts only ten years afterwards, was emphatic that the principal discussions, which led to a lasting peace between the Métis and the Sioux, were actually carried out by Isidore and Jean. Gabriel was present, however, and he remembered long afterwards how at one of the meetings, as he was leaving the lodge where talks were taking place, a Sioux who held a grudge against him hit him on the head with the barrel of a gun and at the same time pulled the trigger; fortunately the gun misfired, Gabriel suffered no more than a bruised scalp, and the Sioux was disarmed and beaten by his own fellows who were not only shamed by this slur on their hospitality but were also anxious for there to be no hitch in securing the treaty. From this time onward the records of skirmishes between the Métis and Indians of any tribe sharply decline, though formal peace with the Blackfoot does not appear to have been concluded until some years later.

About this time Gabriel Dumont became the leader of a small camp of hunters who travelled together even when the great hunts were not in progress. Shortly afterwards a number of Métis bands moved from the Touchwood Hills region and made Fort Carlton their centre. Among them were more than two hundred hunters, who decided to set up an organization for regulating their hunts similar to that of the Red River expeditions. Isidore Dumont, a former leader of the White Horse Plains hunt, would have been the obvious choice for leader, but in 1863 he went to Red River to live with his new wife Angèle Landry and bring up his second family, while his brother Jean went south to the Cypress Hills and lived in the little hamlet of Métis winter houses at Chimney Coulée. There remained no real rival to Gabriel Dumont, and in the summer of 1863 he was elected leader of the Saskatchewan hunt; he was twenty-five. From that time he was the virtual chief of the Métis who wintered in the Saskatchewan region. During the hunt, when his people rode south to join their companions from Fort Ellice and Qu'Appelle in the Cypress Hills, which was now their point of rendezvous, he was the unquestioned leader, wielding as much authority as an Indian war chief in time of battle, and administering the traditional rules of the hunt without favour or fear. Authority had its obligations, among the Métis as in other simple societies, and at each hunt Gabriel would make at least one free run through the herd, dedicating the beasts he then slaughtered to the old and the sick who could not hunt for themselves; it was an example he expected other good hunters to follow, and so the band he led was contented with his leadership, for in the austere terms of prairie living nobody was allowed to want. At other times, when the anarchic Métis community atomized itself into family units, he would spend his time hunting more solitary game than the buffalo, trapping, fishing, trading with Indians for their furs, and guiding the geographers and missionaries and aristocratic travellers who began to wander through the Northwest as the Company's rule in Rupert's Land slowly rotted away.

*

The missionaries Gabriel guided were now bringing other messages than those of religion. They not only sought to convert the Indians from paganism to Christianity; they were also intent on converting the Métis from nomadism to a settled life. It was not merely that they found a stable flock more easy to educate and influence than a wandering one, though that consideration did exist; also, looking with clear outsiders' eyes at the prairie way of life, based so disproportionately on the pursuit of one species of ruminant, they realized that such an existence would not last much longer, because the buffalo could not be hunted indefinitely on the scale of the 1860s without soon becoming extinct. And when the buffalo vanished, the Métis — and the Indians — would have only the land over which they now roamed so freely and so carelessly. But other men were already casting acquisitive eyes on that land. Gentlemen like Lords Southesk and Milton might travel as amateur explorers, intent on regaling the gatherings of the Royal Geographical Society in London with accounts of their adventures in the wilderness, but men like Hind and Palliser, both of whom appeared before the end of the 1860s to carry out scientific explorations, were the representatives of interests in Britain and eastern Canada that saw the prairies not only as a great reserve of land in which to settle the destitute of Britain and even of other European countries, but also in political terms as a region that must be claimed and settled and policed if it were not to fall into the hands of American politicians and speculators. The alternative to American politicians and speculators was all too often to be Canadian politicians and speculators, and this to a degree the missionaries foresaw when they set out to persuade the Métis to settle down and establish at least a right of occupancy to the land they would need when the buffalo vanished.

Already, by 1868, the temporary winter villages of hastily erected shacks usually abandoned in the spring were being replaced by more durable settlements, of which the first was a place, long vanished, that in recollection became known as La Petite Ville, on the western bank of the South Branch of the Saskatchewan, opposite Fish Creek and not for north of the present site of Saskatoon. Here Gabriel Dumont reigned, and it was here that Father Alexis André, who had already preached among the Métis at Pembina, appeared in 1868, "to visit—as he put it—a few patriarchal families of Métis." His was not the first missionary activity in the locality, for downriver at Prince Albert the Presbyterians had already established themselves in 1867. The Presbyterians made little impression on the Indians and less on the Métis, and their mission was to assume importance mainly as a focal point for the white settlers who began to arrive in the 1870s. But Father André, and the other Oblate missionaries who followed him and worked with him, Fourmond and Vegreville and Moulin, became part of Métis life and changed it by their presence.

Father André was a man made for the frontier and its stresses, as tough in fibre as Gabriel Dumont himself, whose friend and later whose enemy he became. He was, like many of the Oblates, "a stocky Breton," as one Quebec admirer described him, "with broad shoulders, muscles of steel . . . an obstinate man, with little constraint or etiquette" but who possessed "an excellent heart and a true zeal." Father André was in fact the French version of the nineteenth century muscular Christian, blunt and impetuous in speech and capable of striking one of his parishioners if he could do it with safety. He cared little for appearances. "This reverend father" — said the Mounted Policeman John Donkin who met him in 1885 — "always reminded me of those priests of the Greek church whom one sees hanging around the wharves at Galata. He wore a lofty cap of beaver, and a greasy cassock very much the worse for wear. In addition he sported an uncared-for beard of iron grey." In spite of its touch of malice, the description was reasonably accurate. But the very qualities that made Father André seem uncouth to the Englishmen and eastern Canadians who reached the Saskatchewan region in the 1880s made him acceptable to the Métis in the 1860s. His willingness to seek them out, to share their life, to bring the simple religious consolations which many of them treasured, were all in his favour, and his straightforward manner and harsh Breton French, not unlike their own rather archaic patois, appealed to men of Gabriel Dumont's character, so that an immediate trust was established between the missionary and the acknowledged chief of the local Métis, a trust that would soon lead to their co-operation in stabilizing the Métis society of the Saskatchewan.

4. Inevitable Change

I t was not long after Father André's arrival at
La Petite Ville that a series of events occurred that were to
transform the primitive little Métis settlements of the far west.
The Hudson's Bay Company sold Rupert's Land to the new
Dominion of Canada without consulting any of its inhabitants,
Indian, Métis, or white. Canadians who had already settled in
the Red River colony began to behave as if they were con-
querors, and even before the territory was transferred, the Canadian government illegally sent in its surveyors to mark out the
land. Having never received legal titles for their river lots, the
Métis were disturbed by these arbitrary actions, dictated by
ignorant and unimaginative politicians in Ottawa. Under the
leadership of young Louis Riel, the miller's son, who had been
educated in Quebec and given a little training in the law, they
set up first a National Committee of the Métis of the Red River
which stopped the Canadian Lieutenant-Governor as he tried
to cross the border at Pembina, and afterwards established a
Provisional Government under the presidency of Riel, supported by a militia of mounted Métis organized like the traditional buffalo hunt, with Ambroise Lépine as its general.

The history of Riel's temporary rule of Assiniboia and of the
negotiations by which that rule came to an end with the creation of the province of Manitoba has by now been often told,
and in any case it is beyond the range of this book. But its in-
direct effect on the Métis communities of the farther prairies is

pertinent, and so is the peripheral role that Gabriel Dumont played.

The news of events on the Red River caused great perturbation among the hunters of the western plains. The Hudson's Bay trader Isaac Cowie was at Qu'Appelle during 1869 and 1870, and in his memoirs, *The Company of Adventurers,* he records how all the independent Métis traders of the locality "and their friends were decidedly in favour of the Riel movement and against the Company, and did everything in their power to bring their fellow countrymen, both Métis and Indians, to their way of thinking." The news from Red River reached Qu'Appelle quickly "and as it was further spread by rumour all over the plains, produced a state of such unrest and excitement that the business of hunting came almost to a stop. Family after family of Métis came in from the plains to the lakes, to hear the latest news and take part in discussing it, and to be at hand to participate in any action taken in sympathy with, or in imitation of their fellows at Red River."

The Hudson's Bay men at Qu'Appelle feared that the local Métis would try to emulate Riel's seizure of Fort Garry by capturing their own fort, with its stores of arms and ammunition, and in their alarm they sent presents of tobacco to the friendly Cree chiefs of the region, who came with their braves and camped near the post during the period of greatest tension. But more influential, so far as the Qu'Appelle Métis were concerned, appears to have been the intervention of Pascal Bréland, a Métis member of the Council of Assiniboia and a leader of the anti-Riel faction among the half-breeds, who happened to be wintering on the prairies. Bréland, the son-in-law of Cuthbert Grant and a loyal supporter of the Company, appears to have played on the rivalry between the Red River hunters, who were supporting Riel, and the White Horse Plains hunters, most of whom were now in the West. His speech left "only a few of the more bitter partisans and extremists disaffected. Some of these rushed down to Fort Garry to share the spoil, but by the time they reached it the settlement had quieted down."

Though there are no similar reports of the situation in the Métis settlements on the South Branch, it is certain that their inhabitants were no less stirred by the news from Red River than those around Qu'Appelle, and that Gabriel Dumont was not only a "partisan" of Riel, but was also one of those who "rushed down to Fort Garry" to offer his support. There is a strong oral tradition among the Métis, particularly in the St. Laurent and Batoche region, of this trip to the Red River; some accounts even say that Gabriel went on two occasions, in 1869 to observe the situation then, and in 1870 to advise Riel to resist, by guerilla warfare, the British-Canadian forces advancing on Red River; it is also said he offered to come with five hundred mounted riders from the plains, and that Riel, who trusted the Canadians, refused his help.

Some writers have cast doubt on Dumont's presence at the Red River, but the evidence suggests that he went at least once. Dumont himself said that he met Riel at Fort Garry on 17 June 1870, and that he said to him, "Si tu fais quelquechose, envois-moi chercher, et je viendrai avec les sauvages." By "les sauvages" he may have meant either the Indians, to whom the Métis applied the word, or, with irony, his own "wild" hunters of the plains, as distinct from the "civilized" half-breeds of Red River. He also told how, when they met in Montana in 1884, Riel did not recognize him at first glance, but knew him immediately he mentioned his name, which can easily be explained by the fact that in fifteen years Dumont had changed from a young hunter to a heavy, middle-aged chieftain, and that at the end of June 1870, when Wolseley's forces were advancing towards Winnipeg, Riel saw many faces, and had too many things on his mind to remember those who appeared out of the distant prairies, offered desperate advice, and then departed.

There is no direct evidence other than Dumont's own accounts regarding this encounter with Riel in 1870, but at least two writers with special knowledge of the times were convinced that it took place. Adolphe Ouimet, a Quebec lawyer who took an active part in organizing Dumont's tour of French Canada in 1888-9 and who was present when Dumont dictated his recollections of the military operations at Fish Creek and Batoche, declared in his book, *La Vérité sur La Question Métisse du Nord-Ouest* (published in 1889 a few months after he met and talked to Dumont) that "Gabriel Dumont was in favour of resistance, and promised to come at the head of five hundred horsemen from whatever place he might be wintering at so as to present a dike to invasion." Father A. G. Morice, the Oblate priest who wrote an important history of the Catholic Church in the West and who knew many of the people involved in both the 1870 and 1885 rebellions, repeated this information, and added that after urging distrust of the Canadian government and making his offer of help, Gabriel Dumont returned to the Saskatchewan because he did not wish to become involved in a disagreement with Bishop Taché, who was less pessimistic in his view of the future and more moderate in his general attitude.

As for the five hundred men whom Dumont is said to have promised to bring out of the wilderness to Riel's support, not only is the offer supported by Ouimet's evidence (repeated by Morice), but there is an unexpected confirmation of it in Isaac Cowie's account, from the Company man's somewhat different point of view, of the events of the time. Cowie remarks that the Hudson's Bay officers in the West had information of a projected Métis action in the spring of 1870, "for, taking a mean advantage of the Company's accommodation in carrying letters for others in their winter packet, a letter containing an offer to put, in the spring, five hundred horsemen in the field to join Riel, was intercepted by Mr. Finlayson at Fort Pelly. Whether these five hundred 'horsemen' were all Métis or composed partly of Indians not so well affected as the Crees, the letter did not state distinctly, but we all wondered where five hundred able-bodied Métis could be found in the Qu'Appelle country."

The answer to Cowie's speculation is that a message on its way to Riel intercepted as far north as Fort Pelly could not have come from as far south as the Qu'Appelle country. It must have come from the region around the junction of the two Saskatchewan rivers, and in that area the only Métis leader capable of making such an offer was Gabriel Dumont. Since he had only between two and three hundred hunters directly under his leadership, he must have relied on support from one of three directions: the Métis of the settlements around Fort Edmonton who followed his uncle Gabriel; the Métis of the Qu'Appelle country who had so scared Cowie and his colleagues; the Indians. Doubtless he thought of all three, for there are a number of facts to suggest that as early as 1870 Dumont had already conceived that alliance of Métis and Indians which

Riel came reluctantly to accept in 1885 as the only hope of the native or half-native peoples of the great plains if they were to save themselves from being swamped by a flow of emigrants moving west from Canada and north from the American territories.

In Ouimet's account of Dumont's activities at this time, he records that, having given his offer to Riel and sensed that if he persisted in advocating resistance he would come into opposition with Bishop Taché, for which he was not yet prepared, Dumont returned to the Saskatchewan and, "foreseeing the events that were beginning to mature, made peace with the Blackfoot against whom he had once made war."

Another French Canadian writer, Auguste-Henri de Trémaudan, in his *Histoire de la Nation Métisse,* tells that after 1870 Dumont visited "toutes les nations sauvages: Cris, Assiniboines, Sauteux, Corbeaux, Coux-Tannés, Arcs-Plats, Têtes-Plats, Walla-Walla, Gros-Ventres, Atchinigans, etc. qui se partagaient les 580,000,000 d'acres du Grand Nord-Ouest afin de mieux consolider les liens qui les unissaient aux Métis." Trémaudan, who displays a tendency typical of the Québecois to sentimentalize the Métis whom in real life they mostly left to their fates, is exaggerating somewhat, especially when he adds that Dumont "enjoyed everywhere such consideration that he could think himself sovereign of this great territory"; he certainly lists Indian peoples of the Oregon Territory whom Dumont could not have visited, since the latter said in 1889 that his trip to fetch Riel in 1884 was the first time he had been as far as Montana. But in more general terms, Tremaudan's suggestion that Dumont at this time attempted to create an accord between the Métis and the Indian peoples of the western Canadian prairies is echoed in Isaac Cowie's description of the situation there after the Red River rising. He claims that the Métis who were discontented with the settlement on the Red River in 1870, and with the way Manitoba was created, "incited the Assiniboines and Sioux along the Missouri to join a general conspiracy of Indians and Métis", and adds that "when the dissatisfaction of the Métis with the Canadian form of government led these to make overtures to the Sioux for an alliance, strong enough to sweep away all opponents from the Qu'Appelle Lakes to Lake Winnipeg, the proposal was favourably considered." He adds that the war plans of this alliance included the capture of Forts Qu'Appelle and Ellice, the raiding of Portage la Prairie and Winnipeg, and the siege of Fort Garry, and that both American traders and Fenians pledged their support.

Given the extent of unrest and intrigue along the international border between the Red River rising and the arrival of the North West Mounted Police in 1874, none of this is impossible, and it is likely that in whatever plotting went on with the Sioux, the Dumonts — who had made the original Métis peace with that tribe — were foremost. The fact that, apart from the Cree, only the Teton Sioux and a few Assiniboines stood beside the Métis in 1885 supports the idea of a long-standing accord with the two latter tribes, doubtless created by Gabriel Dumont during his journeys in the prairies from 1870 onwards. That he kept his contacts alive and well lubricated with gifts of tobacco during the whole period up to 1885 is suggested by reports of the Mounted Police in 1879 that Métis agents had come to Wood Mountain and thence went to parley with both the Blackfoot and the Sioux, including Sitting Bull, who was now in Canadian territory. It was said that Riel, now an exile living in Montana, was one of the Métis who went to Wood Mountain in 1879, but at this time Riel had no contacts with the western Indians, and it is much more likely that the emissary was Gabriel Dumont, keeping his alliances and understandings with the Indian chiefs in good order. Thus he prepared for the clash between the colonizers and the native peoples, which after 1870 he felt to be inevitable.

While Dumont was creating his network of relationships with the Indian peoples, the priests along the Saskatchewan were beginning to stabilize Métis society by creating parishes with mission churches which formed the first nuclei of settlement in the region other than the Hudson's Bay Company forts. In 1871 Father André established the first parish of St. Laurent on the western shore of the South Branch. In 1874 a trader named Stobart established a store beside Duck Lake, and in 1876 a parish was created there. Already in 1871 a Métis trader named Xavier Letendre, nicknamed Batoche, had established a store on the eastern shore of the river, with a ferry operating to

St. Laurent; when in 1881 Father Vegreville established a parish there called St. Antoine de Padoue, the name Batoche (abbreviated from Batoche's Crossing) clung to the place. The Métis began to move towards the focal points provided by churches, stores, and ferries, and in a few years La Petite Ville was deserted as they took up river lots — like those of the Red River and the Quebec of their forefathers — and built their log houses along a few miles of each bank of the Saskatchewan at the point where Batoche and St. Laurent faced each other.

As this process went on, the numbers of Métis in the Saskatchewan country grew steadily by migration from Manitoba as well as by natural increase. Some of those who had taken a more militant role on the Red River in 1869 refused to have any part in the agreement under which Canadian government was extended there, and during the summer and autumn of 1870 between thirty and forty families bundled their possessions into Red River carts and started on the long trek up the Carlton Trail; in 1872 George Grant found a number of these families settled in St. Laurent. Soon afterwards disillusionment set in among those Métis who had chosen to stay in Manitoba. There were even sporadic acts of rebellion, like the minor riot that broke out in White Horse Plains when Lieutenant-Governor Alexander Morris visited the area with a group of land-seeking Mennonite delegates in 1873. But most of the discontented chose, in Lenin's words, to "vote with their feet", or in this case with their loudly complaining cart wheels. First it was the hunters of the Red River band who decided to abandon their custom of wintering in Assiniboia, as much because of the westward withdrawal of the buffalo as from disgust with the Canadian government. But as the decade went on, even Métis of substance and education, including some who had held office under the new government, like Louis Schmidt who was a civil servant and Charles Nolin who actually became for a while provincial Minister of Agriculture, pulled up stakes and travelled west in the hope of finding freedom and undisturbed land in the farther prairies.

It was only gradually that the influence of these more sophisticated Métis began to affect the settlements along the Saskatchewan. At the beginning of the 1870s the villages were still "curious assemblages" like St. Laurent in 1872, when

William Francis Butler visited it, later to describe in *The Wild North Land* the chaos such a place presented in the eyes of those accustomed to the more obvious order of English or even Upper Canadian villages.

> Huts promiscuously crowded together: horses, dogs, women, children, all intermixed in a confusion worthy of Donnybrook Fair; half-breed hunters, ribboned, tasselled, and capoted, lazy, idle, and if there is any spirit in the camp, sure to be intoxicated; remnants and wrecks of buffalo lying everywhere around; robes stretched and drying; meat piled on stages; wolf-skins spread over frameworks; women drawing water and carrying wood; and at dusk from the little hut the glow of firelight through parchment windows, the sound of fiddle scraped with rough hunter hand, and the quick thud of thunder heel as Louison, or Bâtiste, or Gabriel foot it ceaselessly upon the half-hewn floors.

Butler described the Métis with that degree of colourful exaggeration which the Victorians expected of their travel writers, and he obviously viewed them with a crashing condescension and with a sense that — despite the virtues of generosity and hospitality which he admitted — they were "destined to disappear before the white men's footprint. . . ."

In fact, Butler was describing a Métis world that was already passing away, as the nomad hunters began to recognize the inevitability of rooting themselves in land of their own. It was, for instance, in the year of 1872 that Gabriel Dumont, the virtual leader of the St. Laurent Métis, staked out the first land he ever claimed to own. It was a patch of meadowland and aspen and birch woods, broken by marshes and small lakes, and sloping sharply down at its verge about two hundred feet to the eastern bank of the South Saskatchewan. Even if Dumont had wished to make a legal claim, he would not have been able to do so in 1872, since the procedures for acquiring land in the Territories had not yet been formalized, and he established himself as a squatter, though finally in 1883 he would file for homesteader's rights on the land. In 1873 he built his first house, of logs plastered with clay and whitewashed. It was a small house, with a single large room twenty-one feet long by seventeen and a half feet wide, and an attached kitchen fourteen feet square. Around the house, in Métis manner, clustered a huddle of other small buildings, including stables for Gabriel's four horses, and a large semi-underground icehouse for keeping meat and fish during the long winter of the northern prairies.

Gabriel now described himself as a farmer; over the next decade he broke twenty acres of land, grew potatoes and barley, and mowed hay from the meadows for his five horses, though he kept no cattle and sought a variety of ways of living rather than settle too deeply into the routines of agriculture. He never ceased to hunt and fish for long periods of the year, and continued to head the local buffalo hunt, which in the early 1870s was still so productive that Butler recorded six hundred cows killed in a single hunt from St. Laurent in 1872. He also took advantage of the fact that he had settled beside a trail sometimes used as a short cut on the way to Fort Carlton. There, until 1872, the Hudson's Bay Company had kept a scow moored, which travellers were obliged to operate for themselves, as the Overlanders did in 1862 and as George Grant and his party did in the summer of 1872, transporting their carts and wagons by scow while their horses swam around them across the river. Now Gabriel Dumont proposed to replace the scow by a regular ferry.

He started the ferry in the autumn of 1872, and entered into fervent competition with his rival, Batoche, six miles down-river, claiming that his scow was "the best on the river . . . in constant readiness," and that "the road by this ferry is the shortest by twenty-five miles going to or going east from Battleford." He erected a signpost forty miles east, where the Carlton Trail divided, which announced "Gabriel's Crossing" in English, French, and Cree syllabics, and gave the prices he charged; these were the early days of the Territories when English money was still used, and Gabriel collected two shillings for a wagon, one and six for a Red River cart, and six-pence for a horse and rider.

Five years later, in 1878, when the Council of the Northwest Territories had followed the pattern of all governments and begun to bureaucratize matters that previously had been understood between men of honour and good sense, Gabriel had to take out a license, duly given under the seal and signature of the Lieutenant-Governor. This gave him exclusive rights as ferryman over a stretch of the South Branch extending seven miles upriver and three miles downriver from the place now known officially, as well as popularly, as Gabriel's Crossing*, for, as Dumont proudly remarked long afterwards in answer to an official question about his possible aliases, "the half-breeds call me Gabriel!"

Gabriel's scow was a clumsy rectangular craft, twenty-three feet long and twelve feet wide, propelled by oars, on a rope sufficiently strong for the ferry to carry in ordinary weather a load of four Red River carts or two wagons with their horses or oxen. The old rates in sterling were replaced by a new schedule in dollar currency.

5. The maximum rates of tolls chargeable for carrying under this Licence shall be

	Cents
(1) For every single vehicle, loaded or unloaded, including one horse, or other animal, and driver	25
(2) For every double vehicle, loaded or unloaded, including two horses, or two other animals, and driver	50
(3) For every horse and its rider	20
(4) For every horse, mule, ox or cow (not included with vehicle or rider)	10
(5) For every sheep, hog, calf or colt	5
(6) For every passenger in vehicle (except team driver, as above)	5
(7) For every passenger on foot	10
(8) For all articles or goods, not in a vehicle, over one hundred pounds, per 100 lbs.	2

Gabriel was allowed to charge double these rates if he "saw fit" to ferry anyone across between dusk and dawn, but on Sundays between nine in the morning and two in the afternoon he was expected to provide a free crossing for those going to and from church. He was, moreover, expected to keep the

* Today the site bears the name of Gabriel, Saskatchewan, and the bridge that replaced the ferry in 1968 is known as Gabriel's Bridge. There was — and is — only one subarchangelic Gabriel in the folk traditions of northern Saskatchewan. Nowhere in the triangle between Saskatoon, Prince Albert, and Battleford is it necessary to add the surname of Dumont when talking of him.

approaches down the valley sides to the river in good order, so that carts could be drawn up and down them by normal teams of draught animals.

Recollections of Gabriel Dumont in his role of ferryman are rare. Perhaps the most vivid of them, despite its flavour of Ontarian superciliousness, is the account of a certain James Trow, MP, who as Chairman of the Immigration and Colonization Committee of the House of Commons, made a tour of Manitoba and the Northwest Territories in 1877. On a morning early in September, in a thick fog, he and his party approached Gabriel's Crossing.

We arrived at the Ferry, and having no horn, whistled for Gabriel, for we could not see twenty feet in front. The ferryman soon appeared, and made preparations for crossing. The boat was a flat-bottomed scow, roughly put together. Our animals were unhitched, the carriage and cart put in the centre of the boat, the mules on one side, the horses on the other. Gabriel gave instructions by signs and some doubtful French. The mules were very obstinate and troublesome to put on board. He had probably been more accustomed to oxen than mules and undertook to twist the tail of one of the mules. Instantly he received a kick below the ribs, in that portion of the body called by pugilists "the bread basket". Each of our party undertook to row with an unyielding oar, first keeping along the shore and working upstream; fortunately, the wind was favourable, which counteracted the force of the rapid current. The river has a swift current, and is probably over 200 yards in width at low water, with an average depth of 8 to 15 feet. The fee paid Gabriel was $1.50 for ourselves, horses and carriages.

Considering the value of money in 1877, Gabriel must have found his ferry remunerative, since apart from visiting tourists, a regular traffic of freighters made its way along the Carlton Trail, and those going to Fort Carlton and Battleford would be inclined to use his crossing in preference to Batoche's for the miles of road it saved them. Gabriel also made a small profit from the little shack of a store, fourteen feet square, which stood near his house at the top of the approach to the ferry. When Major Boulton saw the store as it was being looted by

89

Canadian soldiers in 1885, it contained only "a few articles, chiefly blacking, braces, strings of beads, and such like, but nothing of value, except a billiard table." The billiard table will appear again in our story; the stock on the shelves was probably especially low when Boulton saw it, since Dumont must have taken away everything of much value in anticipation of the arrival of his enemies, and in any case he had been pre-occupied during the rebellion with matters other than trade. It is likely that before 1885 he carried the kind of varied stock one would have found in any small trading post in the North-west. According to the Mounted Policeman John Donkin, who visited Batoche in 1884, Gabriel then used his store as a kind of saloon, a "smoke den" where "French billiards were played, nauseous hop-beer imbibed, and much violent sedition talked by the half-breed *habitués.*"

To his new occupations as farmer, ferryman, and store-keeper, Dumont added — somewhat intermittently — that of contractor. As government began to tighten its grip on the Northwest, the increased need for year-round communication led to the building of roads, mail stations, and telegraph lines and the improvement of existing trails. The Métis provided the most readily available pool of labour for such tasks, and many of them, giving little thought to the fact that they were facilita-ting the influx of settlers that would threaten their way of life, accepted construction contracts. Even Gabriel Dumont, for all his prophetic insight into the perils of the future so far as his people were concerned, contracted in the spring of 1873 with Lawrence Clarke, the Hudson's Bay Factor at Fort Carlton and local representative on the Council for the Northwest Territor-ies, to build part of a road from the North Saskatchewan, op-posite Fort Carlton, to Green Lake, a post hitherto accessible only by a complicated canoe and portage route. As well as a number of other Métis, Dumont employed John Kerr as the cook for his gang, and Kerr noticed that Clarke treated Gabriel with "much friendliness", a state of affairs that was not to con-tinue.

In later years there were stories that by such various activi-ties during the 1870s and the early 1880s, Gabriel Dumont became a wealthy man, only to lose everything in the rebellion of 1885. In fact, he appears never to have been more than modestly well-off, and that only in frontier terms. He was able to buy his billiard table, and a primitive treadle washing-machine to ease the burden of Madeleine's work, and when the rebellion of 1885 broke out he was in the process of building a new and somewhat larger house to compete with the light green mock-colonial structure his rival Batoche had erected beside the competing ferry. Even so, Dumont estimated the total value of the buildings on his land in that year — which was the peak of his prosperity — at no more than $800. He must have been put to considerable expense employing men to operate his ferry when he was away conducting the buffalo hunts or on contract work, and there were many months when the river was frozen over and the ferry brought no revenue. Besides, Dumont was generous by nature, and his position as a leader among his people gave him an added sense of obligation, so that he often shared his goods and his money with his friends and with those in need. Among the Métis, to this day, there are many stories of his open-handedness, and those who were not Métis also had, like John Kerr, their tales to tell.

Kerr records how, after the road to Green Lake was finished, and all the workers were paid off, he saw Dumont "fill a couple of small sacks with groceries and pork, and hand them to Father André, who was at Fort Carlton that day, for distribution among a few old Métis women who had been left at home at the Mission of St. Laurent, the rest of the population having gone to the hunting grounds." And he tells also how a Métis named Isidore, so poor that he had no horse or cart of his own, worked with his wife for Gabriel Dumont during the buffalo hunt, preparing pemmican and drying meat. One year, en route to the hunting grounds, Isidore's wife gave birth.

"We made camp at noon. Gabriel rode out to where the horses were feeding, picked out a fairly good cart-horse from his own lot, threw the rope over it, brought it into camp, hooked it to a cart, and presented it to Isidore for his wife. . . . Later on he killed enough buffalo to fill the cart with dried meat and pemmican and gave it to them."

"However," Kerr ends his eulogy, "the killing of buffalo and giving them to his less fortunate companions was a common kindness of Gabriel's. I've seen him in one day kill as many as eight buffalo, and not take one for himself, but give them to those who had no fast runners." It was, indeed, no merely impulsive generosity that moved Gabriel to such acts. It was, rather, a deep sense of the need for mutual aid among a people who had lived always on the edge of survival, an almost instinctive recognition that luck and ability must be used for others as well as for oneself. It was the sense of social responsibility that is the corollary of such acts that led Gabriel Dumont during 1873 and the years that followed to play his crucial part in the construction of a political order among the Métis of the South Saskatchewan.

5. The Little Republic
of St. Laurent

Hasty travellers like William Francis Butler were inclined to be so impressed by the anarchic aspects of Métis life between buffalo hunts that they failed to observe the talent for democratic order which so often emerged when it was needed in Métis groups. Butler's fellow officer, Colonel Crofton, who reported to the British War Office at about the same time as Butler travelled in the West, was one of those who recognized the power of collective efficiency that tended to distinguish the Métis at that period from most Indian groups.

Crofton not only remarked that if it were considered expedient to raise an irregular cavalry in the Canadian West (presumably against American as much as Indian aggressors) "there exists in the half-breeds the most eligible material I have ever seen in any country, and I have seen the Risalus of India and the Arabs." He also looked with an unconsciously prophetic eye into the future of the prairies, when he remarked that the "splendid organization" of the Métis "when on the prairies", combined with their superb knowledge of the country and their ability to live off it when necessary, "would render them a very formidable enemy in case of disturbance or open rebellion against constituted authorities."

Crofton was writing fifteen years before actual rebellion in the Northwest, and though the first Métis petition for definite grants of land "in compensation of our rights to the lands of the country as Métis" was signed and presented by eleven

93

Qu'Appelle half-breeds in 1873 (and duly ignored by the Dominion government), the prospect of rebellion seemed far distant in the early 1870s, except perhaps in the minds of a few men like Gabriel Dumont who kept alive the vision of a great alliance of the native peoples to secure and preserve their ancestral rights against the settlers, who were already beginning to find their way along the Carlton Trail in sufficient numbers for Prince Albert and Battleford to develop, from 1874 onwards, into active centres of colonization.

For the present, however, under the guidance of Father André, the local Métis were more intent on regulating their own internal relations with a view to survival as a community. While the nomadic hunters of the prairies had a remarkable tradition of organization when they came together in large numbers for the very specific purpose of killing buffalo, they had developed no organization of their own to regulate their mutual relations in other periods. They were too individualistic in temperament to indulge in unnecessary political exercises, and while they still wintered beside the Red River and at White Horse Plains, they were willing to accept the rather loose government sustained there by the Council of Assiniboia, under the Hudson's Bay Company's auspices, as sufficient to keep the peace and to sustain what few public services were deemed necessary. During the first years when wintering in the prairies began to replace wintering in the neighbourhood of Fort Garry, the camps were too small and too temporary for any form of government to emerge. A few families — usually friends — would share a camp, and matters of common interest would be settled by informal discussion. But as soon as the winter camps were transformed into permanent villages, whose inhabitants were resigned to the distant prospect of a farming existence, then an organization more continuous than the laws and council of the buffalo hunt became an object whose desirability was recognised more clearly by the people of St. Laurent and Batoche than by the Métis anywhere else in the prairies.

There was, before the later 1870s, little pretence of local government in the Northwest Territories. An appointed territorial council had been established in 1872, but it had no structure through which its authority might be imposed, relying mainly on the existing influence of Hudson's Bay officers who were its members or acted as voluntary magistrates. The North West Mounted Police was created in 1873, but it did not appear anywhere on the prairies before 1874, and even then its first task was to establish the frontier as far as the Rockies, to drive out the American traders, and to show the flag and parade the red coats among the Sioux and the formidable warriors of the Blackfoot Confederacy. Not until 1875 did the first contingent of the Mounted Police appear in the region of Fort Carlton; then, ironically, it arrived only in response to the news that the Métis had taken into their own hands the establishment of a political order suited to their needs.

It is likely that the idea of setting up a local government first occurred to Father André and his fellow priest, Father Moulin, who reached Saskatchewan in 1870. Missionaries have always been inclined to encourage the gathering of their flocks into settlements where religious and educational activities can be carried on without difficulty, but both André and Moulin were also sympathetic with the Métis desire to retain their separate identity as a people, and they saw the establishment of self-governed communities as a surer guarantee of such survival than the pattern of alternating dispersal and concentration which, in common with other nomad peoples, the Métis had practiced up to now.

Yet in spite of his forceful character, Father André alone could not have persuaded the Métis to accept his counsel. He needed a man from among them with sufficient prestige and also sufficient insight to win acceptance of his advice, and he found such a man in Gabriel Dumont, who immediately saw the advantages of continuing in all seasons the state of harmony which the hunt organization — tested year after year for as long as he could remember — had created among the Métis in the summer months. Gabriel agreed to call the Métis together so that a scheme of government could be presented, and on 10 December 1873 the people of the South Saskatchewan settlements gathered in a mass meeting outside the church doors at St. Laurent.

The scene must have been rather like that in some of the smaller and more traditional Swiss cantons, such as Appenzell, when the citizens gather each year in the town square to vote their laws. And this was precisely what the people of the South

95

Saskatchewan did on that day. Gabriel Dumont presided over the gathering, and Father André appears to have acted as secretary, for the records of the proceedings of this and later gatherings, now in the National Archives, are in his handwriting.

Out of the meeting emerged a constitution well fitted for the circumstances of an isolated community with a simple culture at the transition point between a nomadic hunting past and an unwilling agrarian future. Though some writers have used the term "provisional government" to describe what was created, this is not a happy definition, since it reminds one of Riel's Provisional Government of the Red River with its echoes of French and American revolutionary constitution-making. The people of St. Laurent described themselves in their proceedings as a "community" and even as a "colony", but never aspired to the dignity of a state or indeed of a province, denying any intention of seeking independence, and stating quite explicitly that "in making their laws, they regard themselves as loyal and faithful subjects of Canada, and are prepared to abandon their own organization and to submit to the laws of the Dominion as soon as Canada establishes regular magistrates with a force sufficient to maintain in the territory the authority of the law." It seems likely, indeed, that at this stage both Father André and Gabriel Dumont were anxious to avoid their actions being associated in the minds of Canadians with the recent events at Red River. There was, in any case, no need to imitate the organization Riel had created to govern the miscellaneous population of the Red River settlements, since St. Laurent seemed to contain no potentially dissident elements. The earlier organization of the buffalo hunt, adapted to the life of a loose group of Métis hamlets, gave a sufficient basis for whatever organization the thousand or so people now living around St. Laurent might require.

The first task was to choose a chief or president and council. Gabriel Dumont was elected president by acclamation, and with him a council of eight described in the records as "Alexandre Hamelin, Baptiste Garriepey, Pierre Garriepey, Abraham Montour, Isidore Dumont junior, Jean Dumont junior, Moyse Walet, Baptiste Hamelin." The two Dumonts in the council were not, as has often been stated, Gabriel's father and uncle, but his brother and his cousin Jean, son of old Jean

Dumont. Since "Moyse Walet" was in fact Moïse Ouelette, Gabriel's brother-in-law, this meant that the Dumont clan was strongly present. Of the other members, Pierre Gariepey, as he was more generally known, was a son-in-law of Cuthbert Grant and a former leader of the White Horse Plains hunt, and Abraham Montour was related to Nicholas Montour, a Métis clerk of the North West Company who had been associated with Grant in 1816, though he had not taken an actual part in the battle of Seven Oaks. The Hamelins had been an influential family on Red River, where one of their members, Salomon Hamelin, was appointed in 1871 a member of the Manitoba Legislative Council. Thus the council elected at St. Laurent in December 1873 represented the rudimentary patrician class that was emerging among the Métis, mainly on the basis of ability in the hunt.

Before proceedings continued, the assembly asked the president and council to take an oath before Father André to carry out their duties faithfully and give judgment according to the dictates of their consciences. Gabriel Dumont answered that he would do this only if the members of the assembly swore to support him and his colleagues in word and deed in maintaining whatever laws might be passed. This was agreed, and the whole assembly went down on its knees before Father André, and, kissing the Bibles that passed from hand to hand, "took the divine word as witness of their firm resolution to sustain their laws and punish justly those who might break them."

Then the assembly proceeded to enact the twenty-eight basic laws of the community of St. Laurent. It is not known to what extent these laws were drafted before the meeting by Father André, Gabriel Dumont, and their close associates, but it seems unlikely that they sprang entirely out of discussion on that winter's day outside the church; most of them were doubtless proposed by the initiators of the meeting. However that may be, the laws as passed presented a code devised with considerable practical wisdom to suit the requirements of a small and simple community.

They recognized, under the councillors, an executive organization of captains and soldiers which would act as a police force for the community, and the first batch of laws related to the responsibilities of the councillors and these officers, laying down that the council should meet at least once a month, and decreeing fines for failures to meet obligations, the highest being three louis (or pounds sterling) for captains who refused to obey orders. There followed a series of laws relating to the functioning of the council as a judicial tribunal, which aimed as far as possible to settle differences between the people by arbitration. Other laws related to contracts, declaring the need for witnesses, and the nullity of agreements made on Sundays. The council was authorized to raise levies of money for public services to the extent of one louis per householder, and to impose corvées for work of importance to the community.

The crimes specified in the laws were those most likely to create dissension in a Métis community. There were clauses imposing penalties for taking other men's horses, for dishonouring girls and refusing to marry them, for lighting fires on the prairie in high summer (after 1 August), for failure to restrain horses that became nuisances or dogs that killed young foals, and for defaming the characters of other members of the community. There was, significantly, no mention of theft (apart from horses), which seems to have been extremely rare among the Métis at that time, or of such violent crimes as assault, manslaughter, and murder. Since it is not to be imagined that the prairies had become peaceful overnight as a result of the meeting at St. Laurent, one can assume that the assembly felt it politic to leave such difficult matters to existing custom, trusting their laws to reduce the incidence of excuses for violence.

There were even, to complete the special concerns of the people of St. Laurent, laws relating to labour relations. An employee (*engagé*) who left his employer (*bourgeois*) before the expiry of his engagement, should lose his wages; a bourgeois who dismissed an engagé without justification should pay him for the entire term of engagement; employers should require their employees to do on Sundays only such work as was absolutely necessary, allowing them time to attend morning services. A further law was of particular interest to Gabriel Dumont: it declared, years before the same requirement was formalized by the Canadian authorities, that ferries should carry without charge people going to and from church on Sundays.

Significant changes in methods of punishment are evident when one compares these laws with the rules of such early buffalo hunts as that of 1840. No corporal punishment was now suggested (and of course imprisonment did not figure in the

Métis view of a just society); even the old punishments by ridicule had vanished, and all punishments were now in money fines, which suggests a society that had proceeded a long way in the direction of a cash economy, largely no doubt through the participation of Métis in the freighting business across the plains and the increase in independent trading. Yet the possibility that for some men the produce of the hunt might still be the only means of living was suggested in a final law which provided that no married man with three animals or less should be forced to give one of them up in payment of a debt; presumably a fine would in this context count as a debt.

Having passed these laws, the assembly proceeded to authorize the president and council to make any supplementary laws or regulations they might consider necessary for the well-being of the community, and then dispersed, to meet again in a year's time.

We have no knowledge of how the council worked, or when it met in the houses of its members, but since there is no record of complaints of its activities from within the community, we can reasonably assume that its proceedings were carried out with good sense and fairness. Gabriel Dumont himself was so pleased by the experiment in self-government that he sent messages to the other Métis communities in the West, around Qu'Appelle and Edmonton, suggesting that they follow suit, and he communicated with John McKay, an English-speaking half-breed in Prince Albert, discussing the possibilities of cooperation in setting up self-government in the Northwest. What his precise thoughts were we do not know, but he may well have had the vision of some kind of federation of communities that would face the Canadian authorities when they came to organize the prairies with the *fait accompli* of a network of local governments already in operation. None of these approaches met with any positive response, with the result that, as George F. G. Stanley noted in *The Birth of Western Canada*: "The history of St. Laurent does not appear to have been paralleled by the other Métis settlements in the North-west. Neither at Red River — if we except Riel's Provisional Government — St. Albert, nor St. Florent de Lebret, did they rise to the same stage of independent political development."

Dr. Stanley adds the comment that "It is quite evident that the Métis attained at St. Laurent, during this period, their highest development, politically, as a distinct race." Certainly the rule of Dumont was characterised by a desire to bring his people into full participation in their own government. He and his councillors had hardly started work when it became evident to them that, now the Métis were beginning to settle down, the possession of land was becoming important to their survival, and might therefore be a great source of conflict between them. Dumont felt that making laws on so important a matter was beyond the discretion which had been granted to the council in December, and he therefore called another general meeting on 10 February 1874, to frame the regulations that would minimize disputes.

The land regulations which the assembly passed recommended what appears to have been a sensible adaptation of Quebec landholding customs to suit the special circumstances of the Saskatchewan region. Each head of family, it was agreed, should have the right to a strip of land a quarter of a mile wide along its river frontage and extending two miles back into the prairie, with grazing rights beyond the two mile limit. For each of his sons over twenty, he could take another plot. Only the owner had the right to cut wood or hay on his land, but areas that could not be cultivated were to be common land, where all the people of St. Laurent could cut wood. Nevertheless, cutting was not to be unlimited; the people of St. Laurent displayed a sense of the importance of conservation in a clause that deprecated the "useless destruction of trees" and decreed that "nobody shall fell more trees than he is capable of using in two weeks" and that if a man leaves felled but untrimmed trees in the wood, any comer shall have the right to trim and square the logs and take them away. Finally, to resolve any disputes that might arise over boundaries, the council was authorized to appoint a commission of three men to visit the land in question and settle the matter.

Exactly a year after the first general meeting, on 10 December 1874, the people of St. Laurent met once again in general assembly, and the president and council surrendered their power. With a due sense of the drama of the occasion, they begged the people to choose others in their places, which would make them happy, since their duties had made them lose much time. Father André countered by "passionately exhorting" the people not only to sustain their laws, but also to continue placing their confidence in "the men who had worked in their interests with complete devotion during the year which had just passed." In view of what happened later between them, it is curious to see André displaying such enthusiasm for Dumont, but he seems to have been quite sincere in his appreciation of the work of the council and not at all anxious to see its members replaced by other men in the community. One suspects that, though for the sake of form the good Father was to declare in 1875 that "without the priest, the laws and rules would be a dead letter," in practice he recognized that the same fate would have overtaken them without Gabriel Dumont and his close friends and relatives at the head of affairs in St. Laurent.

Thanks to Father André's protestations, Gabriel Dumont agreed to carry on for a second year as president of the community, and a council of seven members was now elected, with the two Gariepeys omitted (whether they chose to withdraw or were voted down is not certain) and Baptiste Boyer elected in their place.

This time the assembly voted no new laws and contented itself with ratifying the measures which the council had thought fit to pass during the preceding year. Given a further year of office, and unqualified approval for the first year, the president and council sat down to consider the other problem that loomed as large in their minds as that of land: the fate of the buffalo hunt. By now the most sanguine of the old buffalo hunters, whether Indian or Métis, could not blind himself to the fact that the buffalo had been wastefully killed in the past, and that now, assaulted as they were (particularly in American territory) by enemies of types unknown before, like the sportsmen who killed for mere trophies and the professional hunters who killed only for robes, the buffalo were rapidly declining in numbers. The hunters of St. Laurent had had an especially bad year in 1874, and though most of them blamed the scarcity of buffalo in their hunting grounds on the drought that had burnt up so much of the pasture, there were already those who realized that in sheer numbers the buffalo were declining from year to year.

The new laws for the buffalo hunt which Dumont and his council passed on 27 January 1875 represented an unarticulated compromise between those who still believed that the buffalo

101

would be there forever and that it was the natural right of native people to hunt them, and those who feared that the days of the great hunts were passing away. True, the council was mainly engaged in making tighter and more precise the rules that had governed the hunt for more than fifty years. They declared that each spring at the end of April a general assembly outside the church of St. Laurent would decide the date of departure for the prairie, and that only those who could plead special need would be granted permission to go before that date, and even they on a carefully circumscribed route. The old rules against anybody proceeding, on the day of the hunt, to run the buffalo before the signal from the leader were repeated, and those regarding the defensive circle of carts, sentry duty at night, care about making fires, and unnecessarily firing shots that might scare the buffalo, were strengthened. But for the first time there were also rules forbidding wastefulness, and men were to be fined for leaving unused the carcasses of animals they had killed; it was a measure of conservation that was too slight and came too late to make any significant difference to the fate of the buffalo herd, but it showed an anxiety over the future that had not been present among the Métis in the days when they had often killed a buffalo merely for the tender cuts and had left the rest to predatory animals. The rule among the twenty-five laws of the buffalo hunt voted in January 1875 that has a special interest is Article 23, which declares that any party of Métis in the neighbourhood of the "great caravan", even though they claim to be independent, shall be bound in their hunting by the decisions of the "council of the great camp", and if they do not accept such decisions willingly, they shall be "obliged by force."

It was a reasonable rule for a people whose livelihood depended to a great extent on success in hunting over a region with which they had been long associated. There was no intent of preventing strangers from hunting the buffalo anywhere in the prairie; all the Métis of St. Laurent very sensibly wished to assure was that their own hunting should not be spoilt by outsiders scaring the buffalo before they made their own run, though anyone was welcome to take his place in the line of horsemen and join the run at the appropriate signal, as John Kerr and many other non-Métis hunters on occasion did.

6. The First Clash
on the Saskatchewan

The revision in January 1875 of the rules for the buffalo hunt was — as far as we know — the last public act of the president and council of St. Laurent, for in the following summer an incident occurred that not only brought the council's activities to an abrupt end, but also projected Gabriel Dumont for the first time into actual conflict with the Canadian authorities. It was an incident the newspapers of Manitoba and eastern Canada were to report sensationally, as if it were a major rebellion. One paper, the *Daily Free Press* of Winnipeg, actually anticipated history in a fantasy declaring that Riel had returned, the Cree were on the warpath, a number of Mounted Police had been killed, and Fort Carlton was in the hands of the rebels. All these things were in fact to happen, but in 1885, not 1875; what happened in 1875 was merely a warning which the authorities failed to heed, with the result that the *Daily Free Press*'s story, false when it was printed, would at last come true.

The facts of the case are quite simple, but they are worth recording in some detail, since they describe the first occasion on which the Canadian government was made aware of the emergence of the Métis on the Saskatchewan as a group worthy of consideration.

In mid-June, when the brigade of hunters from St. Laurent was preparing to leave for the prairie, news was brought to Gabriel Dumont that a group of so-called "free hunters" (who in fact appear to have been hunting for the Hudson's Bay Company) had ten days before set off for the hunting ground which the St. Laurent brigade had chosen as its destination. They consisted of Peter Ballendine, a former Hudson's Bay Company employee, Baptiste Primeau, Alexandre Cadien, Theodore Covenant, and William Whiteford. Ballendine and Whiteford were English-speaking half-breeds, but Primeau, Cadien, and Covenant were all Métis from St. Laurent who had taken part in the meetings which passed the laws of the community and accepted the leadership of Gabriel Dumont and his council. They were accompanied by an unspecified number of Indians.

Gabriel Dumont's first act, when he heard of this infringement of the accepted customs of the prairies, was to get a letter written in his name and send it by courier on 17 June to the offending hunters.

My friends,
We are not satisfied that you go so before us, and you are hunting in our Contry.

Therefore all the people of Métis of Carlton pray you to come all at once to our camp. If that agree not to yourselfs, all the cavaliers wil go and bring you to our camp; and if you cause dommage to ourselfs you will pay. That concern especialy the Métis of your camp.

We write to you as frends to advice you. If you wil not believe us, certainely you will pay all the cavaliers who will go and bring you.

Farewell,
Your servants,
all the people of Métis of Carlton
camped in the plain,
Gabriel Dumont.

Considered in the context of Métis traditions, it was a reasonable letter. The hunters to whom it was addressed must have known they were violating their own customs, and Gabriel Dumont was giving them an opportunity to join the "great camp" and to share equally in its pursuit of the buffalo. Quite deliberately, they chose to ignore him, and with forty of his soldiers Dumont rode in pursuit. The account of what happened then, in so far as it has survived in writing, is contained in a letter which Peter Ballendine presented to Lawrence Clarke, the Hudson's Bay Factor at Fort Carlton and recently appointed Justice of the Peace for the Territories, on 12 July, more than three weeks later.

> On the 19th June 41 armed men visited our camp all of them on Horse back and armed to the Teeth with 14 & 16 Repeating Riffles, to take us all to their Camp, and if we refused to go that they would force us to go, and with a little talk one of the leading men got up and said, what is the use of talking, we came here to take them & let us go and do as we said. G. Dummond then said go and drive their Horses and load up their Carts and take them to the Camp. All got up and went to the Tents of our party and Hussled up the things to the Carts. Tents were also knocked down. We told them, they had better think seriously, and that their best plan would be to leave us alone. They then gave a call, Start the Carts, & of course they started. Gabriel Dummond again turned around and said, get into the Carts, the men said they would not go, & that they would not abide by their laws, that they would wait for the Government, and that they Hoped they would get Justice from them. Gabriel Dummond then stopped the Carts & said, Let them pay so much, so they went on and took from the loads what they pleased, and helped themselves.

In a further deposition, made before Clarke, Baptiste Primeau said that Dumont had fined him five pounds, Cadien seven pounds ten shillings, and Covenant a pound, and that the goods taken from the carts were estimated by Gabriel Dumont to equal the fines. Neither the English half-breeds nor the Indians appear to have been affected by Dumont's judgment. Nevertheless, there seems no doubt that Ballendine was principally responsible for making a situation of conflict out of an act which the Métis present knew, despite their protests, to be in accord with their own customary law. It is Ballendine's name that heads the column of signatures and marks on the original letter of complaint, and it was he alone who signed the postscript added in his own handwriting: "We beg to hand you the written summons we received from this party before they reached us by which you will see that they claim the country as their own."

Ballendine received a friendly hearing from Lawrence Clarke, who immediately took his side and that of the delinquent Métis without considering the validity of the customary laws of the buffalo hunt, and sent a report to Lieutenant-Governor Alexander Morris, in which he presented a highly biassed and exaggerated account of what had been going on in St. Laurent. In reading Clarke's assertions, it is well to remember Father André's account of the just and orderly administration of St. Laurent.

Clarke begins by claiming that two-thirds of the people of St. Laurent are linked by kinship and marriage,

> and have assumed for themselves the right to enact Laws, rules and regulations for the Government of the Colony and adjoining Country of a most tyrannical nature, which the minority of the Settlers are perforce bound to obey or be treated with criminal severity.
>
> From this body a Court has been constituted numbering fourteen persons presided over by a Man named Gabriel Dumond who is designated as "President" and before whom all delinquents are made to appear, or suffer violence in person or property. . . .
>
> This court pretends further to have the power to enforce their Laws upon all Indians, Settlers and Hunters who frequent the Prairie country in the lower section of the Saskatchewan, and have levied by violence and Robbery large sums of money of inoffensive persons who resort to the Buffalo country for a livelihood.

Later incidents were to show Clarke as a volatile and intemperate man, given to alarmist statements, yet there seem to have been deeper motives for his activity on the present occasion, and the most important of these was probably a desire to use the incident to propel the Canadian government into giving some concrete support to the authority of which, as local Justice of the Peace, he found himself the powerless personification. It must have been galling indeed to have been given nominal authority with no force to exercise it, while a few miles away in St. Laurent Gabriel Dumont, with no mandate at all from the government, was presiding over courts and disposing what was evidently an efficient corps of irregular police.

But if Clarke's new-found dignity as a magistrate was provoked by the situation, so was his long-standing anxiety as a Hudson's Bay Company officer that any kind of movement among the Métis or the Indians might damage the Company's interests, as a similar movement had done only six years before on the Red River. The Company's posts on the Saskatchewan were, as we have seen, quite indefensible, and as he became aware of Métis discontent building up along the river, Clarke must often have looked forward to the time when the new Mounted Police would find their way into this corner of the Northwest Territories and give their protection to the few remaining years of the fur trade. Undoubtedly he was encouraged in this view by the Company's Chief Commissioner, James A. Grahame, who happened to be at Fort Carlton when Ballendine laid his complaint and who himself took Clarke's report to Winnipeg and delivered it personally to Alexander Morris.

Morris was naturally perturbed when he read Clarke's letter, with its complaint of "being without protective force to compel lawbreakers to respect the Laws of Canada", but, knowing Clarke's proneness to sensationalism, he first consulted James McKay, the Scottish half-breed member of the Territorial Council, who hazarded what was in fact a correct guess, that Dumont and his followers had merely been implementing the traditional rules of the hunt. But even with McKay's advice, Morris could hardly dismiss the memory of the Red River rising; he did not wish to appear responsible for ignoring what might after all be a dangerous situation, so he reported immediately to the Minister of the Interior, and sent an urgent message to Major-General Sir E. Selby-Smythe, the commander of the Canadian militia, who at this moment was travelling the prairies to assess the effectiveness of the Mounted Police (doubtless with an eye to the traditional enemy south of the border). Selby-Smythe was at Swan River with George Arthur French, Commissioner of the Mounted Police, when the message reached him; both men, like Morris, suspected that Clarke's report was exaggerated, and they decided that the best procedure would be to travel to Fort Carlton immediately with a force of fifty men as a "party of observation" which might also be serviceable in halting "the spread of mischievous complications with the half-breeds", an appropriately ambiguous phrase which left open the question as to whether Clarke or Dumont was the source of the mischief.

Selby-Smythe, French, and their party proceeded by forced rides to their destination, covering in eight days the 270 miles across the northern parkland from Swan River to Fort Carlton. They arrived on 6 August, when Clarke, in an attempt to justify himself, caused a few of the Métis who had been involved with Dumont in the arrest of Ballendine and his party to appear before the visiting officers. He reported that they had "begged of me to intercede for them with Colonel French." It is possible that the Métis were overawed by the sudden appearance of the Mounted Police — though their treatment of the same force ten years later suggests that the mood of awe was only temporary. More significant is another sentence in Clarke's letter of 6 August. "They declare that they did not act in defiance of the law, but in total ignorance of having committed any crime and say if their offence is pardoned that in future they will be good citizens and abide by and obey simply those who have the power of enforcing the laws of Canada." It will be remembered that the laws of St. Laurent were always regarded as provisional, to operate until Canadian law should be established in the region, and therefore this answer of the Métis seems consistent with their past actions; they were ignorant of having broken any laws, and with good reason, since in no effective way had the laws of Canada been promulgated in the Saskatchewan region.

Clarke evidently suspected that neither Selby-Smythe nor French shared his grave view of the situation, for he went on to say that, though Dumont, who was still with the hunting party on the prairie, would "be arrested on his arrival and put through the court, at the same time I would advise that he should be leniently dealt with, for I think that the man has acted under the influence of others who should have known better," a sly cut at Father André and the other missionaries, whom Clarke disliked.

Selby-Smythe and French played their hands coolly; after all, they were British officers in the Victorian era of small colonial wars, and even in those terms the affair of St. Laurent seemed pretty trifling. Also, according to Sam Steele, who claims to have been told it by Selby-Smythe shortly afterwards, they had encountered Gabriel Dumont briefly at his crossing on their way to Fort Carlton and had formed their own opinions of the man, an incident they appear to have chosen not to reveal to Clarke. When he had heard Clarke's account and listened to the witnesses assembled for his edification, Selby-Smythe wrote to Morris that "the matter is one in no way requiring military interference", and to Edward Blake, then Minister of Justice, that it did not "demand more than magisterial interference", while French telegraphed to Blake that "the outrages by half-breeds in this vicinity are of a trivial nature", and shortly afterwards wrote to Morris in a way that reflected his disapproval of Clarke's action. "His Honour, and I fear the Dominion Government," he remarked, "have been unnecessarily agitated by the alarming reports received."

Selby-Smythe and French rode off westward with the larger part of their column, leaving Inspector Leif Crozier with a dozen men and overt instructions to arrest Dumont, who had gone back to the plains after meeting them at Gabriel's Crossing, and bring him before Magistrate Clarke. Crozier's confidential instructions may have been different, for he did nothing so rash as to attempt with a dozen men to arrest Dumont in the midst of his hunters. Instead he took Clarke with him to a gathering of the Métis at St. Laurent on 20 August. There Father André and the men of St. Laurent explained why they had set up their local government and how it worked; they argued firmly but unaggressively that they had no intention of doing wrong, and that they believed they had been justified in making their own laws when no kind of government existed. Dumont apologized for anything he had done that might be proved wrong, and offered to make reparation if it were. There is no doubt that Crozier, at the end of the meeting, recognized that according to prairie custom, not yet superseded by any effective Canadian administration, Dumont had not acted wrongly, and, after persuading Clarke that there was no real case for him to try, he dismissed the Métis leader with an admonition to remain loyal and law-abiding. There seems to have been a tacit understanding between the two men that if the council in St. Laurent ceased to exist as a formal body, no objection would be made by the Mounted Police to the retention of traditional rules during the buffalo hunt.

The incident came to an end with a complete vindication of Gabriel Dumont and the Métis of St. Laurent. Commissioner French had persuaded Father André to give him a copy of the laws and proceedings of the community of St. Laurent, and after reading them he repeated his opinion of the "exaggerated accounts given by the Hudson's Bay Company officials regarding the Government set up by these simple hunters." Regarding the laws themselves, he expressed to Edward Blake the view that "on the Prairie such regulations are absolutely necessary", and remarked that "it is not extraordinary, that in a country where no law virtually exists, and where the few Justices of the Peace are Hudson's Bay Company officials inimical to them (as they suppose), settlements should band themselves together for mutual protection." French also expressed the view that all the Métis of the settlement had voluntarily accepted the laws of the community and the government of Dumont and his council, and "this being the case, they have themselves to blame if they find the regulations too severe."

To Lawrence Clarke's vocally expressed consternation, the views of the General and the Commissioner were accepted in Ottawa and even in Westminster. Edward Blake remarked that there was nothing objectionable *per se* in the constitution and laws of the community of St. Laurent, but that the very fact that they had been necessary pointed to the need for "a competent local government and administration of justice." But the final word was spoken by no less a figure than the Earl of Carnarvon, then Secretary for the Colonies, and the episode ended with that Victorian Tory landowner vindicating the policies of Gabriel Dumont and his prairie hunters when he ruled that "it would be difficult to take strong exception to the acts of a community which appears to have honestly endeavoured to maintain order by the best means in its power."

7. Years of Discontent
and Inaction

The council of St. Laurent, as such, ceased to have any active existence after the confrontation between the Mounted Police and Gabriel Dumont in the summer of 1875, but the sense of mutual dependence out of which it had sprung did not diminish nor did the principle of group action entirely die away. Indeed, it tended to be preserved as the isolation of the farther prairies drew to an end during the final years of the 1870s and the early years of the next decade.

Already, in 1875, a district headquarters of the North West Mounted Police was established at Battleford, and in the same year Gabriel Dumont provided the services of his ferry for teams exploring possible routes for the Canadian Pacific Railway. Two years later, in 1877, Fort Battleford would be built and would become the capital of the Northwest Territories, a seat of authority very close to the centre of Métis activity in the region. And even before that, Lieutenant-Governor Morris would arrive to conclude, with the chiefs of the Cree and the Chipewyans and the Assiniboines, gathered at Fort Carlton and later at Fort Pitt, the sixth of the treaties between the government of Canada and the Indians of what had once been Rupert's Land. It was the last treaty but one on the prairies; Treaty 7, with the nations of the Blackfoot Confederacy, would be signed in the following year, and then a conclusion would be reached to the pattern of agreements by which the rights of the plains Indians were limited to reservations that were mere fragments of their former territories, now made available for the flood of settlers who were expected to arrive when the railway finally linked the prairies with central Canada.

It was indeed high time some accord were reached, for the Indians, even more than the Métis, were disturbed at the intrusion of strangers into their territory; they recognized the growing population of white men of various kinds in the Northwest as a danger not only to their traditional way of life, but also to the diminishing buffalo herds that were their main source of the means of existence. For food and dress, for shelter and even fuel, the peoples of the plains had depended on the buffalo through a past longer than tradition itself, and the dwindling of its numbers left them bewildered and angry. Already certain bands of the Cree had impeded the building of the telegraph line in this region, and in 1875 had refused to allow a Geological Survey team to proceed. Missionaries like the Reverend George McDougall, and leading Métis like Gabriel's father and uncle, Isidore and Jean Dumont, were recruited as intermediaries who enjoyed the respect and trust of the Indian peoples, and eventually, on 23 August at Fort Carlton and on 9 September at Fort Pitt, the Indian chiefs came to hold their parleys with Lieutenant-Governor Morris and his attendants and to sign the treaties.

The Fort Carlton ceremony was carried out on a hill some distance from the Hudson's Bay Company's post, and it was attended by a great deal of traditional Indian pomp, which Alexander Morris described in his report:

> The view was very beautiful: the hills and the trees in the distance, and in the foreground, the meadow land being dotted with clumps of wood, with the Indian tents clustered here and there to the number of two hundred.
>
> On my arrival, the Union Jack was hoisted, and the Indians at once began to assemble, beating drums, discharging firearms, singing and dancing. In about half an hour they were ready to advance and meet me. This they did in a semicircle, having men on horseback galloping in circles, shouting, singing and discharging firearms.
>
> They then performed the dance of the "pipe-stem", the stem was elevated to the north, south, west and east, a cere-

112

monial dance was then performed by the Chiefs and head men, the Indian men and women shouting the while.

They then slowly advanced, the horsemen again preceding them on their approach to my tent. I advanced to meet them, accompanied by Messrs Christie and McKay, when the Pipe was presented to us, and stroked by our hands. After the stroking had been completed the Indians sat down in front of the Council tent, satisfied that in accordance with their customs, we had accepted the friendship of the Cree nation. I then addressed the Indians in suitable terms, explaining, that I had been sent by the Queen, in compliance with their own wishes and the written promise I had given them last year, that a messenger would be sent to them.

The negotiations took place in the presence of many spectators, including a number of leading Métis who were as near to a "third party" as could be found in the prairies; Isidore and Jean Dumont were among those who placed their marks on the treaty as witnesses. Gabriel Dumont was also present and, indeed, it was on this occasion that John Kerr — who was a member of Morris's party — saw him for the last time, "when I handed him a keg of Hudson's Bay Company rum — and . . . Gabriel did full justice to the offering."

The terms offered under this treaty were more generous — "more onerous" was the phrase significantly used by David Mills, then Minister of the Interior — than those of the previous treaties. In addition to the customary allocations of land at the rate of a square mile for every family of five; to the initial presents of $12 a head and the wretched annuities of $5, plus medals and flags and suits for the chiefs; and to the few tools and agricultural implements incorporated in the earlier treaties; the bands of the area covered by Treaty 6 secured a few extra trifles — horses and buggies for the chiefs themselves and medicine chests for their people — but they also gained two more important concessions. The first allowed — in the case of Indians who settled down on a reservation — for a three-year grant of provisions. The second moved into potentially broader obligations, since it provided for aid to the Indians, including rations of food, in the event of either pestilence or famine.

Even these terms were accepted only grudgingly by some of

the chiefs, such as Beardy, whose camp at Duck Lake bordered on the territory of Gabriel Dumont and his Métis followers. They were even rejected by a few, notably the Cree Big Bear; at this time Big Bear was a minor chief, but his refusal to settle on a reservation for years after 1876 made him a potent focus of discontent in his own tribe and even among the Assiniboines. Big Bear in 1876 laid great stress on the fact that the treaty contained no provision to prevent the hanging of Indians, but his later actions suggest that he realized more clearly than his fellow chiefs the extent of the surrender which the Indians made when they signed the treaty, and the slight benefit they were likely to gain from it.

Big Bear, of course, was to be proved right in his apprehensions; equally right from another point of view was David Mills, who from the detachment of Ottawa foresaw the difficulties which the pestilence-and-famine clause might create for the Canadian government. He expressed his great regret that Morris and the other Commissioners should have agreed to it, "as it may cause the Indians to rely upon the Government instead of upon their own exertions for sustenance, especially as their natural means of subsistence are likely to diminish with the settlement of the country."

Mills believed that the Indians should be squarely presented with adjustment to the agrarian life as the only way to avoid the consequences of the destruction of the buffalo, and that to promise free gifts of food beforehand would not avert famine, but would tend to make it more certain. It was an honest if somewhat harsh point of view, to be echoed within our own generation by those who have objected with some logic to the imposition of a welfare pattern of existence, with its consequent erosion of traditional skills and initiatives, on the Eskimo hunters of the Barren Lands. Certainly a policy based on Mills's views could have been no more disastrous than that followed by his successors in the Conservative government of 1878, who adhered nominally to the provisions of the Indian treaties but in practice neglected their implementation to a criminal degree.

Those successors, on whom a heavy burden must be placed when we come to assess responsibility for the events of the 1880s in the Northwest, were Sir John A. Macdonald, who in 1878 returned to power with the avowed intention of completing the

Canadian Pacific Railway and opening the West to settlement, his Cabinet minister Sir David Lewis Macpherson, and his bureaucratic subordinate, Lawrence Vankoughnet. Macdonald retained the Ministry of the Interior and the Superintendency of Indian Affairs as well as the Prime Ministership until 1883, and Macpherson was Minister of the Interior from 1883 until the end of 1885. Thanks to Macdonald's excessive preoccupations and Macpherson's expansive inefficiency — the poet Charles Mair once described him with notable felicity as "a huge cloak-bag of pomposity and conceit" — matters in the Northwest during this vital period fell largely into the hands of the permanent officials involved. Of these the Deputy Minister of the Interior from 1882 to 1885, A. M. Burgess, was a man of such impenetrable nonentity that his name did not surface as the author of any initiative — either good or bad — relating to the Northwest, while the Deputy Superintendent of Indian Affairs, Lawrence Vankoughnet, into whose hands Macdonald entirely committed relations with the native peoples of the prairies, was a bureaucrat of a kind still — alas — common in Ottawa, totally devoid of the imagination needed to understand the attitudes and predicaments of either Indians or Métis and governed by a passion for petty economy which was nothing less than disastrous at a time when insight and generosity might have made the essential differences in a situation where the choice was literally between peace and war.

It was not a matter of men wandering unwarned into a perilous situation. After all, the Northwest was in the forefront of Macdonald's National Policy, as the territory through which the railway would finally knit the Canadian nation into an operational whole, the territory into which would eventually flow the millions of settlers who would give solidity to the link between the original eastern provinces of Confederation and the outpost of British Columbia beyond the Great Divide. There was no excuse to be made for a Cabinet that encouraged a programme of western expansion without making itself acquainted with the needs and the aspirations of the peoples already living in the West, and particularly of the Métis whose initiative as a people wishing to secure their own security and freedom had both delayed the accomplishment of Canadian aims in Manitoba and strongly modified the form that Canadian rule would eventually take when the first prairie province was created. Yet as the years slipped by towards 1885, the rulers of Canada acted as if they were virtually ignorant of the true situation developing in the Saskatchewan country as the decline of the old hunting economy assumed a disastrous impetus.

It was an ignorance that sprang less from lack of information about the facts than from what appeared to be an invincible failure to interpret them properly. Nobody in Ottawa seems to have formed a clear idea of the consequences of the virtual extinction of the buffalo that became yearly more certain, nor was there, until it was already too late, any real understanding of the possible consequences of the fact that the Métis claim to aboriginal land rights, unlike that of the Indians, had not been satisfied.

As early as 1873 the warning signals began to sound, with the petition of the Qu'Appelle Métis. In 1874 John McKay informed Alexander Morris of the anxiety of the settlers moving into the Prince Albert district — at this time about fifty families, mainly of English half-breeds — to "know how the land is to be laid out," and also of the concern which the Métis of St. Laurent were showing to have their own holdings legally secured to them. In the conclusion to his report on Treaty 6, Morris himself in 1876 drew the attention of Alexander Mackenzie's government to what he regarded as the two urgent outstanding questions in the Northwest: the conservation of the buffalo and the provision of land for the unsettled Métis. On the first point he declared his view that "a few simple regulations would preserve the herds for many years," and urged the need for appropriate legislation. On the second point he remarked:

> There is another class of the population in the North West, whose position I desire to bring under the notice of the Privy Council. I refer to the wandering half-breeds of the Plains, who are chiefly of French descent, and live the life of the Indian.
>
> There are a few, who are identified with the Indians, who live with them and can properly be treated as Indians, but there is a large class of Métis who live by the hunt of the Buffalo and have no settled homes. I think that a census of the numbers of these should be procured, and while I would not be disposed to recommend their being brought under

the Treaties, I would suggest that land should be assigned to them and that on their settling down, if after an examination into their circumstances, it should be found necessary and expedient, some assistance should be given them to enable them to enter upon agricultural operations.

Morris sweetened his recommendations with a word of gratitude to the Métis. "On this occasion as on others I found the half-breed population, whether French or English, generally using the influence of their relationship to the Indians in support of our efforts to come to a satisfactory arrangement with them." But, curiously, he did not mention the situation of the Métis who already, at St. Laurent and Batoche, had staked their land, built their houses, begun to rear crops and had formed their own local government — the people from whom in years to come the movement of protest and eventually rebellion on the Saskatchewan would originate.

The conservation of the buffalo was the first of Morris's aims to be implemented, though it turned out to be an abortive achievement. Father André and Commissioner French of the Mounted Police had also been urgent in their pleas for some kind of legislation to halt the destruction of the already diminished herds. Ottawa typically shrugged off responsibility, David Mills as Minister of the Interior ruling that it was a matter to be decided by the Council of the Northwest Territories, and in March 1887 the Council passed an Ordinance that, if it had been sustained, might have preserved the buffalo in fair numbers until the day when the spread of agriculture and ranching would have confined their dwindling remnants in the few wild and hilly areas that were comparatively useless to the farmer. The Ordinance forbade such traditional but wasteful methods of killing as the use of pounds or leaps, and the slaughter of buffalo merely for amusement or "solely to secure their tongues, choice cuts or peltries." A hunter must make use of at least half the flesh of any beast he killed. More important for the future of the herds, the killing of cows was allowed only between mid-August and mid-November, and it was forbidden to kill calves under two years old. There were provisions allowing travellers to kill the buffalo under circumstances of great need, and during certain winter months the closed season on cows was relaxed, for Indians only.

The Ordinance failed partly because the very people for whose benefit it was conceived were opposed to it, and partly because it could never have succeeded — given the open nature of the international frontier — unless the Americans had been willing to take similar conservation measures. Despite the concessions given to them, the Indians objected because they regarded the buffalo as a gift from their Manitous with which the white men had no right to interfere. Dumont and his fellow Métis, though they had introduced conservationist measures into the rules of their own buffalo hunts, objected to legislation that discriminated in favour of the Indians and denied them what they regarded as their equal rights as natives of the prairies.

The anger aroused by the Ordinance was indeed so vocal that in the following year the Council repealed it, and the buffalo were abandoned to the irresponsible mercy of the hunters. In 1879 the Americans are said to have assisted the elimination of the buffalo in Canada by lighting fires along the border which burnt a black path hundreds of miles long that prevented the beasts from returning on their northerly migration. The herds that remained in the United States were killed off by commercially organized hunters for their robes alone. As for those in Canada, there is a poignant group of reports in the *Saskatchewan Herald* (published in Battleford and the first newspaper of the Northwest) relating to the autumn of 1881. On 31 October the *Herald* remarks that "Most of our half-breed hunters are off to the plains for buffalo meat." Less than a month later, the paper reports: "Some of our hunters have returned from the plains with light loads of meat. One venerable buffalo was shot about seventy miles from here." When one compares that single venerable buffalo with the great herds that Paul Kane had seen along the Saskatchewan less than forty years before, the tragedy of the destruction of a species becomes vividly immediate. Yet another note in the *Saskatchewan Herald* for 12 November underlines just as poignantly the disturbance of the ecosystem which the unrestricted hunting of the buffalo brought about, for it tells how the packs of buffalo wolves, deprived of their natural prey, were now haunting the neighbourhood of Battleford and endangering cattle. Soon the wolves also would be destroyed, by bullets and strychnine. Not only a human way of life with its attendant culture, but also a whole series of natural relationships came to an end when the buffalo left the prairies.

In his old age, Gabriel Dumont gave 1880 as the last year he rode out to the plains at the head of the St. Laurent buffalo hunt, the great cavalcade. It may have been 1881, for his recollections of dates were not always sharply accurate, but it could hardly have been later. At last, the historic buffalo hunt, with its splendid organization and its discipline of an ordered anarchy, with its line of leadership running back from Gabriel to Isidore Dumont, and then to Pierre Gariepey and Jean-Baptiste Wilkie and finally to Cuthbert Grant, the original Warden of the Plains, had come to an end. But the cohesion of the Métis people, which had been exemplified in the hunt organization and also in the little republic of St. Laurent, did not come to an end. It had been born of the harsh necessities of survival in the plains, which demanded a combination of mutual aid and individual resourcefulness, and it continued in other forms because the need for solidarity persisted when the guarantee of security for the Métis was transferred from the buffalo herd to the land the buffalo had once grazed, which by cultivation and pastoral use might provide the livelihood formerly gained from hunting.

In this situation it is not surprising that Gabriel Dumont soon re-emerged into leadership of the Métis who lived in the villages of the South Saskatchewan. The character of these communities of the far prairies was changing rapidly during the 1870s, partly through the decline of the buffalo hunt as the basis for a way of living, and partly through the steady influx of Manitoba Métis who found life no longer possible in the changed world of the Red River Valley. Some of them were hunters who had found it impossible to follow the buffalo in the environs of the upper Missouri Valley to which the Red River expeditions had formerly resorted. Many of these men put down fragile roots in winter camps just north of the border, near the Qu'Appelle Lakes or at Wood Mountain or in the

Cypress Hills, and still attempted to hunt southward into American territory. But in 1879 the American army went into action against them once again as four companies of cavalry rounded up four hundred families of Canadian Métis and released them only on condition that they agree to hunt in the country where they were domiciled and nowhere else. The question, in hindsight, seems a nullity, since by 1881 there would be very few buffalo left on either side of the border, but it posed a choice to those Métis who still favoured the nomad life; some of them moved into the still fairly free and wild territory of Montana in the United States, where Louis Riel tried with no great success to educate their children. Others remained in the small and unorganized Métis encampments of the southern Canadian prairies, trading and hunting what game survived the great slaughter. But many made their way north to Batoche, St. Laurent, Duck Lake, and the settlements in the Touchwood Hills, where the wilder, younger, and more discontented of them became adherents of Gabriel Dumont in his increasingly intransigent attitude to the Canadian authorities.

These nomads mingled, in the Saskatchewan area, not only with Gabriel's already partially settled followers, but also with a quickly growing group of more sophisticated emigrés from the Red River: the men who had tried to farm there but had failed in competition with the more aggressive Canadians and even in some cases had lost their land by fraud, and the others who had thought themselves men of some consequence on the Red River until they became disillusioned by the completeness of Canadian domination, such as Louis Schmidt and Michel Dumas, who arrived in 1880, and Riel's cousin, Charles Nolin, who, after living briefly in the Touchwood Hills, settled at Batoche in 1882. As Louis Schmidt remembered, 1882 was the year in which "a strong immigration of Métis from Manitoba came to reinforce our groups."

Men like Schmidt and Nolin, with education and some political experience, in other circumstances might well have challenged Dumont's leadership of the local communities, but Schmidt was a man of indecisive character, while those who treasured the memory of the Red River rising were distrustful of Nolin, who had opposed Riel and had gained political office as a reward. Besides, none of these men was present when, in 1877, Dumont re-emerged to lead the Métis in stating their wishes and their grievances.

Their first act was to take up again a matter that had already been discussed by the council of the community in 1874: the provision of a school. If they were not legally entitled to raise a tax of their own for a school, the Métis, doubtless encouraged by Father André, decided to ask the government for help, and petitioned the North West Council in 1877 for a grant in aid of education. Though the government was slow to act, it was this petition that eventually, in 1880, resulted in an Ottawa decision to grant aid in the construction and furnishing of school houses anywhere in the Northwest Territory, and also a proportion of the salaries of teachers. It is significant that Dumont and his Métis followers, most of them as illiterate as he, should have recognized the importance that formal education would assume in the new world that was coming upon them and should have made it the subject of their first representations to duly constituted government as now established in the western prairies.

The next concerns of the Métis of St. Laurent and its surrounding settlements were representation in the governing body of the Territories and, of course, the question — by now perennial — of land. These were freely discussed in the mass meeting held outside the church door of St. Laurent on 1 February 1878, under Gabriel Dumont's chairmanship, with his cousin Alex Fisher acting as secretary. The assembly, doubtless partly inspired by the concessions its participants had seen made to the Indians under Treaty 6 at Fort Carlton, asked for assistance with seed grain and agricultural implements, for scrip and land grants given to heads of families on the same basis as they had been given to the Métis in Manitoba, and, as a matter of urgent necessity, "that the Government should cause to be surveyed, with the least possible delay, the lands occupied and cultivated by the half-breeds or old residents of the country, and that patents therefor be granted to them." The meeting also asked that the Métis, who still outnumbered whites in the Territories, be given representation on the Council, which at present consisted only of the new Lieutenant-Governor, David Laird, of the Commissioner of the North West Mounted Police, and of the two stipendiary magistrates, all of Angloceltic ancestry and background.

Dumont forwarded the petition to the Council at the end of February, and sent copies to other Métis communities, with the result that in June a similar memorandum was submitted by 151 Métis from Prince Albert and its environs, and later on petitions were sent by the half-breeds of St. Albert near Edmonton and of the Cypress Hills, the latter bearing 269 signatures.

The first response to the urgings of Gabriel Dumont and his fellow Métis was the appointment of a Métis member of the North West Council. But the government was unwise enough to choose a man with a record of obedience rather than a man who represented current Métis feeling. Pascal Bréland, the appointed Councillor, had served faithfully on the Council of Assiniboia under the Hudson's Bay Company, had used his influence against Riel both on the Red River and in the Qu'-Appelle region when the question of concerted Métis action came up there in 1870, and, with the support of the Canadian authorities, he had been elected to the first Legislative Assembly of Manitoba. He was now an old man, living as a merchant in the Cypress Hills, which gave an excuse to include him in the governing body of the territories. Bréland was not ignorant of the problems that disturbed the prairie peoples, and on a few occasions he did present them insistently enough to convince his fellow councillors, but in any confrontation he had always been on the side of authority, and most of the Métis had by now come to distrust him. His standing was certainly slight in comparison with that of the Dumonts and their connected clans, headed by the immensely popular Gabriel with his fame as a hunter and his proven ability as a leader in both the hunt and the village community. But though Gabriel Dumont would have been a more acceptable councillor for the Métis than Bréland, it is doubtful if he could have been more effective in changing official policy far enough to avoid the conflict that eventually took place. For the land question, as I have suggested, led to disaster not from lack of warnings on the part of people who knew the West, but from the failure to heed them in Ottawa and especially the failure of the Conservative government that came into power in 1878 and remained there throughout the critical years up to 1885.

One of the warning voices was that of Alexander Morris, the retiring Lieutenant-Governor who in June 1878 remarked privately to Hector Langevin, soon to be a member of the incoming Macdonald government, that "It is a crying shame that the half-breeds have been ignored. It will result in trouble and is most unjust." The North West Council passed in August of the same year a resolution calling for immediate attention to be paid to the question of Métis lands, and in September the new Lieutenant-Governor, David Laird, urged on the government "early action with relation to the claims set forth." The Deputy Minister of the Interior at this time, but unfortunately not for much longer (he retired in 1881), was Colonel J. S. Dennis, who had played a notable part on the Canadian side in the events at Red River during 1869 and 1870, and on the basis of past experience he was well aware of the perils involved in the present situation in the Northwest. In a memorandum to his Minister, who as Sir John A. Macdonald happened also to be Prime Minister and therefore the very fount of policy, he recommended that the half-breed claims should be immediately attended to, and that special inducements should even be offered to persuade them to settle down and accept training in farming and cattle raising. He thought that if the land question were dealt with imaginatively, what was now a situation of potential conflict could be turned to advantage in establishing peace in the West.

> The immediate effect would be, assuming that the Half-breeds themselves are willing to give it a trial, that we should have the whole of this element in sympathy with the Government in dealing with the plain tribes of Indians. In this way we should attract to our side a moral power which in the present critical relations of the various tribes of Indians towards each other and towards the Government would prove of the greatest value to the Dominion. . . . The undersigned . . . is of opinion that further means should be adopted to cultivate and maintain relations with the In-

123

dian and halfbreed populations calculated to attach them to us and to convince them that the Government is desirous of fulfilling its obligations to them in the utmost good faith.

Dennis was not content with expressing his own opinions, which showed a sensible assessment of the potential value of Métis friendship to the Canadian government; he sent copies of his memorandum to Lieutenant-Governor Laird, Archbishop Taché, and the Anglican Bishop McLean. They all virtually agreed in a point of view that was expressed most eloquently by the Archbishop, whose involvement in Métis problems extended over more than thirty years since he arrived on the Red River as a missionary in 1845, and who remembered with a certain lingering bitterness the dishonesty — as it appeared to him — of Macdonald's actions after the settlement of the Red River question in 1870. He began by warning the government that "the Halfbreed element in dissatisfaction would form a standing menace to the peace and prosperity of the Territories." He went on to summarize with admirable clarity and forthrightness the alternatives that lay before the government.

The formidable Indian question has not yet arisen in our midst, owing largely to the influence of the Halfbreed element. The disappearance of the buffalo and especially the extension of the settlers into the Indian country, are preparing difficulties which may be avoided, I hope, but which would otherwise involve such terrible and expensive results that it is the duty of all the friends of the Government and of the country to do all in their power to prevent such misfortune.

The result depends in a great measure on the way the Halfbreeds would be treated. Friendly disposed, they will mightily contribute to the maintenance of peace; dissatisfied, they would not only add to the difficulty, but render the settlement of the country the next thing to an impossibility.

The Halfbreeds are a highly sensitive race; they keenly resent injury or insult, and daily complain on that point. In fact, they are daily humiliated with regard to their origin by the way they are spoken of, not only in newspapers, but also in official and semi-official documents.

It is desirable that the Halfbreed question should be

decided upon without any further delay. The requisite legislation ought to be passed in the coming session of the Legislature. . . . There is no doubt the difficulties increase with delay.

The warnings that Macdonald, as the Minister responsible for the Northwest Territories, received from men as different in their outlooks as Alexander Morris, Colonel Dennis, and Archbishop Taché, were to be repeated, in startlingly similar forms, during the whole period of tension that extended to the early months of 1885. Priests and policemen, traders and casual travellers, continued to send their cautionary messages, too numerous to quote in this particular context, so that the Conservative government, which inherited in 1878 the problems of the unsettled prairies, could never have honestly argued that it failed to act from lack of warning.

Nor did it fail to act for lack of legislative sanction, since the Dominion Lands Act, which was passed on 1878, specifically envisaged a situation in which the special claims of the Métis would have to be considered, and actually laid down how they could be satisfied, since Clause 31 of the Act gave authority to the Governor-General-in-Council, meaning in practice the Dominion Cabinet, "To satisfy any claims existing in connection with the extinguishment of the Indian title, preferred by half-breeds resident in the North-west Territories outside the limits of Manitoba, on the fifteenth day of June, one thousand eight hundred and seventy, by granting land to such persons, to such extent and on such terms and conditions, as may be deemed expedient." Clearly, under the Act, Macdonald was authorized to make any arrangement that would satisfy the Métis and assure the peace of the Northwest. The land regulations which the people of St. Laurent framed for themselves in 1874, allowing half a square mile of land to each head of family, suggest that their demands would not have been high. But Macdonald, doubly responsible as Prime Minister and Minister of the Interior, never seriously attempted to ascertain or to satisfy these demands.

When we turn from the level at which men of national standing, with a knowledge of the Northwest, warned an unresponsive government, to the level of the Métis themselves, it is easy to understand their mood of bewilderment, building into resentful frustration. They had moved into the far west in pursuit of the old free life of the *coureurs de bois*, and they had seen that life coming to an end with the death of the buffalo herds. Persuaded by their priests, and by leaders like Gabriel Dumont, they had accepted the inevitability of settlement, and had assumed that their claims to the lands on which they settled beside the deserted rivers of that great empty country would never be challenged.

But they were to be faced, as we all are, by the imperatives of change and by the perishability of all earthly paradises. By acting as guides and freighters, they even contributed to the destruction of their own Eden, bringing in the settlers and gentlemen hunters and government officers who would completely transform their world. Then, having acted as go-betweens and witnesses for the Indian Treaties, they were to discover that, since they themselves had obtained no similar treaties, the land not allocated for Indian reserves was to be treated by the Canadian government as its domain, to be allocated at will. Under the general provisions of the new land law and its attendant regulations, the prairies were to be surveyed according to the American quadrilateral system. Complex agreements with the Canadian Pacific Railway and the Hudson's Bay Company meant that in many areas alternate sections would not even be available to homesteaders but would have to be bought by those who were unfortunate enough — in terms of the law — to have squatted on them, while other areas, under the act, were to be reserved for schools. Although the government had the power to ignore any of these circumstances in satisfying the claims of the Métis, it showed no sign of making any use of that power.

Even those Métis — Gabriel Dumont among them — who were lucky enough to find the land they had chosen at least in part available for homesteading, were faced with the fact that — unless they had instructions to the contrary — the government surveyors who were beginning to move through the west would be inclined to ignore the traditional predilection of the French half-breeds for long and narrow river-front lots. All such concerns, however, were subsumed in the major anxiety; year after year, as inaction continued, every Métis remained legally a squatter, with no title to his land, and this at a time when strangers in growing numbers were moving into his country. These strangers, moreover, were not merely the English half-breeds or the Canadian or immigrant settlers, who shared with the Métis their anxieties over delays in obtaining title to occupied land, but the agents of land speculators attempting to secure large areas of land over the heads of the present occupiers. One group of speculators, calling itself the Prince Albert Colonization Company, is actually said to have attempted to secure title to lands occupied by Métis farmers around Batoche and St. Laurent. One would assume that no well-informed land company would involve itself in so potentially explosive a manoeuvre, but the very remoteness and irresponsibility of this syndicate of profiteers must have given it, in the minds of the simple hunters and farmers of the Saskatchewan, a menacing impersonality rather like that which emanated disconcertingly from the government in Ottawa, so deaf to appeals, so blind in its actions.

Since, until the rebellion had become virtually inevitable in the early months of 1885, Macdonald gave no evidence of his comprehension of the situation in the western prairies, we must assume that he never even imagined how his appearance of indifference might affect the Métis, already disillusioned with the results of the pact between Riel and the Canadian government in 1870. Yet Sir John had enough experience to recognize the situation that was developing. As George Stanley has remarked: "There may have been excuses for Sir John A. Macdonald in 1869; there were none in 1885. For the problem which had faced the Prime Minister was the same one that had faced him earlier; the problem of conflicting cultures, of reconciling a small primitive population with a new complex civilization." Macdonald's failure on each occasion is all the more surprising and reprehensible when one remembers that he himself, a Highlander one generation removed, belonged by ancestry to the clans that at Culloden stood in defence of a primitive culture against a complex civilization in the same way as Gabriel Dumont and his people were preparing to stand on the Saskatchewan.

Against Macdonald's fatal indifference and incomprehensible inertia, and against the growing invasion of their territory

127

by an alien world, the Métis did not even have the meagre protection offered to the Indians by their treaties. All they could do was to attract attention to their plight by agitations in which they were often supported by the priests and by members of the local government, and, later on, by English half-breeds and even the white settlers. But the original initiatives came from the Métis of St. Laurent, and the vital force among the Métis of St. Laurent was Gabriel Dumont. Some writers have suggested that, after he appeared in 1882, Charles Nolin took over the leadership of the French-speaking Métis on the South Saskatchewan, but Nolin was in fact a discredited man who led at best a small faction of Manitoba emigrés, and the only man who inspired a general loyalty among the Métis, and whose voice was always sought, remained Gabriel Dumont.

It was he — in 1880 — who raised an agitation against new regulations that would have imposed a toll on all wood cut from crown lands, as a result of which the Territorial Council withdrew the tax. And he was foremost in the activities during 1881 which resulted in petitions sponsored by both Father André and Lawrence Clarke being forwarded to the Territorial Council, as a result of which, on 8 June, the Council presented to Ottawa, accompanied by a request for action, the renewed Métis demands for land and scrip. By the autumn of that year, in spite of the final opening of a Land Office in Prince Albert, anxiety over the validity of their occupation of what had appeared to be free land had spread to the white settlers, many of whom realized that instead of owning their farms, they were in fact — or at least in law — squatters on land arbitrarily set aside for schools or for the profit of the Hudson's Bay Company. At a meeting of Prince Albert settlers — mainly Canadians and English half-breeds — on 8 October, the demand was made that all persons who had been settled on their lands for three years and had fulfilled the normal homestead requirements of residence and cultivation should be granted patents, irrespective of the present regulations. But those who attended the meeting did not forget their Métis neighbours, and passed a resolution demanding that the half-breeds' rights in the soil as sons of Indians should be recognized, as it had been recognized in Manitoba.

The grievances of the Métis did not prevent them from

Dumont at Fort Assiniboine, May 1885.

GLENBOW-ALBERTA INSTITUTE

BATTLEFORD HISTORIC PARK

SASKATCHEWAN GOVERNMENT PHOTOGRAPH

SASKATCHEWAN GOVERNMENT PHOTOGRAPH

TOP LEFT: Big Bear after the rebellion.

TOP RIGHT: The rectory at Batoche with bullet holes below the top window.

ABOVE: The cemetery at Batoche. In the background the rectory and church of St. Antoine de Padoue.

volubly demonstrating their loyalty to Queen Victoria when Viscount Lorne made his viceregal progress across the prairies in the late summer of 1881. The buffalo hunters and their wives, mounted and in their gayest clothes, gathered at St. Laurent on 22 August, the day his arrival was expected, planning to greet him with songs and salvoes. But Lorne's progress through the Touchwood Hills and over the Salt Plain was slower than planned, and on the next day the Métis dispersed. Lorne and his party actually arrived at Gabriel's Crossing on the morning of 25 August, and Gabriel himself was there to supervise the ferrying over of the whole company with their eighty horses and nineteen wagons, all transported in a high wind by his single scow. Then, with the other Métis of Batoche, he formed a mounted escort that accompanied the viceregal cavalcade as far as Duck Lake, where Lawrence Clarke presented an address of welcome on behalf of the whole population of the region, and to Fort Carlton, where Lord Lorne held an Indian council the following morning, with the Dumonts on hand as intermediaries and spectators, and then boarded the steamer *Northcote*, which had recently begun to ply the Saskatchewan, for a voyage downriver to Prince Albert, and thence back upriver to Battleford, from which he would proceed by land to the Rockies.

Demonstrating what were essentially feudal loyalties was one thing. Demanding one's rights from arrogant parliamentarians was another, and the glitter of the viceregal visit by the great Queen's son-in-law did not prevent either the Métis or the other inhabitants of the Saskatchewan region from pressing for a just settlement of their land claims. On 4 September 1882, Gabriel Dumont's signature — or rather his carefully drawn mark — appeared at the head of forty-five other names on a petition in the handwriting of Charles Nolin, protesting against the land regulations that forced them to pay for land they already occupied if it happened to fall in the unevenly numbered sections that were not available for homesteading. They asked to be exempted entirely from the homestead regulations, and requested a type of survey adapted to their needs and their traditional predilection for long and narrow river-fronting lots rather than square quarter-sections. They ended in proud peroration: "Having been so long regarded as the masters of this country, having defended it against the Indians at the cost of

129

our blood, we do not consider that we are asking too much when we call on the government to allow us to occupy our lands in peace and to exempt us from the regulations by making free grants of land to the Métis of the North-west."

Like all the other petitions, like the renewed pleas from Archbishop Taché and Father André, from the Territorial Council and from individuals like Lawrence Clarke who were not especially sympathetic to the Métis claims but who saw the consequences of scorning them, this appeal fell on deaf ears. The government appeared unmoved.

On the bureaucratic level it insisted that surveys must go forward on the system already laid down, and that there would be no exception to the regulations: this in spite of the provision in the Dominion Lands Act which specifically provided for discretionary exemption in the case of the Métis from the general provisions of the Act.

On the political level, Macdonald and his colleagues presented an almost unbelievable record of procrastination. In April 1882, to quote one of the salient episodes which make up that record, the Department of the Interior proposed an amendment to the Lands Act that would have allowed patents to be issued to those who had already fulfilled the requirements in terms of occupation and cultivation specified in the homestead regulations; through some inexplicable lapse into dilatoriness, the amendment was never presented to Parliament. Then, moving at the tortoise-like pace that marked his treatment of political situations he found embarrassing or distasteful, Macdonald, at the end of 1882, finally acknowledged that there might be a situation to be investigated, and proposed to send to the West a special delegate, Lindsay Russell. Russell, however, was incapacitated by an accident, and it was not until early in 1884 that the first representative of the Ottawa government, an Inspector of Dominion Lands named William Pearce, who spoke no French, arrived in the area. Pearce investigated the claims of those who could or would speak to him in English, though not entirely satisfactorily, since many remained disgruntled after the government had acted on his recommendations in April 1884. But, using his lack of French as an excuse, he did nothing about the Métis claims, and left the matter to the bilingual Dominion Land Agent in Prince Albert, who went to St. Laurent in May 1884. Only in October of the same year did the Agent send his report to Ottawa, where it was promptly mislaid, and not resurrected until February 1885. By that time, action on it was already too late, for the Métis, calling Louis Riel back into Canada to advise and inspire them, had taken their own direction.

8. The Coming of Riel

Who first thought of inviting Riel to leave his refuge in Montana, and journey far north to the banks of the Saskatchewan, is a matter of argument among the Métis people and of confusion to historians. It is certain that Riel had for some time been aware of the situation on the Saskatchewan River. His own home at St. Peter's Mission on the Sun River, where he taught the local children, might have seemed distant from events in the Canadian prairies, but he had not lost interest either in his people or in the great land to the north where he had made his mark on history, and rumours of what was happening on the Saskatchewan reached him through his wandering Métis neighbours who maintained contacts with hunters and traders north of the border. Sometimes, also, Métis from the Saskatchewan found their way south and visited him. One of these was Philippe Garnot, who kept a kind of inn for travellers in Batoche and who later became Riel's secretary; he visited Sun River in 1882, and told Riel of the political situation in the Northwest Territories and of the plight of the Métis. It is not recorded that Riel at this time offered any advice.

Later, in July 1883, Riel himself left Montana on a trip to the Red River, and there he met his young relative Napoléon Nault, son of André Nault, the man on whose land in 1869, by placing his foot on a surveyor's chain, Riel had made the first symbolic act of Métis refusal to accept unconditionally the transfer of power in the Canadian West from the Hudson's Bay Company to the newly formed Dominion. Napoléon Nault had moved to the Saskatchewan, where he found Dumont's bluff independence more agreeable than Charles Nolin's political deviousness. Nault also talked of the plight of the Métis, and it is likely that by this time, with his mystical sense of the importance of coincidence, Riel was becoming impressed by the way in which history seemed to be repeating itself in shaping the fate of his people, and was relating this pattern of destiny to his own sense of being endowed with a God-given mission. At the trial in Regina of Riel's associates in the 1885 rebellion, one of the prosecution lawyers was to suggest that on this occasion Nault and Riel actually plotted that Dumont should be persuaded to suggest inviting the leader of the 1869 rising to solve the present problems of his people, but there is no evidence that supports this allegation.

Even on the question of who in St. Laurent or Batoche first proposed inviting Riel, the record is indefinite. Louis Schmidt, who took no actual part in the 1885 rebellion, later laid claim to the credit. During the summer of 1883 Schmidt had served as secretary for another mass protest meeting in St. Laurent, this time presided over by Pierre Parenteau, a veteran of 1869; but as an educated and ambitious man he was drawn towards the minuscule metropolis of Prince Albert, where he became a lawyer's clerk and eventually entered the Land Office as a government official. He relates that in January 1884, when he was going to Prince Albert to take up his legal employment, he ran into Baptiste Arcand, one of Dumont's close associates, who was on his way to a meeting between the French and English half-breeds. "In talking with him, I suggested to him the idea of getting Riel to come and help them with their claims. His influence would unite them, and their demands would have a better chance of being accepted. This idea took root and the English halfbreeds freely joined with the French in putting it into execution."

There is no evidence that directly corroborates Louis Schmidt's statement, and Gabriel Dumont almost two decades afterwards credited neither Schmidt nor Arcand with any part in the bringing of Riel; he declared, in 1903, that the idea was brought forward at a meeting in the house of his father Isidore by the English settler Andrew Spence, who declared: "There is only one man capable of helping us, and that is Riel."

It is possible that Schmidt may have originated the idea of bringing Riel which was mentioned by Arcand to Spence and repeated by him at a later meeting. But there is a great deal of reason to believe that, even if Napoléon Nault had not entered into any understanding with Riel, it was he who activated the idea at the vital meeting where the Métis chiefs made their decision to support an appeal to their former leader and that — in a way I shall later explain — Dumont's memory of the actual sequence of events was defective.

The meeting took place on 22 March 1884 in the house of Abraham Montour. It was called to discuss proposals for common action among Métis, English half-breeds, and white settlers that had come from W. H. Jackson, the secretary of the Settlers' Union, a militant liberal whose disgust with the Macdonald government was pushing him near the edge of rebellion. About thirty Métis were present, including Gabriel Dumont, Charles Nolin, Maxime Lépine, Michel Dumas, Napoléon Nault, and Jean-Baptiste Boucher. The meeting marked Dumont's return to a militant role after a period of relative withdrawal when he appears to have thought the Métis cause might be better served by literate men with some knowledge of the law, such as Nolin and some of the other emigrés from Manitoba, and to have occupied himself recreating his life after the termination of the buffalo hunt. But even if he himself was able to establish title to part of his land, and to build up — in Métis terms — a reasonable standard of living on the wreck of the old hunting life, Dumont was not the kind of man either to evade a struggle or to forget the plight of those among his fellow Métis who now had neither the produce of the hunt nor the certainty of securely held land to compensate for the loss of the buffalo. And, for their part, the other leading Métis realized that they alone could not speak for their people, and that without Dumont's support it would be impossible to achieve the ambitious plan of an alliance with the other local groups, which both Nolin and Maxime Lépine (the son of Riel's lieutenant in 1869, Ambroise Lépine) had become convinced was essential if any impression were to be made on the Canadian government.

By 22 March Nolin and Lépine had already convinced Dumont of the need for collaboration between the three malcontent groups, and the three men went together to the meeting at Montour's. The meeting was attended by some thirty men, varying in attitude from younger activists like Napoléon Nault and Damas Carrière to comparative conservatives like Charles Nolin and Xavier Batoche (the richest man in the village named after him) and to patriarchs of the nomad past like Pierre Gariepey and the elder Isidore Dumont. No English-speaking settlers were present, nor was any of the priests, and those who attended took an oath of secrecy to which eight put their signatures and twenty-two their marks; it was still mainly a community of men schooled not in letters but in the lore of the hunt and the wilderness.

A general discussion took place, which embraced not only the proposals that had come from Jackson, but also other ways of demonstrating to the Canadian government the resolution of the Métis to gain their rights. It appears to have been at this meeting that the possibility of armed rebellion was first broached, not at this time by Dumont, who was still willing to try more pacific means, but by some of the younger and more impatient men. It was also on this occasion that Napoléon Nault suggested the involvement of Louis Riel, and in doing so crystallized a thought that had doubtless begun to form already in the minds of many of his associates. Riel had once forced the Dominion government to come to an agreement with the Métis, and he was not to blame if the government had failed to keep its promises. Perhaps he could now advise the people of the Saskatchewan how to persuade the deaf men in Ottawa to listen to their complaints and satisfy their grievances.

There was as yet no idea of doing more than asking Riel's advice; the thought of accepting him as a leader in an active way had not yet occurred to anyone, except perhaps Nault. Gabriel Dumont immediately took up the proposal to consult Riel; it was a way of assuaging his sense of impotence in the present situation, and it gained general acceptance. So did the proposal to collaborate with the English half-breeds and the white settlers, and a general open-air meeting of the Métis community was called for mid-April outside the house of Isidore Dumont senior, who had now moved back from the

135

Red River and was living near St. Laurent. It is significant that the space in front of the church was no longer regarded as an appropriate meeting place; the Métis leaders appear to have realized that they were starting on a course along which the priests might not be willing to accompany them.

Gabriel Dumont and Baptiste Boucher were delegated to visit the outlying settlements around Prince Albert to assure that the French-speaking people of the area would be thoroughly represented, and on 28 April several hundred men gathered and stood for hours in the melting snow outside old Isidore's log house as they discussed and passed a series of seven resolutions which not merely reiterated their own demands for a more representative Territorial Council and for land titles, but also blamed the government for its neglect of the Indians, thus pointing to a common grievance between the two native peoples and to an alliance yet to be achieved — or at least to be brought into the open. It appears to have been at this meeting that Andrew Spence advocated inviting Riel, perhaps unaware that the Métis leaders had already discussed the idea among themselves. The meeting elected a committee of six to prepare a draft Bill of Rights to be submitted on behalf of the Métis to a general meeting of all three groups early in May. Dumont was a member of the committee, and it was proposed that he and Nolin, respectively the most influential and the most literate of the Saskatchewan Métis, should take the document personally to Ottawa, travelling by way of Montana so that they could seek Riel's advice.

The general meeting of delegates from all three aggrieved communities took place on 6 May in the Lindsay Schoolhouse, between Batoche and Prince Albert. Andrew Spence took the chair at this meeting, and Dumont was one of the five official Métis representatives. The meeting was in general agreement about the unendurable procrastinations and the apparent indifference of the Dominion government. But the unanimity began to crack when the question of consulting Riel was raised, and it was only Spence's eloquent advocacy that quelled the misgivings of many English half-breeds and white settlers. The original Métis proposal for Dumont and Nolin to go to Ottawa by way of Montana was abandoned on the grounds of expense, and a resolution was finally passed:

We, the French and English natives of the North-west, knowing that Louis Riel made a bargain with the Government of Canada in 1870, which said bargain is contained mostly in what is known as the "Manitoba Act", have thought it advisable that a delegation be sent to said Louis Riel, and have his assistance to bring all the matters referred to in the above resolutions in a proper shape and form before the Government of Canada, so that our just demands be granted.

Two points in the resolution should be noted. It does not say specifically that Riel will be invited to come to the North-west, though this was understood by the time the committee appointed by the meeting made its selection of the delegates, for the Catholic Bishop Grandin, who was visiting Prince Albert at the time, noted that "Our poor métis . . . have sent a deputation to Louis Riel to bring him back as their leader with a view to opposing the government." The other point worth observing is that the resolution is specified as representing the "French and British natives of the North-west", which embraces half-breeds of both languages but excludes most of the white settlers; doubtless, while the half-breeds were fairly unanimous in their willingness to involve Riel, the white settlers were not, though some of them undoubtedly contributed to the funds that were collected to pay the expenses of the trip to Montana, a fact which Sir John A. Macdonald later distorted when he claimed that the trip had been subsidized by the "white speculators" of Prince Albert.

The three chosen delegates were all half-breeds, Gabriel Dumont and Michel Dumas representing the French-speakers and James Isbister the English-speakers. Louis Schmidt had been suggested, but as he had just been appointed to the Land Office, he decided not to go; the fear of losing his government appointment would in fact keep Schmidt on the verge of events throughout the coming period of agitation and rebellion. Moïse Ouelette, Gabriel Dumont's brother-in-law and a member of the original Métis council of St. Laurent in 1873, accompanied the party unofficially, and two other men from St. Laurent, Calixte Lafontaine and Philippe Gariepey, visiting relatives in Lewiston, Montana, accompanied the party most of the way.

Already, in April, Dumont had sold his ferry — though not his house and land — to Philippe Garnot, and therefore he had no pressing concern to hold him in Batoche; his friends and relatives agreed to look after his family in case of need, and he looked forward to this journey of nearly seven hundred miles that would take him into territory he had never seen before.

The party set out on 19 May, Dumont driving an ordinary four-wheel wagon, and Ouelette and Isbister each driving two-horse buggies. They slipped away quietly, not wishing to attract unduly the attention of the authorities, but their departure and their mission were known to Father André, who did not approve, and also to Lawrence Clarke, who on the day afterwards wired to Lieutenant-Governor Dewdney and sent a long letter to James A. Grahame, the Governor of the Hudson's Bay Company in Winnipeg, who forwarded it to the Ministry of the Interior, where it had no effect and was presumably filed as another example of Clarke's well-known alarmism, though in fact — in part at least through Clarke's own ill-considered actions — the fears it expressed would actually be fulfilled.

Clarke claimed that at one of their meetings — perhaps he had heard reports of the secret gathering at Abraham Montour's — the Métis had passed a resolution that "the halfbreeds do not recognize the right of the Government to the North-west Territories." He went on to discuss the delegation that was travelling to Montana: "The delegates so appointed — names: Gabriel Dumont, Moïse Ouelette, Michel Dumas, and James Isbister — left yesterday for Montana to carry out the objects of their mission."

Clarke — one of the few local people who failed to take seriously the importance of the land question to the Métis — remarked that there were now some seven hundred adult Métis males in the district, and that they were increasing each year by migration not only from Manitoba, but also from the southern prairies around Qu'Appelle. "These men," he continued, "are not farmers, merely cultivating small patches of land little larger than kitchen gardens. They live by hunting and fishing. Their occupation as hunters was ended by the disappearance of the buffalo, and there is not sufficient overland freighting going on in the country to afford labour to one third of their number, hence they are getting poorer year by year. This in reality is the real source from which this agitation arises, although pretended grievances against the Government are rushed to the front."

One passage, which Clarke presumably based on what he heard being said in and about the Hudson's Bay posts, suggests that the Métis were already thinking in terms of an alliance with the Indians, the alliance that Dumont had prepared on his journeys to the various tribes of the plains in the years since 1870. "These men avow," says Clarke, "that the Indians are in sympathy with them. The French Halfbreeds are closely related to the plain Indians and there is danger of the Halfbreeds persuading the Indians to join them should an uprising take place. The Indians have no arms or ammunition, it is true, but both arms and ammunition in considerable quantities, belonging to the defunct Saskatchewan Military organization, are scattered throughout the country without protection and could be seized at any moment."

Clarke recommended that the arms and ammunition should be collected, that the Mounted Police in the area should be reinforced, and, claiming he shared this view with Father André, that Dumont and his companions should be shadowed so that, if Riel came back with them and crossed the border, he might be arrested. Clarke's warnings and recommendations, like the petitions of the Métis themselves, provoked no action whatever on the part of the Dominion government, for Macpherson, now Minister of the Interior, was as accomplished a pigeon-holer as Sir John A. Macdonald himself; in fact he would continue for a whole year afterwards to deny that any Métis grievances really existed.

Meanwhile Dumont and his companions rode southward, averaging more than forty miles a day over terrain that was often rough and trackless. They easily evaded the patrols of the Mounted Police, and in Canada their journey was facilitated by the help and hospitality of the Blackfoot, to whom Dumont was known by name even when he was not personally acquainted with the members of a particular band. He and his companions struck south through the Cypress Hills, the old haunt of whisky traders cleared out a decade before by the police on their first march into the prairies, and crossed the border near Fort Assiniboine, reaching the Missouri at the old trading centre of Fort Benton. It is said that the Gros Ventre Indians south of the border, who had never reached any agreement with the Canadian Métis, stopped the travellers and tried to exact tribute from them in exchange for permission to cross tribal territory, and that Dumont, who shone in situations of this kind, managed to talk a way through without payments of any kind being made.

From Fort Benton they travelled up the Missouri to its confluence with the Sun River, which they followed to Fort Shaw and thence to St. Peter's Mission, fourteen miles beyond it. They reached the mission at eight o'clock on the morning of 4 June, and, stopping at one of the little log houses, were told that Riel was in the church attending mass, as was his regular habit. Dumont asked an old woman who was standing near them to go in and tell Riel that there were some visitors who wished to speak with him urgently. Riel emerged from the church, and Dumont went forward to meet him. According to Dumont's account, Riel shook his hand, and held it long in his own. "You seem to be a man from far away," he said; "I do not know you, but you seem to know me." "Indeed I do," said Gabriel, "and I think you should know me as well. Don't you remember the name of Gabriel Dumont?" "Of°course," Riel answered, "I remember it very well. I am happy to see you again. But excuse me; I must go back to finish hearing the mass." And he directed them to his cabin down the road, where his wife would give them hospitality.

When Riel returned and heard of the deputation's mission, he appears to have been surprised and flattered, and then he said something so curious that it remained in Dumont's memory ever afterwards. "God wants you to understand that you have taken the right way, for there are four of you, and you have arrived on the fourth of June. And you wish to have a fifth to return with you. I cannot give you my answer today. Wait until tomorrow morning, and I will have a decision for you."

The next morning – 5 June – Dumont and Dumas accompanied Riel to the mission church to confess and receive communion. Then they went back to join Isbister and Ouelette at Riel's house, and Dumont asked for a decision. "Fifteen years ago," Riel answered, "I gave my heart to my nation, and I am ready to give it again. But I cannot leave my young family behind. If you can arrange to take us all, I will go with you." He had, as well as his wife, a son of four and a daughter of two. "There will be no difficulty," Gabriel answered. "With our three vehicles we shall have room for you all." Riel said he could not leave for several days, since he had to wind up his employment as a teacher. They agreed to wait, and Riel then sat down to write a letter which he gave to Dumont.

Dumont handed it to Michel Dumas, who had the benefit of a missionary education. It was a curious but characteristic document that he read aloud to his fellow delegates, in which Riel's contradictory capacities for exaltation and self-doubt were both exemplified, and in which his reawakening sense of mission was — as always — mingled with a desire to gain the material rights which he felt had been denied him in 1870.

Riel began by referring to their long journey and the credentials they had brought, afterwards said to include letters from prominent citizens of Prince Albert, which were later destroyed to avoid compromising their writers in culpability for the events of 1885. He continued,

Your invitation is cordial and pressing. You ask me to accompany you with my family. I could make my excuses and say no. Yet you await my decision, so that all I have to do is to make my own preparations, and the letters you bring assure me that I would be welcomed by those who have sent you as if I were returning to my own family. Gentlemen, your visit honours and pleases me, and your role as delegates gives it the character of a memorable event; I record it as one the happiest occasions of my life. It is an event my family will remember, and I pray to God that your deputation may be one of the blessings of this year, which is the fortieth of my existence.

Let me speak briefly and frankly. I doubt if any advice I could give you while on this alien soil concerning matters in Canada would be of much use beyond the frontier. But there is another aspect of the matter. According to Article 31 of the Manitoba treaty, the Canadian government owes me two hundred and forty acres of land. It also owes me five lots which are valuable because of their hay, their wood, and their nearness to the river. These lots belonged to me according to various paragraphs of the same Article 31 of the treaty to which I have referred. Directly or indirectly, the Canadian government has deprived me of these properties. In addition, if the Canadian government were to examine the matter, it would soon see that it owes me something more than that.

These claims which I have on the government retain their validity in spite of the fact that I have now become an American citizen. In your interest therefore and in mine as well, I accept your friendly invitation; I will go and spend a little time among you. Perhaps by presenting petitions to the government we shall be able to gain at least something. But my intention is to come back here soon, in the coming autumn.

He went on to talk of the friendships he had made among the Métis of Montana, and of his desire to be of assistance to them, and reiterated his intention to return among them, this time specifically naming the month of September. There is no sign that at this moment he had any other than a modest notion of the role he would play in Canada.

The delegates were not only impressed by the sincerity of Riel's reply and pleased by the welcome he and his shy young Métis wife Marguerite extended to them. They were also moved by the conditions in which they found him living. "Usually, when visitors enter the dwelling of a very poor man," they would say in the report they presented on returning to the Saskatchewan, "they experience a rather painful feeling, but on entering M. Riel's house, our impression was different. The humble condition of his home reminded us of the times in years past when he had the chance to enrich himself and indeed to make a considerable fortune; it also reminded us how far, despite everything, he was strengthened by confidence in his nation. We know how he worked for Manitoba and how he struggled on behalf of everyone in the Northwest, and having seen how little he had worked for his own benefit, we have returned, after a long journey of almost fourteen hundred miles, with double the confidence we had in him when we left to seek him out in a strange land."

On 9 June Louis Riel taught his last class at St. Peter's Mission, and felt he had honourably fulfiled his obligations to the priests. On the morning of 10 June, Gabriel Dumont led the little cavalcade along the banks of the Sun River at the beginning of the long and now much slower journey back to Batoche; a Red River cart had been added to carry the scanty possessions of Riel and his family.

At Fort Benton they halted for a day to rest the horses and buy supplies, and Riel attended mass and then talked to Father Eberschweiler, the local Jesuit priest, and asked his benediction. Eberschweiler was doubtful of Riel's mission, and at first refused, but when Riel returned the next morning, he agreed, and Riel went back to fetch his companions so that they could be blessed together. Isbister, Ouelette, and Dumas all refused; only Dumont agreed to go with Riel and his family. It was an occasion both men remembered with great emotion. Riel, writing from his prison cell in Regina when the Northwest Rebellion had been fought and lost, described it to Archbishop Taché. "The holy priest put on his surplice, made us kneel at the altar rails, took his vessel of holy water, and sprinkled on us the divine blessing. While he was blessing us, with his approval and permission I offered the following prayer to God. 'Dear God, bless me according to the light of your Providence which is loving and without measure. Bless me with my wife, with our little son Jean, with our little daughter Marie Angélique, and with Gabriel Dumont.' "

Gabriel composed his own prayer as he rode away that morning, which afterwards every night and morning he said as an invocation after his other prayers, for this prairie warrior was as punctilious in his religious observances as any mediaeval knight. "Lord, strengthen my courage, my faith and my honour that I may profit in my life from the blessing I have received in Thy Holy Name." After the rebellion, when he became an exile in Montana, Dumont revisited Father Eberschweiler, and told him that he attributed his escape from death as a favour from God because of the father's blessing. For all the anti-clericalism that his experiences were to teach him, Dumont never lost the simple faith that the Métis had inherited from their French forefathers.

The way back to Batoche was uneventful. There were no

police waiting at the border, and none were seen on the whole journey. Riel's children were intermittently sick, and this slowed the party's progress over the hills just beyond the border and the prairies that were already becoming dusty with summer, the deserted prairies where only the crop of bones reminded the travellers of the departed buffalo. June passed into July before they reached the parkland beside the South Saskatchewan, with its green and fragrant poplar woods and the jade-pale barley springing in the little Métis fields above the river. About fifteen miles from Batoche, at Tourond's Coulée, which the English called Fish Creek, they were met on 5 July by a column of sixty Métis horsemen, cheering and shouting their welcomes, firing salvoes from their muskets and Winchesters, singing the old proud songs of Pierre Falcon. They escorted the travellers to Tourond's farm, where fifty wagonloads of older people, women and children were gathered around the whitewashed log buildings. The wild young men were there, anxious to see the man who in his exile had become a legendary emblem of defiance, and so were the patriarchs of the dying prairie life, like old Isidore Dumont, and Patrice Tourond, and the giant Toussaint Lussier, whose strength had become almost proverbial throughout the plains from the Assiniboine to the Athapaska. Riel was moved to tears when he saw so many companions of the Red River days, forced to leave their homes in Manitoba for an equal uncertainty in the far prairies. There was a moment of tension when he came face to face with his cousin Charles Nolin, who had opposed him in 1869, but this was eased by Dumont's genial assurances of Nolin's present devotion to the Métis cause, and, for the moment at least, the old rivals seemed to be reconciled.

From Tourond's farm, the party proceeded the ten miles north along the high banks of the Saskatchewan to Gabriel's Crossing, and there they halted for the night, as Madeleine welcomed the Riels into her house, and the rest of the company camped in their tents outside. On the next morning, the cavalcade rode north to Batoche, where the village straggled on the land towards the river, below the hill where the church and rectory of St. Antoine de Padoue had recently been built, and where they still stand to this day, the sole survivors of the settlement Riel first saw on that summer morning of 1884.

Here another crowd of people — English half-breeds as well as Métis — had gathered to welcome Riel, and Dumont went to ask Father Moulin to allow the church to be used so that Riel could speak to his well-wishers. But by the time the church was opened so many people had been drawn by the news of Riel's arrival that it was too small to hold them all, and it was out of doors that he spoke to them, of their rights and of the agreement made in 1870 with the Dominion government which he believed guaranteed them. His attitude, as it would continue to be, was based on the idea that the Northwest would only become part of the Dominion after a treaty had been concluded between two equal nations, the Métis and the Canadians.

In Batoche Charles Nolin, who did not come destitute from Manitoba, had built a house that was second only in size and style to that of Xavier Batoche, and a great deal more palatial, with its double storeys and its verandah, than the log-walled simplicities of Gabriel's Crossing. Nolin offered his hospitality to the visitor — as Riel still thought himself — and his family, and Riel accepted.

9. The Great Agitation

Gabriel Dumont's life during the months following the arrival of Louis Riel shows the same kind of alternation between withdrawal and action as we have already observed in earlier periods. Though an admirable leader of his own community, and in the limited world of the buffalo hunt with which he had been familiar since childhood, he had no feeling for the complexities of politics where they extended into a world beyond his direct and personal knowledge. Not merely his illiteracy, but also his very immediate way of apprehending experience, made him uneasy in such activities as the organizing of petitions to distant and faceless bureaucrats and politicians, and though he would involve himself where it seemed necessary in such tasks as serving on committees and laboriously tracing his mark on documents, he preferred to leave these matters to people who at least gave the impression of being more politically adept and practiced.

During 1883, as we have seen, Dumont seemed inclined to allow men like Nolin and Michel Dumas to direct the Métis agitation and establish the initial contacts with English half-breeds and with white settlers, though he was careful to retain his own personal links with the Indians. After Riel's arrival, in the early summer of 1884, there was another period in which for most of the time Gabriel stood watchful in the shadows, as other men seemed to direct what went on. This period corresponded roughly with the four months when Riel lived in the house of Charles Nolin, before he moved in with Moïse Ouelette and thus, at least physically, into the ambience of the Dumont clan and of the Métis of the Saskatchewan country, as distinct from the Manitoba emigrés. Indeed, it would do little injustice to the events if one were to divide Riel's time at Batoche into a Nolin period and a Dumont period, the first marked by a fever of political agitation, leading nowhere, and the second by the acceptance of the idea of physical resistance, leading to war and — through Riel's indecisiveness — to disaster.

Nevertheless, though he stepped into the background once Riel had arrived, Dumont did not lapse into a total retreat from political activity. He was present to offer the report of the delegation to Montana at the meeting held in Charles Nolin's house on 8 July. On that day delegates arrived from as far away as Prince Albert and Fort Carlton, and the general atmosphere was one of harmony among the various groups of malcontents and of confidence inspired by Riel's platitudinous exhortations to unity. Three days later, Dumont was one of the party accompanying Riel to a broader meeting, once again in the Lindsay schoolhouse, where the creator of Manitoba presented himself formally to a non-Métis audience and, by finding the right balance of perfervid eloquence and essential moderation, won over the white settlers so successfully that Canadians who had actually been his opponents on the Red River came to offer their allegiance.

Even the priests were reassured. Father Fourmond of St. Laurent, more favourably disposed than most of his colleagues, was impressed by Riel's appearance of dedication, and the shrewd and distrustful Father André, who appears to have regarded with jealousy anyone who challenged his own self-appointed role as protector of the Métis, admitted to Lieutenant-Governor Dewdney that, though he was "no friend of Riel" and had regarded the prospect of his arrival as a danger to peace, he no longer felt any apprehension.

If I can believe the reports I have heard, Riel is acting peacefully and speaking wisely; he has blamed Charles Nolin in strong terms for having refused to present Your Honour with an address. . . . You will receive alarming reports on the pretended dangers Riel's arrival is about to cause in this country; do not believe a word of them. Those who make such reports would be happy to see you commit some unconsidered action. They will write to you and advise you to have Riel arrested. For the love of God, do no such thing without having sufficient reasons to justify it. . . . I tell you sincerely — and this is my firm conviction — that there is no trouble to be feared if you leave Riel in peace; but if you or any other officer should create difficulties for him or try to have him arrested, it is almost certain that there will be trouble and the Métis and the Indians will make common cause. While Riel comports himself peacefully, why disturb him and excite the anger of the people?

Having advised Riel that it would be unwise and provocative for him to accept an invitation to address a meeting at Prince Albert, where many of his former enemies were living, André afterwards changed his mind and urged Riel to go, which he did on 19 July. He was so well received that it was necessary to expel only one Orangeman for creating a disturbance, which his fellow Canadians did with alacrity.

For the time being, Riel was caught up in a circle of enthusiasm among all the various communities, and Dumont's name appears seldom during July and August except as a voiceless member of a group like the central executive committee of French- and English-speaking half-breeds, on which the Métis were represented mainly by the older men, and on which, out of twenty members, only Dumont, Michel Dumas, and Maxime Lépine could be regarded, on the basis of their later action, as militants.

Nevertheless, time and events were playing into the hands of such activists. Crops were poor that summer in St. Laurent and Batoche, and the consequent economic tightening gave an edge to discontent. Despite renewed cautionary messages from the police and the priests, politicians and civil servants in Ottawa showed no sign of moving towards a settlement of the Métis grievances. Meanwhile the introduction of so many factions into the task of making a single great petition to Ottawa resulted in an apparently endless series of meetings and hence to an apparently endless series of delays. The need to impress or — if it were necessary — to frighten Ottawa resulted in the extension of the agitation to include even malcontent Indian chiefs from as far away as Battleford and Qu'Appelle, whom Riel met in July and August, an action which lost him some of his white supporters, but which showed a veering towards Dumont's old idea of an alliance of all the native peoples, Indians as well as half-breeds of whatever origin.

The first occasion on which the edge of militancy began to show itself decisively, and on which, significantly, Dumont began to appear again as an influence on events, was the visit in September of Bishop Grandin of St. Albert to St. Laurent. He was accompanied by Amadée Forget, secretary to Lieutenant-Governor Dewdney, who had come with a roving commission to discover as much as he could by talking to the ordinary Métis in their own language — or rather in one of their two languages. He also appears to have been empowered to offer at least prospects — if not promises — of patronage to leading Métis, and this is by no means unlikely, for Sir John A. Macdonald seems always to have preferred a devious to a straightforward solution to any political problem; after all, one binds a man more securely by persuading him to accept a bribe than by granting him his just rights.

However, it was not Forget who interested Riel and his associates. They were concerned with the lack of help from the Catholic clergy during their campaign, in comparison with the considerable support Riel had received from priests on the Red River in 1869-70 and the encouragement Dumont had received from Father André between 1873 and 1875 in establishing the council of St. Laurent. Though up to the late summer of 1884 the joint campaign had generated much enthusiasm in the region, and had been conducted so far with impeccable legality, the priests — who might have been of considerable assistance — had remained aloof, and seemed to be discouraging the more pietistic of the Métis from becoming involved, so that it was being said among the Protestants, as James Isbister told Riel, that "your clergy are doing their utmost to break the existing unity between the French and English half-breeds." The situation was not in fact quite so simple as that, since a conservative reaction had built up after the success of Riel's July meeting in Prince Albert, and many of the white settlers who had then received him with enthusiasm were experiencing second thoughts.

Whatever the reason, Riel and his associates were beginning by the first days of September to feel that the movement was losing impetus, especially as there had been a fiasco late in August, when Sir Hector Langevin, Minister of Public Works, had come to the Northwest, with the proclaimed intention of visiting Prince Albert, where the malcontents planned to greet him with a manifesto of their grievances. Langevin got wind of their plan, and never appeared; Dumont, who did not put his mark on the manifesto, must have thought his scepticism justified.

The meeting which Riel, Dumont and some of the other Métis leaders sought with Bishop Grandin was designed to involve the church more deeply in the movement; its eventual effect would be to hasten the final estrangement between the priests and the Métis, an estrangement that even today has not completely vanished. On 1 September, a written address was presented to the Bishop as he was about to bless the bell that had just been installed in the church at Batoche. Grandin agreed to a meeting so that he could be made aware of the grievances of the Métis, and on 5 September he arrived at the church of St. Laurent, accompanied by Fathers André, Fourmond and Vegreville, and also by Amadée Forget.

It was left for Riel to make the political statement which laid down point by point what the Métis under his guidance were seeking, including better land laws, financial compensation as natives of the Northwest, and better treatment for their relatives, the Indians. But it was Dumont who opened the meeting with a speech whose simplicity did not disguise his deep emotions. He spoke of the deliberate absence of the priests from the gatherings of the Métis, and of how this absence aroused uneasiness among the members of the community, who contrasted it with Father André's support of their actions in 1873. He assumed that the intentions of the Métis must be either misinterpreted or misunderstood by the good missionaries, but whichever was the case, clerical aloofness could not help but harm the cause. He begged Grandin to guide them and to enlighten them on the attitude of the church, and ended on a conciliatory note by remarking that they would listen with as much docility as ever to what the Bishop had to tell them.

It was clear from his manner that Dumont had reached a point of inner crisis, in which a consciousness of the need to move towards decisive action conflicted with his desire not to break with the priests, and it is significant that among the events of that day Grandin found most disturbing a later conversation with Dumont which led him to remark: "I fear our poor Métis are making mistakes, and that we shall be blamed for it." Watching the scene with the acute eye of an outsider, Forget was moved to remark to Dewdney that perhaps the "most alarming" feature of the situation, "considering the religious nature of the half-breeds, is their loss of confidence in their old missionaries, such as Fathers André, Fourmond and Moulin."

On the next day, Forget stayed the night with Joseph Vandal, whose house was near to Gabriel's Crossing, and Dumont came over to give him a written version of the demands which Riel had already advanced the previous day in the church at St. Laurent. He went on to describe the sense of frustration that had led him and his people to send for Riel, as a man who seemed to be more politically adept than they. He carefully delimited Riel's role from his own. "We need him here as our political leader. In other matters I am the chief here." He seemed intent on presenting himself as more influential, in the sense of commanding the ultimate loyalty of the Métis, than more voluble leaders like Nolin, Dumas, and Lépine. He made a point of emphasizing the common interests of Indians and Métis, and the bonds between them. "They are our kin," he said, "and when they starve they come to us for help, and we have to feed them. The Government does not treat them properly." An ominous suggestion of the direction in which Dumont's thoughts were turning occurred when he told Forget that the Métis would resist any attempt by the authorities to arrest Riel. There was even a touch of hidden menace in the sentence with which he ended his remarks. "We want to see the Indians fed, to have our rights recognized, and to keep Mr. Riel as our leader, but we do not want to create any disturbance." His implication was not that disturbances would fail to occur, but that when they did the blame would lie with the government.

The main result of the meeting between the Bishop and the Métis leaders was the creation under Grandin's patronage of a confraternity known as the Union Métisse de Saint-Joseph. It was inaugurated at St. Laurent on 24 September, with much ceremony, including a sermon by Father André, a special canticle composed and sung by Father Fourmond, and a speech by Riel. It had been hoped by the clergy, and perhaps to an extent by Riel himself, that the Union would serve as a means of reconciliation, a channel by which priests and laity might communicate and the influence of the church be brought to bear in a beneficial way on the solution of Métis problems. But there was another side of Riel's mind which interpreted the Union politically, and even as he acknowledged loyalty to the Pope and Queen Victoria, he declared that the new organization was a recognition of Métis nationhood. In practice, the Union was to provide a framework of organization in which Métis political militancy could be fostered under the guise of religion, and within which Riel could develop among his more sympathetic followers the heretical religious notions he was already nurturing.

Grandin and Forget clearly understood that the Métis were reaching the point when frustration would break out in violence, but it was impossible to transmit their sense of urgency to the men in Ottawa, though Lieutenant-Governor Dewdney, who was responsible for local peacekeeping, had sensed the need for urgent action ever since he had heard the news that Riel was to be brought from Montana. He persuaded the Commissioner for the Mounted Police to strengthen the Prince Albert unit and to place a small detachment at Fort Carlton, which was as near as the police could approach to St. Laurent and Batoche without giving the appearance of provocative action.

Dewdney rightly decided that any attempt to restrict Riel's movements at this stage would be self-defeating, but he sent agents to keep a watch on the agitations that were going on among the various groups of malcontents. Most police informers feel they have to produce evidence of criminal activity, even when none exists, to justify their continued employment, and Dewdney's were no exceptions to the rule. In September they reported that an uprising of Indians and Métis could take place in a few weeks, if not a few days, and Dewdney hurriedly sent a French-speaking stipendiary magistrate, Charles Rouleau, with Hayter Reed, the Assistant Indian Commissioner, to investigate. Rouleau and Reed found the reports highly exaggerated, though Rouleau cautioned that a great deal of harm might ensue if the half-breed claims were not satisfied. Such reports seemed to confirm Sir John A. Macdonald in his procrastinatory complacency, for the Prime Minister chose this time to wire to Dewdney: "I suppose . . . there will be no trouble until winter sets in & the roads closed." He added that "Sir David Macpherson will take the Half Breed question and endeavour to settle it this winter," but added with a tired cynicism that "no amount of concession" would stop people from "grumbling and agitating."

It was in this inauspicious atmosphere that the various aggrieved groups in the Prince Albert district finally agreed on their demands and assembled the points into the grand petition to the Dominion Government; on 16 December the document was sent off to the Secretary of State in Ottawa, J. A. Chapleau, under cover of a letter signed by the white settler, W. H. Jackson, as secretary of the joint committee, and the English half-breed Andrew Spence as its chairman. The name of neither Riel, nor Dumont, nor Nolin appeared on this letter; it was considered politic to de-emphasize the Métis participation in the agitation. The petition asked virtually for what had been obtained by Riel fifteen years earlier on the Red River, with the addition of some concessions relative to the special circumstances of the western prairies. The petitioners asked for a responsible provincial government elected by ballot, for representation in the Ottawa parliament and in the Dominion cabinet, for scrip and land patents for the half-breeds, better treatment for the Indians, a modification of the homestead laws, a reduction of railway tariffs to satisfy the white settlers, and a railway to Hudson's Bay. Chapleau acknowledged the petition, and a copy was sent to the Colonial Office in London, which did not prevent Sir John A. Macdonald from blandly denying in the following March any knowledge of the existence of such a document.

Week after week, the people of the Northwest waited for a reply, shifting from optimism to pessimism and back, according to how they interpreted the actions of the authorities. As soon as the petition had been sent, Father André endeavoured to persuade Riel that his duties were ended, but Riel brought up the question of his unsatisfied personal claims on the government, for lost land in Manitoba, for the hardships of an unjust exile. He talked wildly of a total debt to him of $100,000, but hinted to André and D. H. MacDowall, the local member of the Territorial Council, that he might accept $35,000. André and MacDowall thought that they might persuade Riel to accept $5,000 or less as the price of departure, though it is possible that, while appearing to be willing to leave, Riel was in fact merely humouring his visitors and asking a high sum precisely because he did not intend to go. However, the question was rendered academic by the fact that Sir John A. Macdonald, who had willingly paid to get Riel out of Manitoba in 1870, suddenly developed scruples of an uncharacteristic delicacy about settling the problems of the Northwest by means of a cheap bribe; he probably knew Riel well enough to understand that the bribe would be rejected.

Meanwhile, Riel stayed at Batoche, and by many small signs the restless and apprehensive people of the region where the two Saskatchewan rivers flowed together came to realize that they were living in the shadow of a storm. Charles Mair, the poet who had played an active part on the Canadian side during the Red River rising, had gone to live in Prince Albert, where he had found himself on this occasion in sympathy with the Métis. But after trying in vain to convince Macdonald and Macpherson of the perils created by their indifference and immobility, he had left the Northwest with his family as early as September 1884, convinced that unless the government changed its policies a rebellion was inevitable. Mair would have appreciated the significance of the curious note that on 9 January 1885, appeared in the *Saskatchewan Herald* of Battleford.

> The Indians have always been in the habit of paying their compliments to their white brethren by calling on them on News Year's day, and this was one of the few occasions on which their women were allowed any freedom from the drudgery that makes their life. This year, however, they all stayed on their reserves, and even those who are living about town paid no visits.

Among the Métis, this was the time when Riel began to appear, as one of the police reported, in "the role of a religious reformer", talking of the decline of Rome and putting forward the notion he had developed during his exile, that the ultramontane Bishop Bourget would be the new Pope, heading a revitalization of Christianity, a new Counter-Reformation. And on a less exalted level, the temper of the Métis was shown in a stormy incident on 27 January, which demonstrated the rising influence of the activists seeking a confrontation with the Canadian government. Nolin had tendered for a government contract to construct a telegraph line, and it seemed likely that he would be successful. Riel and Dumont called on him and asked him to withdraw his tender to show that the Métis were not satisfied with the Government's procrastination. Nolin, who turned hostile witness at Riel's trial later in 1885, declared that Riel talked during this January meeting of raising an army among the Métis of Montana, but there is no other confirmation of any such plan; however, as Nolin himself talked of the need for violence before violence materialized (and then retracted), it is possible that some such talk did go on, and that Nolin expressed more agreement with Riel than he later admitted. Certainly Dumont, who himself at a later time of defeat thought of returning to the Saskatchewan at the head of the Montana Métis, would hardly have opposed the idea.

On the very day after the meeting of the three men, if one is to believe his evidence, Nolin "received a telegram", in reply to one sent by MacDowall to Ottawa, which "said that the Government was going to grant the rights of the half-breeds." In fact, his evidence appears to have distorted both the sequence of events and also what actually happened. It was not until 2 February that MacDowall wired to Ottawa saying that among the Métis there was "great discontent at no reply to representation" and ending "I anticipate no immediate danger but urge Government to declare intention immediately." Macdonald — who in the meantime had received another stormy letter of warning from Father André — wired to Lieutenant-Governor Dewdney — not to either Nolin or MacDowall — on 4 February saying that the government had decided to "investigate claims of half-breeds" and that a commission of three would be appointed to carry out "enumeration of those who did not participate in grant under Manitoba Act." Dewdney transmitted the substance of the wire to Nolin, thus by-passing both Riel, whom the French half-breeds regarded as the leader of their nation, and Dumont who was their undisputed local leader, and fastening on the man whom the Dominion officials — not without justification — felt to be the weakest link on the chain of Métis resolution. No mention was made of Riel's claims, which Macdonald had decided to disregard as a kind of extortion, nor was there any promise that after the investigation had been completed the Métis claims would actually be satisfied.

This telegram, with its lack of any specific commitment on the part of the government, and its transmission through Nolin instead of through the real leaders of the Métis, marked the vital turning point in the events beside the Saskatchewan river as winter moved into the fateful spring of 1885. As we have seen, there was already a group among the Métis — at most a few dozen men — who had decided that some kind of violent demonstration was the only way to convince the politicians in Ottawa of the gravity of the situation and the genuine resolve of the Métis to change it. Gabriel Dumont, whose wise and temperate government of the commune of St. Laurent between 1873 and 1875 had demonstrated his sense of social responsibility, was not originally among them. As he had shown in 1875, he was willing to accept the fact of Canadian sovereignty as long as it seemed compatible with the freedom of movement that was so precious to the Métis and with the security in terms of assured land holdings which they needed now that the buffalo had vanished from the prairie. But as the months passed, with the agitation and petitioning that had filled 1884 bringing no better result than Ottawa's vague talk of another commission of enquiry, his patience came to an end. He was too realistic to hope that he and his fellow half-breeds could win a long war against the Canadians, even if his long-cherished dream of an alliance with the Indians came into being, but he did believe — as he had believed in 1870 — that a well conducted guerilla campaign might cause the Dominion government enough trouble to force it towards genuine negotiations and equally genuine concessions.

It was Dumont's acceptance of the need for insurrection that more than any other factor decided the course of events in February and March 1885. After the contents of Macdonald's telegram became known, he apparently told Riel that their year of work had been wasted, and the only way to redeem the fortunes of the Métis was by drastic action. The government felt that it could ignore petitions; it would respond — as it had done in 1870 — only to decisive deeds. Dumont was too little experienced in politics, and Riel was already too exalted by his sense of fulfilling a divinely ordained mission, for either of them to listen to the reasonings of Father André, who pointed out that both the Red River rising of 1869 and the St. Laurent commune of 1873 had taken shape in regions with no viable government in operation, and were validated by this fact, but that now there was an established government and — however much the Métis may have disliked its methods — they could not set up a rival state except as an act of rebellion and therefore, in the eyes of the law, of treason. Both men had loyalties — Riel to his own vision and Dumont to his own people — that were more than any theoretical loyalty to a government in unknown Ottawa led by the hated Sir John A. Macdonald. And so, when the fatal telegram arrived from Sir John A. Macdonald on 4 February, and Riel banged the table and shouted: "Within forty days Ottawa shall have my answer," both he and Dumont knew what the answer would be. But Dumont was ready to follow his choice of action to the end, since that was in the buffalo hunting tradition by which he had always lived, while Riel was not prepared for the inevitable consequences of the same choice, and so by his indecision destroyed what chance Dumont may have had of drawing some degree of success out of a forlorn hope.

A last speculation on Dumont's motives — before we watch him moving into action — is appropriate. Neither he nor his family stood to gain anything in the way of personal benefits from an uprising. Gabriel had secured the better part of his chosen land as a homestead under the land regulations, and he enjoyed a security of existence and even a level of income and living above that of most of his neighbours — benefits that the call to arms could only shatter. His father and most of his brothers had already received land on the Red River, or scrip in compensation, so that they did not stand to gain any great material benefits. They chose to fight because their freedom and pride as a people seemed to be threatened, and that has been the motive of all the resistance movements which in history have gained more lustre than common wars.

10. The Provisional Government of the Saskatchewan

Whan was said in Batoche, between Riel and Dumont, and among the Métis in general, during the days after Macdonald's telegram arrived, is not known in much detail, yet it is clear from what happened on 24 February, the first day to emerge with any clarity from that time of confusion, that the Métis community, and others in the region who shared similar hopes, were shocked and bewildered by the lack of any positive response to the petition whose requests had seemed to them so reasonable and on which they had placed such hopes. Certainly the leaders must have discussed the situation at length before they called a meeting on the evening of the 24th in the church of St. Antoine de Padoue at Batoche. The object of the meeting was to communicate the contents of Macdonald's telegram to the people and to discuss its implications, but it seemed to be generally understood that whatever happened would have momentous consequences, and among those who were present in the crowded church, from which Father Moulin had prudently removed the monstrance, were three of the local priests, Fathers Moulin, Fourmond, and Vegreville. Inspector Gagnon of the Prince Albert detachment of the Mounted Police also arrived, but, seeing that his presence would not be welcome in the church, he decided to stay outside.

Riel began the meeting with a tirade against the government for its ruthless taking of the West from the native peoples, and its unwillingness to consider the complaints of its victims. Then he broke off to announce in a quiet voice that it was time for him to depart. His task had ended. The petition had been sent. An answer had been received. A commission would enquire into the grievances of the Métis. And he would go back to his neighbours in Montana, as he had originally planned to do. It would be no great loss to the Métis in Canada, since his past record had harmed their cause, and the government had refused out of an old enmity to accept him as the spokesman for the people on the Saskatchewan.

There is no means of knowing whether Riel was speaking in full sincerity, or whether he was playing a role to test his popularity. If the latter were the case, he was completely successful, for almost everyone in the church joined in the cries of protest, and though the loudest shouts came from Dumont and other members of the group dedicated to action, there is no doubt that Charles Nolin, who later claimed that Riel stage-managed the whole affair, was almost equally insistent. When Riel — clearly hinting at more extreme measures than hitherto — asked the people if they were willing to accept the consequences of his continuing leadership, they professed themselves, with no dissentient voice, ready to do so. There seems to have been no actual talk at this meeting of armed rebellion or illegal action, doubtless because the priests were present, but the fact that Riel had been urged to remain, and had agreed, must have suggested to many of the participants that something more drastic than sending useless petitions to the government was about to be adopted.

The first sign of the new tactics came a week afterwards, when Riel stood on the church steps at St. Laurent and said there was a possibility that the Métis might have to resort to force. On the next day — 2 March — he rode into Prince Albert, accompanied by Damase Carrière and Napoléon Nault, to see Father André. Since Father André had sponsored Dumont's local government at St. Laurent twelve years before, Riel asked for the priest's permission to form a provisional government by midnight. André refused, and from this point he set himself actively to combat Riel and Dumont and try to persuade as many Métis as possible to adopt a stand of neutrality in the conflict which he feared was about to begin. The following day, 3 March, a meeting was held at Halcro, near Prince Albert, for

a discussion between the Métis and the English-speaking malcontents on what should be done in response to the government's action. Riel and Dumont arrived at the head of some
sixty Métis, most of them carrying arms, and during his speech
Riel declared that the Mounted Police were trying to arrest
him, but that "these" — pointing to the armed Métis — "are the
real police." Needless to say, no common decision was reached
at the Halcro meeting, and afterwards most of the white settlers
who had hitherto supported Riel began to withdraw from association with him, and the English half-breeds prepared to
adopt a neutral stance in the event of trouble between the Métis
and the police. Thus the first result of the forceful policy that
Dumont advocated and Riel appeared to adopt was the fright-
ening away of potential allies, accompanied by a deepening of
the existing rift between Riel and the clergy.

But the impetus of events and passions could not be halted,
and two days later Riel and Dumont called a secret meeting of
the leading Métis. Those who attended were Joseph Ouelette
and his son Moïse, Isidore Dumont, Pierre and Philippe
Gariepy, John Ross, Augustin Laframboise, Calixte Lafontaine,
and Napoléon Nault. Of the eleven present, at least five were
Dumonts or linked to them by marriage, which suggests that
now there was talk of action the old Saskatchewan clans of
hunters who had dominated the earlier council at St. Laurent
were once again moving into leadership. This was the meeting
at which the decision to resort to armed action was made, and
sealed in a curious oath which united the religious and the
patriotic passions of the Métis people. In a document heavily
embellished with pious phrases, the participants engaged themselves "to save our souls by making ourselves live in righteous-
ness night and day in all things and in whatever place we may
be," and "to save our country from wicked government by taking up arms whenever it shall be necessary." All signed or put
their names to the oath.

Then Dumont and Riel went with it to Charles Nolin's
house. They told Nolin that they had decided to take up arms
and to raise the people against the government, but that before
all else they meant to fight for the glory of God. One can imagine that, in their exhortations, Dumont's emphasis was on
the arms and Riel's on the deity. They then asked Nolin to

sign the oath. Nolin had no intention of placing his signature on so compromising a document; on the other hand he had little inclination to offend Dumont and Riel in their present rather menacing mood, so he suggested that if they were serious in their desire to work for the glory of God, it would be better to hold a novena — nine days of public prayers and confessions — after which the Métis should be able to act according to their consciences, which the Holy Spirit would doubtless illumine.

After some discussion, Riel and his associates agreed, and both Nolin and the priests thought they had won time. The novena, it was agreed, should commence on 10 March, and carry through to the 19th, which by coincidence happened to be the day of St. Joseph, patron of the Union Métisse. Given the emotional tension that existed in the Métis settlements, it is not surprising that the novena was well attended, a fact which led Fathers Vegreville and Fourmond to believe that it would be successful in curbing the militants. The Mounted Police took a less roseate view of the situation, basing their views on some very significant developments reported by their spies. The Métis were refusing to carry freight, since Dumont did not want them to leave the country. They were unwilling or frightened to accept government employment. Dumont and some of his associates were talking of taking Fort Carlton. Men were getting their arms ready for use, as if they were about to start on one of the vanished buffalo hunts, and they talked of getting more arms from traders in Montana. On 14 March, Superintendent Crozier, now in charge at Prince Albert, warned Commissioner Irvine that a rebellion could be expected "at any moment", and that some of the whites seemed to be in sympathy with the movement. Lieutenant-Governor Dewdney wired to Ottawa urging immediate surprise action; in his view the Métis "are like Indians, when they gather and get excited it is difficult to handle them, but if they are taken unawares there is little difficulty in arresting the leader." As a result of these messages, the government took the initiative in terms of action; on 15 March, Commissioner Irvine of the Mounted Police was instructed to move as quickly as possible from Regina in the direction of Prince Albert with a force of a hundred men; he set out early on the 18th. The *Saskatchewan Herald* reported from Battleford, where the mood among the local Indians provoked anxiety:

"Incipient rebellion. Riel and his friends are on the move, and so are the police."

By the time Irvine actually set forth, the Métis leaders were already riding around the countryside gathering their followers. The mild Father Fourmond, who throughout the months of agitation and petitioning had been much more sympathetic to the Métis cause than his fellow priests, unwittingly precipitated the crisis. From the beginning, the militant leaders had been using the novena, which attracted many Métis to St. Laurent, as a means of dramatizing their conflict with the Government, and on Sunday, 15 March, they attended mass in force, with Riel, Dumont, and such warlike lieutenants as Lépine and Carrière at their head. Fourmond rather tactlessly chose the occasion to preach on the sin of resistance to established authority, and ended by threatening to withhold the sacraments from any Métis who took arms against the government. His words precipitated the open breach between the Métis rebels and the church, for Riel rose from his place in the congregation to denounce the priest for playing politics and sowing discord by using threats against those who wished to fight in defence of "sacred rights". By thus intervening, Riel made it clear that he and his followers would act if necessary in defiance of the church as well as of the state, and except for those who had in some way committed themselves to oppose — or perhaps rather to evade — rebellion, like Charles Nolin and Louis Schmidt, the majority of the Métis seemed to be in sympathy with Riel in his sharp delimitation of the area in which the church could influence the actions of his people.

Immediately after mass, Dumont began to go among the men who had attended, urging them to gather at St. Laurent on 19 March. This would be the final day of the novena, and also the day on which William Henry Jackson, secretary of the white Settlers' Union, would be received into the Catholic church. Jackson, drifting already near the breakdown that would eventually overtake him, had become completely devoted to Riel and was now his secretary. It may have been their variant forms of instability that attracted the men to each other, yet it was partly also Riel's extraordinary charismatic magnetism. And when one considers this Upper Canadian Methodist falling under Riel's spell so far as to change his faith, it is not surprising that the Métis themselves should at times have seemed faithful beyond the bounds of reason to the leader who had given them pride in themselves as a people, so that even a man so earthy and so definite as Dumont would follow Riel's lead even against his own better judgment of the situations in which they were involved together. However, there remained an essential difference between their approaches, and while Riel stressed the religious aspects of the gathering on 19 March, Dumont told the Métis to be sure of bringing their guns with them.

But neither he nor Riel was content with merely exhorting the Sunday congregation. They began, in the bitter cold of that March of 1885, a recruiting expedition through the whole region around Batoche, St. Laurent, and Duck Lake. Dumont rode to One Arrow's reserve to the east and demanded the allegiance of the Indians there; he knew already that Chief Beardy at Duck Lake was friendly. Then the party started in a southerly direction, with Dumont rousing all his neighbours around Gabriel's Crossing and Fish Creek. After staying overnight at Tourond's Farm, they rode back on the 18th in the direction of Batoche, where John Willoughby, a doctor from Saskatoon, met Dumont riding north and then found Riel in the house of a certain Rocheleau, uttering prophesies about the god-fearing peoples who would come to the prairies at his invitation, and declaring that it was time for the Métis to ignore the procrastinations of the Dominion government and take the rule of the country on themselves "or perish in the attempt." Willoughby was in no way molested, though he might easily have been acting as a spy for the government, but he was aware of the excitement that vibrated in the air of the little riverside hamlets. Indeed, that very day the Métis were to be provoked into a mood of anger and fear that made the whole region under their control unsafe for anyone who was neither a half-breed nor an Indian.

Once again the author of trouble appears to have been the Hudson's Bay factor, Lawrence Clarke, whose alarmist reports in 1875 had been responsible for the unnecessary confrontation of that year between Dumont and the Mounted Police. Clarke had been to Winnipeg, where he had heard of Irvine's projected departure from Regina with police reinforcements, and

163

he was returning to Fort Carlton through the highly excited Métis settlements. At Batoche's ferry he encountered a group of Métis, including Napoléon Nault and Michel Dumas, and an exchange followed of which there are several accounts, including Clarke's own denial — which his past record makes one doubt — that he said anything at all.

In a letter written a few days after the incident, Riel claimed that Clarke had said five hundred policemen were on their way to arrest the Métis leaders and disperse their followers. Hillyard Mitchell, the trader from Duck Lake, who was sympathetic to the Métis grievances but opposed to rebellion, reported that what he had been told led him to believe that "Mr. L. Clarke of the H.B.C. is the cause of the whole excitement, viz. on Wednesday he, on driving from Grey, stopped at the Settlement on the South Branch, and told the people that the Government was sending 500 Police from Troy to fight the half-breeds. The people, of course, got excited and said they were going to fight the said 500 men. And they are now waiting at Batoche expecting them to arrive." Dumont's recollection in 1902 of the incident was, surprisingly enough, less sensational, and it may be nearest of all to the truth. He claimed that when Clarke arrived at the Batoche ferry, he said to the Métis he encountered there, "Well, are you still holding meetings?" "More than ever," was the answer: "We're holding them almost every day!" "Fine! Fine!" answered Clarke: "But it won't go on much longer. Eighty policemen are on their way. I ran into them at Humboldt, and tomorrow or the next day Riel and Gabriel Dumont will be picked up!"

Dumont's account gives much more accurately the number of police on their way under Irvine, and the conversation, as he reports it, has just the tone of sardonic meanness that seemed to characterize the reactions of Lawrence Clarke to the fact that the power and prestige of Hudson's Bay factors had withered away forever. But even if Clarke acted foolishly and then tried to defend himself with equally foolish denials, one should not exaggerate his responsibility for what eventually happened, for it is obvious that by this time the militant leaders of the Métis had already decided on armed resistance, and that they welcomed the news that the Mounted Police had moved first, which enabled them to proceed with their plans, on the rather specious

164

excuse that they were acting in self-defence. Certainly Nault, Dumas, and the others who had listened to Lawrence Clarke took his remarks seriously, and hurried to tell Riel and Dumont.

Accompanied by the sixty or seventy men they had gathered around them during the day, Riel and Dumont immediately rode into Batoche, and on the way called at a small store kept by George Kerr. Dumont entered the store to demand whatever arms and ammunition Kerr might have in stock. As luck would have it, they acquired prisoners as well, for John Lash, the Indian agent at One Arrow's reserve, and his interpreter, William Tompkins, had just arrived to buy a sack of potatoes, and Dumont immediately took them prisoner. The taking and holding of hostages was a traditional factor in prairie warfare, and at least in the early days of the rebellion that was now beginning the acquisition of a number of captives to be used in bargaining with the Dominion government was an element of strategy on which Riel and Dumont were in agreement. George Kerr was set free after he had surrendered six shot guns, a keg of powder, and some rifle cartridges, but a couple of days afterwards he too was made prisoner. Riel earnestly explained his plans to all the captives, yet it was Dumont who played the most conspicuous part in these actions. George Kerr remembered him as appearing "to be in command of the whole outfit, as they say in this country", while others remarked that though Riel seemed to exercise an overall influence, the Métis took their immediate orders from Dumont, who was now in his element, the black-and-white world of action, where cunning and courage, the virtues of the plains fighter and the buffalo hunter, once again had their places.

From Kerr's store, the insurrectionaries went on to the church of St. Antoine de Padoue. Father Moulin met them at the door, and when he protested at their appropriation of the church for secular purposes, Riel jeeringly shouted: "The priest is a Protestant!" and, loudly proclaiming that "Rome has fallen!", he led his followers into the building, where he spoke to them on the situation that had arisen, and promised that provisional government would be established. It was agreed that the actual formation of the government should be left until the next day, when more of the Métis would be gathered to celebrate the end of the novena. Dumont left to carry out the immediate defensive tasks, which consisted of cutting the telegraph lines to north and south, and of going to the other non-Métis store in the immediate locality, kept by Henry Walters, where they took other prisoners and appropriated the arms and ammunition, which the proprietor was reluctant to surrender.

From all accounts, on this first day of active rebellion considerably less than a hundred of the Métis — mostly the militants under the influence of Dumont, Nault, and Carrière — were involved. By the next day many more had arrived in Batoche, partly in response to the earlier call to gather at the end of the novena, and partly because of the news that their leaders were imperilled and needed protection. Some of them were armed with Winchester repeating rifles, others with shot guns and old unreliable trading muskets. A few Indians had arrived from One Arrow's and Beardy's reserves, some of them armed merely with bows and arrows. Xavier Batoche — sensing the approach of an actual conflict between the Métis and the authorities — had discreetly departed for some winter trading down river at Fort à la Corne, and Riel appropriated his house — the best in the village — as a dwelling and headquarters. Outside it, on 19 March, the second Provisional Government of Riel's career was established by popular vote. Several of the prisoners were allowed to attend, as if the Métis leaders wished to act in the presence of witnesses from the outside world; among them were William Tompkins, the interpreter, and his cousin Peter Tompkins, who had been captured trying to repair the telegraph lines which Dumont's men had cut.

The meeting was conducted by Riel and Dumont, whose methods of election were somewhat arbitrary. Riel nominated Dumont as "Adjutant-General of the Métis nation . . . at the head of the army," and the assembly dutifully ratified the choice by its applause. Then it was left to Dumont to pick the councillors, in their turn accepted by acclamation. Riel himself refused any official position; he was an outsider, and preferred being prophet to being president. The government, he argued, should represent the actual people in rebellion, should emerge from among them, and he suggested a title that would emphasize the emergence; the council should be called the Exovedate, and its members Exovedes, meaning those picked out of the flock. Inappropriate as it might seem to confer on a crowd of belligerent prairie hunters a name derived from a Latin word (*ovis*) meaning a sheep but also a simpleton, the suggestion was accepted because no-one in the audience wished to admit that he did not know its meaning. Old Pierre Parenteau was picked as nominal President, and the twelve members Dumont chose for the council included his brothers-in-law, Moïse Ouelette and Baptiste Parenteau, as well as his close associates, Damas Carrière and Maxime Lépine. Charles Nolin, who was appalled and terrified by the proceedings, was named Commissaire without being consulted, and the whole group of councillors and officers declared itself the "Provisional Government of the Saskatchewan" (to be called by many Métis "le petit Provisoire" to distinguish it from Riel's Provisional Government of the Red River sixteen years before). William Henry Jackson was chosen as secretary, but within two days his mind became so obviously unhinged that he was replaced by Philippe Garnot, the diminutive inn-keeper of Batoche.

Dumont lost no time establishing his military command. He picked the house of Norbert Delorme, a member of the Exovedate, as military headquarters, since his own farm at Gabriel's Crossing was too far from the centre of activities. As principal lieutenants he named Joseph Delorme and Patrice Tourond. Then he proceeded to organize his miniature army, now about three hundred men, according to the traditional ways of the buffalo hunt. Ambroise Champagne and Patrice Fleury were appointed captains of scouts, to patrol the east and west banks of the river respectively; each of them had ten men, picked from among the best riders. Then ten captains of the fighting companies were chosen. Having set up his organization, Dumont advocated the raising of the Indians and an immediate attack before the government forces had time to establish themselves; the campaign should begin with surprise assaults on Fort Carlton and Prince Albert, and the capture of the stores of arms and ammunition in these places.

Riel disagreed; however violently he might talk when no specific action was involved, he lacked the plainsman's willingness to accept without qualm the fact that war meant fighting. It was a first contest in the Council of the strength of two wills, and Riel used the respect he inspired among the Métis to win a reluctant agreement from even its more militant members, so that it was Damase Carrière, one of Dumont's associates, who seconded a compromise resolution that Fort Carlton should if possible be taken without bloodshed, but that "in the event of our being forced to fight, justice will compel us to resort to arms."

The first act of the Provisional Government was not, indeed, one of war, but an example of that familiar activity of insurrectionary administrations, the political heresy trial. Charles Nolin, together with William Boyer and Dumont's old hunting companion, Louis Marion, had refused to take up arms for the Métis cause. They were arrested and brought before the Council. Riel proffered the accusation of treason against Nolin, and he was formally condemned to death, but allowed to repent, knowing that the price of his life would be to act as Riel's tool. Dumont's attitude towards the proceedings is not clear, though he must have concurred in the verdict, but after the rebellion he made a curiously understanding remark: "Nolin a eu peur, et on n'est pas maître de la peur." ("Nolin was afraid, and one is not the master of fear.")

On the following day, Riel sent his ultimatum to Superintendent Crozier at Fort Carlton. Unofficial communications had already been established through Hillyard Mitchell of Duck Lake, whom Dumont and the other local Métis regarded as the most friendly of the white traders on the Saskatchewan. Mitchell visited the Métis leaders, urging them to go no further on the path of rebellion, to which advice they replied with bitter recriminations against Sir John A. Macdonald, and he also sent a note warning Crozier to make no kind of demonstration, since this would only further enrage the Métis, and probably bring in the Indians on their side. Later on Mitchell — one of the few people in this drama for whom one's admiration is consistent — went to Fort Carlton in the hope of finding a way to keep the peace. Crozier asked him to return to Batoche in the company of Thomas McKay, a half-breed Hudson's Bay official who had just arrived at Fort Carlton with a contingent of armed white volunteers raised in Prince Albert.

McKay was hardly the best of envoys. He was resented by the Métis because of his loyalty to the Company, and also because he had held aloof from the peaceful attempts to win justice over the past year; to this day, ninety years afterwards, old people in Batoche and St. Laurent mention his name with distaste. It is also possible that his reception was affected by the fact that Riel and Dumont already knew that the English half-breeds who had worked with them up to that point were undecided about their line of action. Certainly they regarded McKay as a traitor to the cause of the native peoples, and they subjected him to the ordeal of a mock trial, with Gabriel Dumont presiding, seated on a syrup keg, Philippe Garnot acting as court clerk, and Riel in his customary role of the bitter accuser. Dumont was particularly angry because McKay had never involved himself in the cause of the Métis before this occasion, and now presumed to advise them to surrender to the police. McKay was let go after this sinister little comedy, but Riel and his associates refused to leave Batoche and discuss the situation with Crozier. Dumont doubtless remembered a past discussion with Crozier that had done no good to the cause of the Métis, and Riel feared being led into a trap. Instead, the Council concocted an ultimatum, which was signed by all the Exovedes, as well as by Riel, Dumont, and the reluctant Nolin.

> You will be required [Crozier was informed] to give up completely the situation which the Canadian Government has placed you in, at Carlton and Battleford, together with all government properties.
>
> In case of acceptance, you and your men will be set free, on your parole of honour to keep the peace. And those who will choose to leave the country will be furnished with teams and provisions to reach Qu'Appelle.
>
> In case of non-acceptance, we intend to attack you, when tomorrow, the Lord's Day, is over; and to commence without delay a war of extermination upon all those who have shown themselves hostile to our rights. . . .
>
> Major, we respect you. Let the cause of humanity be a consolation to you for the reverses which the governmental misconduct has brought upon you.

Charles Nolin and Maxime Lépine were delegated to carry the message to Fort Carlton; they were given a personal note of instruction from Riel himself, in which the actual formula to be used by Crozier was laid down: "Because I love my neighbour as myself, for the sake of God, and to prevent bloodshed, and principally the war of extermination that threatens the country, I agree to the above conditions of surrender."

In fact, Crozier did not surrender, and the Métis did not attack Fort Carlton on 23 March, the day their ultimatum had specified. Undoubtedly one of the crucial factors in the situation was the lingering reluctance of the English half-breeds to define their own position in the coming strife; it was not until 24 March that they decided to send yet another futile petition and to remain strictly neutral in any fighting that might follow. This decision strengthened Crozier's position, and so resolved the first of those might-have-been situations between Dumont and Riel which make the Northwest Rebellion such a fascinating phenomenon to the speculative historian. For if Riel had agreed to Dumont's plans, there is a fair probability that the ill-defended positions of Fort Carlton and Prince Albert would have been taken without difficulty, with Battleford to follow shortly afterwards, and that the English half-breeds would have joined the winning side. As it was, the Métis were left to face their first battle alone. It was a battle which Riel had not foreseen, and which Dumont fought.

11. The Battle of Duck Lake

The most thoroughly authenticated account which Gabriel Dumont gave of the Northwest Rebellion was dictated by him in December, 1888, less than four years after the events he described, to Benjamin de Montigny, then recorder of Montreal; on 14 January 1889 it was read to Dumont in the presence of seven witnesses, including two doctors and three lawyers, one of whom was Adolphe Ouimet. Enough of it is confirmed by other accounts of the same incident for us to accept the whole as an authentic account of events remembered with the particular accuracy one often encounters among illiterates.

"On the 25 March 1885 . . . ," Dumont begins, "since the Mounted Police had shown themselves on the far side of the river, I asked Riel to let me take thirty men to pillage the stores of those in Duck Lake who were opposed to us."

Dumont had been reproaching Riel for giving too many advantages to his opponents, whose spies were moving into Métis territory, and having gained agreement he rode over and appropriated the contents of Hillyard Mitchell's store. Then, establishing Duck Lake as an outpost, he sent scouts on the road towards Fort Carlton, and during the night arrested the deputy sheriff of Prince Albert, a certain Harold Ross, and a surveyor named John Astley, who were acting rather amateurishly as scouts for Crozier; the two men were added to Riel's store of hostages, while their horses were appropriated as mounts.

By the time the excitement over this incident was over, and Dumont and his men were stabling their horses, the dawn was breaking, and then the cry went up: "The police are coming!" Superintendent Crozier, warned by Hillyard Mitchell that the Métis were likely to occupy Duck Lake, but unaware that they had already done so, had sent a detachment of fifteen police and seven Prince Albert volunteers, under Sergeant Stewart and Thomas McKay, with a number of sleighs to fetch some government provisions that had been stored on Mitchell's premises.

Dumont and about thirty of his men, including his younger brother Edouard, immediately set off and intercepted the police party. There followed a noisy battle of insults, with a couple of misfired shots and little harm done to anybody.

Thomas McKay described the Métis as "very excited . . . yelling and flourishing their rifles." Dumont claimed that he knocked over with the barrel of his Winchester a policeman who threatened to shoot him. Then his own gun went off by accident and he became engaged in the shouting match with Thomas McKay, who cried out: "Look out, Gabriel!"

"I answered him: 'Look out yourself! I'll blow your brains out!' I threw myself on him. . . . I jabbed him in the back with my rifle. McKay kept on protesting, 'Look out, Gabriel!' and I repeated, 'Look out yourself, or I'll finish you off!' and I followed him with my gun.'"

According to McKay, "Dumont talked very wildly; he wanted us to surrender. He said it was my fault that the people were not assisting them, and that I was to blame for all the trouble."

Sergeant Stewart quickly decided that this was no occasion for valour, since the police were obviously outnumbered, and the least resistance would have led to a fight. The best they could hope for was to escape unhurt, and so, without firing a single shot, he and his party turned their sleighs, and hurried back to Fort Carlton, speeded by a salvo over their heads from Dumont and his young men, who then returned to Duck Lake, delighted at having forced the police into an ignominious retreat.

But, as Dumont remembered, "we had hardly let our horses out to feed than we again heard someone shouting, 'The police are coming!'" For in Fort Carlton the ignominy of Sergeant

Stewart's retreat had been felt immediately by Crozier and his fellow officers. They realized that if the news spread before the defeat were redeemed, the Indians and perhaps even the Métis in other centres would cease to fear the power of the police, and rebellion might proliferate. They felt even more the blow to the pride of the force.

Crozier had two alternatives, to attack at once, or to wait until Commissioner Irvine should arrive with his reinforcements. Later he was to be officially blamed for not waiting, but apart from the fact that he was an impetuous man, with an almost neurotic sensitivity about his honour, his situation was complicated by the mood of the Prince Albert volunteers, zealous amateur soldiers until the first shot was fired, and much inclined to criticize anything that seemed like hesitancy among the professionals. Even more unfortunate was the presence of Lawrence Clarke who, with his usual penchant for creating needless trouble, insisted that the Métis should be taught an immediate lesson. Such influences outweighed any impulse of caution that Crozier might otherwise have felt. He led the whole garrison of Fort Carlton in an immediate assault on Duck Lake.

Crozier's minuscule army consisted of fifty-six Mounted Police and forty-three Prince Albert volunteers, most of the latter with no battle experience whatever. Some were mounted; some rode on sleighs. They took with them a seven-pound cannon. Meanwhile, the news of the first encounter had reached Batoche and St. Laurent. The Métis had converged on Duck Lake, so that three hundred of them were concentrated there, including Louis Riel and the unhappy Nolin, as well as a number of Cree Indians from the two nearby reserves.

Upon hearing the news of the return of the police, Dumont set off immediately with an advance guard of twenty-five men to pick a suitable ambush; he had no intention of making a frontal attack, since the police would be better armed than his men and perhaps also better trained for a parade ground battle. He chose a spot about two miles from Duck Lake. When one visits the site today, it seems unimpressive because of the lack of striking natural features. But there was a low elevation overlooking the road, plenty of low bush, a gully through which men could creep unseen and shelter from cannon fire, and over on the right a log house which Dumont immediately sent a few men to occupy; it was a good enough combination for a guerilla tactician of Dumont's quality, particularly as most of his men, being hunters, were good marksmen. His one problem was that the younger Métis were green in warfare; the day of Duck Lake broke a virtual peace among the peoples of the prairies that — largely through Dumont's truce-making abilities — had lasted half a generation.

Some of Crozier's scouts were English half-breeds, familiar with the ways of prairie warfare, who detected the Métis manoeuvre, and Crozier ordered his men to halt, prepare a barricade with their twenty sleighs, and get the cannon ready for action. Already the Métis had formed a semi-circle that threatened the police on both flanks; reinforcements were arriving, led by Riel, who brandished the crucifix he had appropriated from the little church at Duck Lake.

There are confused reports on how the fighting started and on who fired the first shot, but a general reading of the accounts suggests that at the first encounter Isidore Dumont, Gabriel's elder brother, went forward with an old half-blind Indian chief named Aseeweyin, waving a white blanket as if for a parley. Joseph McKay, the half-breed interpreter, was ahead of the main police column, with Crozier close behind him. McKay went towards Dumont and Aseeweyin. It seems likely — though the accounts say nothing of this — that the Métis and the Indian intended to transmit a demand from Gabriel Dumont for surrender, in accordance with the Exovedate's original ultimatum. Aseeweyin began to talk in Cree to McKay. He was unarmed, but McKay carried a rifle and had a revolver in his belt. "Where are you going with so many guns, grandson?" said Aseeweyin. He reached for McKay's pistol (or his rifle — the accounts vary). McKay fired at him, and at the same time Crozier shouted to his men, "Fire away, boys!" In the volley that followed, Isidore Dumont fell dead from his horse. Gabriel believed that McKay shot him and that the half-breed had "an interest" in killing Isidore. Only Crozier's account, which was obviously written with the intent of clearing himself of as much blame as possible, maintained that the first shot was fired by the Métis.

Once blood had been spilt, battle was inevitable. Dumont was enraged at his brother's death, and intent on revenge, and

Crozier and McKay had barely time to reach their barricade of sleighs before the Métis, by now carefully disposed by Gabriel with a group of especially good marksmen in the hut on the right, began to fire from all sides. Riel exhorted them, fearlessly exposing himself, waving his cross, and shouting "In the name of God who created us, answer their fire!" In the midst of this excitement Charles Nolin, who had accompanied Riel unwillingly, seized a sleigh and escaped unobserved from the Métis ranks, hardly drawing rein until he reached Prince Albert, where he was treated as a suspect and immediately put in the local lockup by the side to which he was seeking to desert.

Once the shooting began, we fired as much as we could [Dumont remembered]. I had used up the twelve shots in my Winchester, and I had just reloaded it to start again, when the English, scared by the number of their dead, began to retreat. It was about time, for their cannon, which up to then had prevented my men on foot from descending the hill, had been silenced because in loading it the gunner had put in the shot before the powder. My footmen now began to surround them. That first part of the battle had lasted about thirty minutes. [During that time the volunteers and the police had lost ten men killed, and thirteen had been wounded, two of them fatally.]

In their flight the police had to go through a clearing, and I quickly laid an ambush for them, saying to my men: "Courage! I am going to give the redcoats a few shots that will make them jump in their carts!" and then I laughed, not because I got any pleasure from killing, but to encourage my men.

Since I was so anxious to pick off the redcoats, I did not think of keeping cover, and a ball came and furrowed the crown of my head, so that there is still a deep scar to be seen; I fell from the saddle, and my horse, which was also wounded, jumped over me in its attempt to escape. We were then about sixty paces from the enemy. I tried to get up, but the blow had been so violent that I could not stand. When Joseph Delorme saw me fall down again, he shouted out that I was dead. I said to him: "Courage! While you still have your head you are not yet dead!" I then told Baptiste Vandal to take my cartridges and my famous rifle, which had a range of eight hundred metres.

Throughout the battle, this Delorme stayed at my side, fighting like a lion. Yet before it began, he had said to me: "I have never been under fire before. If I show any fear, keep me at it and do not spare me!" While we were fighting, Riel was there on horseback, exposing himself to the bullets with no other weapon than the crucifix that he held in his hand. [Riel was following Métis traditions, acting in exactly the same way as the unarmed missionary priests during earlier prairie battles like that of Grand Coteau.]

As soon as he saw me fall, my brother Edouard ran forward to drag me into the ravine, but I told him to go instead to our people who seemed to be discouraged by my fall. We rallied and reassured them, and they shouted with joy and began to fire again. It was then that my cousin August Laframboise fell close by me; only a few moments before I had been telling him not to expose himself so much. A bullet had hit him in the arm and gone through his body. I dragged myself over the ground towards him, saying to myself: "At least I can say a little prayer for him," but in trying to make the sign of the cross with my left hand, since my right side was paralysed, I fell down on my side, and I said to him, laughing: "Cousin, I shall have to owe it to you! . . ."

When Riel saw Laframboise fall, he said to me: "Uncle, I am going to have our men advance on foot." I told him he would be sending them into the wolf's mouth, and that he would do better to keep up the courage of the men in their present posts.

At this point the enemy began to flee, and my brother, who had taken command after I fell, shouted to our men to follow them and finish them off. Riel begged him, for the love of God, to kill no more of them, saying that enough blood had already been shed.

Gabriel agreed with his brother Edouard, but he was unfit to argue the point effectively with Riel, and Crozier and his men escaped without further harm.

The police took their own dead with them, and left on the

battlefield the corpses of the dead volunteers. They also left behind five wagons, eight uninjured horses, a dozen rifles and some ammunition, together with Lawrence Clarke's cap of wild cat skin, with which modest booty the victors returned in triumph to Duck Lake, where Riel formed the little army into two ranks, and called on them to "Shout three times, Long live Gabriel Dumont!" and to thank God "who gave you so valorous a leader!" Swaying feebly on his horse, to which his men had tied him, Dumont nodded wearily in acknowledgment to the cheers and the *feu de joie* that followed. The Métis had lost only five men killed, including the two shot at the beginning of the engagement, and three had been wounded, including Dumont.

Afterwards, with the air of a drunken man, and with blood still seeping down over his face, Gabriel demanded to see the prisoners, and talked loudly in Cree of killing them. Whether he was partially deranged from the concussion of the wound, or still angry for the death of his brother and his cousin, it is impossible to be certain, but at least one of the prisoners, Peter Tompkins, later testified that after having ordered the prisoners out, "Gabriel Dumont . . . did not seem to act as a man as though he wanted to kill prisoners very bad. He just simply ordered them out, and then he seemed to quit there when he had ordered them out."

He seems, indeed, to have acted as much from confusion as from anger or malice, and after his wound had been dressed in Hillyard Mitchell's personal room at the store — using Hillyard Mitchell's personal toiletries — and he had rested, he showed a different side to his nature. He went to Riel to talk about the bodies of the volunteers which the police had left behind them in their flight. It was hard, he said, "to leave exposed to the dogs the bodies of our enemies who perhaps bore us no more ill will than we bore them." He suggested sending one of the prisoners to Fort Carlton, with a message offering a safe conduct; Riel agreed, and some days later a party came from Prince Albert to collect the bodies, which Dumont had carefully stored in a vacant house where the frosty air preserved them.

*

177

It became a habit among Canadian commanders during the Northwest Rebellion to minimize their own shortcomings by praising Dumont's capabilities, and Crozier was no exception; doubtless, as he led his badly mauled little force back through the snowy woods to Fort Carlton, he was already composing in his mind the report in which he would say that the rebels "had their dispositions most skilfully made". For he was facing an encounter almost as intimidating as that he had just left; he would have to meet the disapproval of his superior, Commissioner Irvine, who was on that very afternoon hurrying from Prince Albert with eight-three policemen and twenty-five more Prince Albert volunteers. Irvine had taken it for granted that, knowing reinforcements were on their way, Crozier would not commit his men to battle in a territory so favourable to the Métis, who knew it as intimately as the Indians, and he was shocked and angry to arrive in time to celebrate the first defeat suffered by the Dominion's forces in its western territories, and the first outbreak of actual physical insurrection in the country since the pre-Confederation uprisings of the 1830s in Lower and Upper Canada.

"I cannot but consider it a matter of regret" — he declared in the neutral language of official reports — "that with the knowledge that both myself and command were within a few miles of Fort Carlton, Supt. Crozier should have marched out as he did, particularly in the face of what had transpired earlier in the day. I am led to believe that this officer's better judgment was over-ruled by the impetuosity displayed by both the police and volunteers."

Temporarily in command of what scanty forces the Dominion could muster near the forks of the Saskatchewan, and out of touch with the small outlying forces up the North Saskatchewan at Battleford, Fort Pitt, and Edmonton, Irvine was forced to consider the untenability of his present situation. With his own column, the survivors of Crozier's forlorn venture, and a number of refugees from nearby farms, he had more than two hundred people cooped in the dilapidated and indefensible Fort Carlton, whose surrounding hills made it, as one of the volunteers remarked, "a beautiful spot for sharpshooters to pot us as we walked about." Trying to anticipate the moves of the Métis, Irvine decided that it was likely they would either attack

Fort Carlton, where the defenders would be at a complete disadvantage, or descend on Prince Albert, which had almost no defenders and whose capture would be of great strategic as well as moral advantage to Dumont and his forces. The one thing he did not expect them to do was nothing.

However, it was Riel's religiosity rather than Dumont's military calculations that prevailed, and the Métis at Duck Lake spent 27 March praying for the souls of their own dead, whom they buried two days later at St. Laurent. Irvine had time to make his plans, and he decided to abandon Fort Carlton and to concentrate on the defence of Prince Albert, which was the principal white settlement in the locality. The 27th was spent in preparing for the evacuation, and the police were allowed — over the protests of the now discredited Lawrence Clarke — to loot the Hudson's Bay stores, on the pretext that otherwise they would fall into the hands of the Métis. It was proposed to sink under the ice of the Saskatchewan the provisions that could not be carried away, or to spoil them with paraffin, but before this task could be completed a fire broke out in the buildings. The official explanation was that hay spread out for the wounded to lie on had ignited near a stove, but there is no witness to the actual happening, and the fire may well have been set by Dumont's troop of six scouts who were hovering on the hills outside. Certainly the defenders were thrown into such a panic that they made no attempt to put out the fire but immediately set off in the early morning darkness, anxious to flee from the circle of revealing flames.

Dumont had anticipated their retreat, and as soon as his scouts told him the first wagons were setting out through the steep gulley that leads up the hill near the fort — even today it seems a natural spot for an ambush — he suggested to Riel that he might attack Irvine's column in a large spruce wood through which they must pass on their way to Prince Albert. "We could have killed a lot of them," he remarked, and indeed it is likely that, attacked at night in country unfamiliar to most of them, very few of Irvine's party would have survived to join in the defence of Prince Albert. "But Riel, who kept us constantly on the leash, was formally opposed to the project."

Once again, Riel's restraint and his lingering dreams of a treaty without further bloodshed, gave respite to the enemy, and

Dumont, who realized that strategic as well as tactical advantages were being given away, raged inwardly even as he did his best to calm the restlessness of his young captains and their men. He and they had to be content with riding over and taking formal possession of the deserted Fort Carlton, where his scouts had saved the store and most of its contents, though the warehouse had been burnt completely. They then returned to Duck Lake and ransacked the remaining stores, after which, according to Dumont, "Riel made us leave Duck Lake, having burnt down all the buildings except the mill." Here Dumont's memory played him false, for according to the minutes of the Council, meeting at Duck Lake on 31 March, it was he who proposed, with Lépine seconding, that they should return across the river to Batoche, and there prepare to do battle with a further contingent of three hundred and fifteen police who — they had been told — would be marching northward to attack them.

The very idea that their enemies would come in small numbers and could be dealt with piecemeal is illustrative of the almost complete failure on the part of Dumont and the other Saskatchewan Métis to understand the forces that the Dominion might eventually array against them. Nolin and Schmidt had some conception of the eventual probabilities, and so had the priests, though Riel by now was caught in his apocalyptic visions in which the forces of good would defeat his enemies, no matter how numerous their armies of evil. But Dumont and his associates had never seen anything larger in the way of Canadian forces than the troop of less than three hundred men who had ridden west in their red coats on the original western march of the Mounted Police in 1874. They still thought in terms of traditional small scale prairie warfare of the kind waged between bands of Indians and buffalo hunters, and the tales that drifted over the prairies of the success of such methods against Custer's regulars only nine years before at the battle of Little Big Horn seemed to confirm their attitude. And indeed, if the police had merely come in small groups like Irvine's command, each contingent could have been eroded by able guerilla attacks, and the Métis might have held on for years of mobile warfare.

Such a prospect was undoubtedly in Dumont's mind — as

the prospect of early negotiation was in Riel's mind — during the short period of peaceful tension along the South Saskatchewan, as Irvine dug in at Prince Albert after a march hastened by fear of Dumont and his men, and the Métis waited at Batoche for the next move of their opponents. But already the situation was changing into something quite unlike the erratic Indian warfare the prairies had known in the past, and Dumont would need all his undoubted resourcefulness to meet it.

For at last, having remained indifferent for so long, Sir John A. Macdonald had been spurred into action. It was almost as if he were waiting for the situation to become irrevocable before he recognized it, for on 26 March, the very day of the Duck Lake fight, he stood in the House of Commons and declared: "We are quite unaware of the approximate cause of the half-breed rising under Riel" — this in spite of the spate of warnings which for the past seven years had come to him from local officials, from members of the North West Council, from missionaries, policemen, and traders, from men as varied in their attitudes — but united in their apprehensions — as Archbishop Taché and Alexander Morris, and Charles Mair.

In fact, even before the battle of Duck Lake, without having made any attempt to solve the Métis problem by concession or negotiation, Macdonald had already set in motion the primitive military apparatus of the Dominion and in doing so had started Canada on its first war fought without assistance from British troops — a little war and a shameful war, but indisputably our own.

On 23 March, four days after the Métis established their provisional government, Lieutenant-Governor Dewdney had arrived in Winnipeg and had wired to Macdonald of the possible need for the militia to go northwest from Winnipeg and of the desirability of placing a competent officer in charge. Macdonald had immediately instructed Major-General Frederick Dobson Middleton, a walrus-like British Blimp in command of the Canadian militia, to proceed to Winnipeg. Meanwhile Dewdney had asked for full discretion in dealing with Riel, adding, on 24 March: "In the event of mission failing, must have a large force at command who are sufficiently strong at first blow to overcome the half breed and Indian population."

181

Macdonald decided to reject the idea of a mission and to rely on military force. On the 27 March, General Middleton arrived in Winnipeg, having travelled through the United States; he immediately set off with the 90th Rifles, the Winnipeg militia regiment which had been hastily mobilized, and established his headquarters at Qu'Appelle, the nearest railhead to Batoche.

All through Canada, in the days that followed, in Quebec as well as in Ontario and Manitoba, young Canadians were struggling into unfamiliar uniforms and marching to stations for a bitterly hard trip over the uncompleted Canadian Pacific Railway to fight in the distant prairies against men they did not know and with whose grievances they were unfamiliar. It was an army, however ramshackle, that Dumont had called into being with his victory at Duck Lake, not another contingent of police.

And meanwhile, all along the Saskatchewan, the Indians of whose alliance Dumont had long dreamed were stirring into rebellion or watching the play of fortune between their Métis kinsmen and the white intruders.

12. Hesitant Warfare

Though the Indians of the North Saskatchewan rose within a few days of the Métis of Batoche and St. Laurent, and links were sustained between the two groups, the rebellions went on separately, so that the Canadian forces operating against them would eventually be divided into three virtually independent expeditions, one against the Métis and the other two against the leading rebel Indian chiefs, Poundmaker and Big Bear. Only a few Crees from the reservations of the South Saskatchewan and a few Sioux, faithful to old treaties with the Dumont clan, would gather to play their parts in the battle of Fish Creek and in the defence of Batoche. The Indian risings have been narrated in detail elsewhere — e.g., in Stanley's *The Birth of Western Canada* and in Norma Sluman's *Poundmaker* — and in the context of Dumont's life they have significance only in so far as he helped to incite them, and in so far as the actions and inactions of the Indian chiefs affected the outcome of the Métis struggle.

If one consults the documents, and especially those presented in evidence at Riel's trial, it seems as though Riel was foremost in inciting the Indians; it was he who signed the written messages that were sent to them and which were later brought up against him in court. But this is clearly one of the instances in which documents actually distort history because they leave out the unwritten contacts between the illiterate, who in the Northwest Rebellion included most of the principal

183

actors, and especially Gabriel Dumont and the Indian chiefs. The letters signed by Riel to satisfy his own sense of controlling the situation give us no idea of the extent to which they merely confirmed the fact that the Indians and Dumont were already in contact through oral messages and exchanges of gifts. Moreover, Riel did not arrive at Batoche until the early summer of 1884 and did not meet the Indian chiefs at Duck Lake until the end of July that year. All the contacts previous to that date were made by Dumont, and it is unlikely that Riel could have established later contact except through Dumont, who was linked by relationship or alliance or non-aggression treaty with most of the Indian bands between the Touchwood Hills and the Rockies. Riel's defenders — or those at least who seek to present him as a good man led astray by a bloodthirsty Dumont — have been inclined to make a great deal of this fact. They have portrayed Riel as being reluctant to call in the Indians because he feared the "horrors of Indian warfare", and have suggested that he was persuaded against his better judgment by Dumont. Trémaudan, for instance, in his *Histoire de la Nation Métisse dans l'ouest Canadien*, claims that "Riel was always opposed to employing the Indians. However, he could not stop Gabriel Dumont from sending an 'end of tobacco' as he put it in his picturesque language, to persuade the tribes to join him." Such an argument fails to take into account the fact that Riel did not sign his letters to the Indians under duress, and that he did succeed — as we shall see — in stopping Dumont from actions that were much more urgently important to the Métis cause even than the rising of the Indians. It is not unfair to Riel to insist that he did favour calling in the Indians, though he doubtless did not bargain for such episodes — immensely damaging to the Métis as well as to the Indian cause — as the massacre of whites by the Cree and the Assiniboines at Frog Lake on 2 April. But Indian leaders like Poundmaker and Big Bear were equally concerned to avoid this kind of incident; far from inciting such bloodthirsty and fanatical white-haters as Wandering Spirit, the principal culprit in the Frog Lake massacre, they did their best to restrain their followers from indiscriminate violence.

For all the rebel leaders with any vision, whether Poundmaker and Big Bear among the Indians, or Dumont and Riel (in his less exalted moments) among the Métis, recognized that the day when they could sweep the white man from the prairies was gone, if it had ever existed. What they hoped was that a strong alliance of the native peoples, willing to take decisive action, could force the Dominion government to negotiate, could assure the Métis a fair position in the new order of the prairies, and could gain the Indians something better than the starvation which by 1883 had in many areas been the result of the treaties, coupled with the ill-considered economies by which Lawrence Vankoughnet, supported by Sir John A. Macdonald, had cut down on the expenditure of the Indian Department on rations at the very time when the full effects of the disappearance of the buffalo were being felt.

The aim of the rebel leaders was shown by the eagerness of both Métis and Indians to gather hostages. Dumont took prisoner virtually every non-Métis person who strayed into the Batoche area after 18 March, and his hastily conceived plan at Duck Lake was devised with the hope of surrounding Crozier and his men and offering the alternative of extermination or surrender. Dumont and Riel calculated that they would accept the latter and provide the Métis with enough prisoners to promote effective bargaining with Macdonald; only the sharp eyes of Crozier's half breed scouts prevented the complete encirclement of the police on this occasion. Big Bear also, after the massacre at Frog Lake had taken place against his will, was intent on obtaining hostages instead of killing white people, and for this reason he took prisoners at Fort Pitt rather than allowing another slaughter. An effective alliance of all the Indians and the Métis, if it could have held all the white people of the prairies hostage, might indeed have forced Macdonald to send envoys ahead of his soldiers. Events, and Riel's hesitancies, were to make such an alliance impossible.

There is no doubt that Dumont tried hard to cement such a working accord among the prairie peoples. If he was little in evidence at Batoche during the early part of the agitation after Riel's arrival from Montana, this was partly because he was moving among the Indian reservations of the area, and there is no doubt that he was mainly responsible for the Indian chiefs making Duck Lake the site of their gathering at the end of July, which Riel attended to talk to Big Bear, Poundmaker,

Red Pheasant, and the other malcontent tribal leaders. It was also due mainly to Dumont's influence that the grievances of the Indians began to figure prominently during the later months of 1884 in the demands that were being put forward by the joint agitation of the Métis, the English half-breeds, and the white settlers.

Dumont's account of his actions after the Duck Lake fight leaves no doubt that, even if letters to the Indians, who could not read them, were written by Louis Riel, the actual messengers were sent out by his Adjutant-General, and they bore oral messages from Dumont that would carry much more weight with the Indians who knew him and his reputation than Riel's missives could do. As a result, within a few days of the battle of Duck Lake, the defeat of the Mounted Police was known throughout the western prairies, and it was in response to this news that the Stoney Indians in the Eagle Hills and the Crees on the Battle River and at Frog Lake rose in rebellion. All these Indians had smoked the tobacco which Dumont had previously sent to them, and therefore felt obliged to fight on his side. Poundmaker, even before the Duck Lake fight, had returned a message that "he and his men would remain sitting on their heels, ready to stand up again at the first signal," as indeed they did, moving to besiege Battleford.

Dumont was also successful with a mission to the Teton Sioux, survivors of Sitting Bull's army, who had been allowed to settle on a reserve at Round Prairie to the south of Saskatoon. François Vermette and Napoléon Carrière were sent on this mission, and found Charles Trottier and a number of other Métis living among the Sioux. The whole party, led by the Sioux chief White Cap and comprising sixty Indians and a dozen Métis, set off for Batoche. The "Orangemen" of Saskatoon, as Dumont called them, tried to persuade White Cap and his party to turn back, but they continued on their way, and "arrived at Batoche singing and shouting war cries; some were on horseback, others in carts, and several on snowshoes." They established their camp at Batoche on 10 April and were joined by a few other young Sioux who had travelled from the Cypress Hills to fulfill the treaty obligations to the Saskatchewan Métis which their fathers had contracted at Devil's Lake a quarter of a century before.

This was the sum of Dumont's achievements in building a

functioning alliance. Though his agents visited the most powerful chiefs of the prairies, the Blackfoot Crowfoot, the Cree Piapot, and even Sitting Bull, all of these chose to remain neutral. It has been said often that they did so because of the persuasions of powerful Catholic missionaries, like Father Albert Lacombe who was living among the Blackfoot, but it is much more likely that they were cautiously watching the turn of events. They had observed that, despite the victory of Duck Lake, Riel had allowed a stalemate to develop between the police, strongly entrenched in Prince Albert, and the Métis at Batoche, and they were waiting to see what action Dumont would take to counter the advance of the Canadian militia into the territory. The younger Blackfoot were eager for action, and the people of Calgary expected to be attacked, but Crowfoot restrained his braves.

In the same way, most of the Métis outside the Batoche-St. Laurent region remained neutral. Apart from the few who came with White Cap from Round Prairie, and another handful whom Edouard Dumont fetched from Fort à la Corne (including young Elie Dumont but not Xavier Batoche — who insisted on staying away), there were no recruits from outside, though the men of a small Métis encampment at the mouth of the Turtle River, 150 miles northwest of Batoche, led by Joseph Jobin and Athanase Falcon, joined Poundmaker's Crees in the siege of Battleford. Dumont sent half a dozen Métis from Batoche, led by Norbert Delorme and José Arcand, to strengthen contacts with Poundmaker and Big Bear. The Turtle River and Batoche Métis allied themselves with the more restless young braves of Poundmaker's camp, and helped to sustain the warlike spirit among his people. Ironically, there was another group of Métis who had settled down to farm at Bresaylor, northwest of Battleford on the Saskatchewan, and these wished to have no part in the rebellion. Led by Delorme and the "loyal" Métis, the Indians took them prisoner, and though — thanks largely to Poundmaker — none of them was harmed, they remained captive until the end of the fighting. The larger Métis settlements outside Batoche, at St. Albert and Lac Ste. Anne, at Qu'Appelle and Wood Mountain, adopted the same attitude as the great Indian chiefs; they remained neutral until the shape of events became clear.

It is possible that all the Indians and all the Métis might

have been moved into action if Dumont had carried out the strategy he had devised to hamper the small Canadian army, less than six thousand strong, that came into the prairies to deal with the rebellion. Of that six thousand, a column of eight hundred men, with artillery and with Captain Howard's famous Gatling gun, was selected to march north towards Batoche. Other columns were sent via Swift Current and Edmonton to deal with Poundmaker and Big Bear respectively, and the rest remained at the base of Qu'Appelle.

Middleton started north from Qu'Appelle on 6 April, proceeding slowly, since troops and supplies would still be joining him, and reaching Clarke's Crossing, about forty miles south of Batoche, on the 17th; he had covered a hundred and eighty miles in eleven days. At Clarke's Crossing he stayed another six days to await the soldiers who would complete his contingent, and to divide the column into two parts, one of which would proceed on each bank of the South Saskatchewan.

Dumont was fully informed of these developments, for he had sent scouts as far south as Qu'Appelle, and one of his spies, Jérome Henry, was actually employed as a teamster in Middleton's column. Every move of the militia was seen by the elusive and extremely mobile Métis scouts and reported by an efficient system of couriers; their task was not difficult, for these were the days before the Boer War and universal khaki, and Middleton's men marched in bright uniforms with less idea of the art of camouflage than Macbeth's enemies who attacked him disguised as Birnam wood.

Dumont and his captains had worked out a strategy of guerilla harassment that would undoubtedly have been as efficient as his information service. He proposed to send his men riding to the southeast so that they could blow up the railway tracks, destroy the bridges and prevent supplies and reinforcements reaching Middleton and his army. He also — as he said — "proposed we go ahead of the troops, harass them by night, and above all prevent them from sleeping, believing this was a good way to demoralize them and make them lose heart." Undoubtedly such tactics would have been extremely effective with the kind of green soldiers — the clerks and shopmen of Montreal and Toronto and Winnipeg — who were marching fearfully into the wilderness as the major part of Middleton's army. "I am sure," said Dumont, "we should have made them so edgy that at the end of three nights they would have been at each others' throats." Undoubtedly he was right. An effective campaign of destroying the railway and of night attacks on Middleton's column would not only have held up its advance by demoralizing the Canadian militia; it would also have brought a dividend of arms and ammunition that was urgently needed, for though Dumont said that at this time he had three hundred and fifty men capable of fighting, he had rifles for only two hundred of them.

Perhaps the most ironical aspect of the situation was that the possibility of such attacks as Dumont planned was precisely what made the Canadians most anxious. On the day of the Duck Lake battle, the Indian agent Hayter Reed wired to Dewdney: "The force coming to our relief should be cautioned that the rebels are good shots and will attempt to surround them in wooded country." His message was passed on. And shortly afterwards, on hearing that Middleton was slowly nearing the Saskatchewan, Sandford Fleming — who had travelled the country with George Grant in search of a route for the Canadian Pacific Railway — wrote urgently to the authorities in Ottawa: "The country the General is approaching is exceedingly favourable for the Indian and Half-Breed style of fighting. It is broken, covered with clumps of wood and brush, and altogether admirably adapted for ambuscades. It is quite evident that the rebels who know every part of the country will be best suited for a surprise." Even Middleton at first feared such attacks, but allowed himself to be lulled into confidence by an old hunter turned guide (and perhaps an agent of Dumont) who assured him that the Métis would be too superstitious to attack by night!

Thus everyone — Dumont and his men and his opponents — was prepared for the kind of guerilla warfare he had planned: everyone except the most important figures, Middleton and Riel, and Riel opposed it with all the rational and irrational resources he could command. He argued that with the police occupying Prince Albert in strength, the Métis could not afford to divert large numbers of men to harrying Middleton. He told Dumont that guerilla tactics were too much like Indian warfare, and that night attacks might involve firing on French

Canadians who had joined Middleton's column. Dumont protested that, French or English, he could hardly regard them as friends if they came to fight against him, but Riel replied: "If you knew them, you would not want to deal with them in that way." Riel was also concerned about Gabriel himself, to whom he was genuinely attached and who had not yet recovered from the wound — unattended by any physician — that he had received at Duck Lake. "If anything happened to Dumont," he noted in his diary of the time, "it would not only be a misfortune for his friends, but an irreparable loss for the army and to the nation. If my Uncle Gabriel were cured of his wound I should be more willing to see him start on an expedition of this kind."

But there were other matters that at this time occupied Riel's troubled mind. The forces of darkness might be marching on Batoche, but that did not exonerate him from the responsibility of turning the Métis capital into a citadel of light, and during the brief days between the Duck Lake battle and the arrival of Middleton's army there were important theological questions to be decided that might well affect God's willingness to intervene miraculously on the Métis side. "Old Rome" had to be deposed, and the priests put under protective arrest. The libels against the Almighty promulgated for centuries had to be set right, and a resolution was passed by the Exovedate declaring that eternal punishment was an idea incompatible with the concept of a merciful god, and therefore Hell could not be everlasting. Another resolution transferred the Sabbath back to Saturday, and yet another removed the pagan names of the days and replaced them by such titles as Christaurore for Monday, Viergeaurore for Tuesday, Josephaurore for Wednesday. When the priests protested, Riel declared that papal infallibility had come to an end and that he had been chosen as the Holy Spirit's delegate in the reformation of the Church. As for the properly religious way to deal with one's enemies — personified for the moment in Middleton and his men — Riel and the members of the Exovedate under his influence rejected Dumont's advice in a resolution declaring that "It would be better to watch well their moves, to let them come when they please — under the Almighty Hand of Divine Providence — and when they are near enough to strike, and then to work until, with God's and Christ's help, we have conquered them." Complete success, it was added, could come only through petitioning "our Lady, the Blessed Virgin Mary."

It has been suggested, especially by George F. G. Stanley in his *Louis Riel,* that Dumont had no interest in such matters. "He was a man of action," says Dr. Stanley, "not a man anxious to indulge in or understand abstract ideas, particularly those of a theological bent. He wanted to be about, moving." It is true that Dumont wanted "to be about, moving." And yet, though he did not vote on the question of renaming the days of the week, he did give his voice to limiting the duration of Hellfire and to shifting the Sabbath to Saturday. And, in the face of his very shrewd military judgment of the situation, he allowed his decisions as Métis general to be over-ruled by Riel.

Why he did so has always been difficult to explain. It is too easy to picture him as the simple hunter beguiled by a charismatic and literate leader. For Dumont had his own charisma, and his lack of literacy had not prevented him from acting as a decisive and intelligent leader of his own people in past years. Therefore we have to dismiss immediately any suggestion that Riel hypnotized him. Dumont's own explanation is — on analysis — much less simple than it first appears. "I yielded to Riel's judgment" — he said — "although I was convinced that, from a humane standpoint, mine was the better plan; but I had confidence in his faith and his prayers, and that God would listen to him." There was obviously a division within Dumont between the highly practical hunter and warrior, who never really abandoned his view of the appropriate strategy for the situation, and the pious Métis in whose eyes Riel had become a substitute for the missionaries who had lost credit by refusing to support resistance to the established government. The balance between these two opposing views was tipped partly by Dumont's almost feudal sense of fealty (he had accepted Riel as his leader and found it dishonourable to deny him even when he was wrong) and partly by a bond of affection that sprang up between the two men, expressed on Riel's side by a feeling that Gabriel, who had become his friend during the months since they had ridden together from Montana, in some degree shared the blessedness that in his exalted moments he felt descending on himself. There is an illuminating note in the diary of thoughts and visions Riel kept at Batoche :

> I saw Gabriel Dumont. He seemed weakened, and was ashamed. He did not look at me; he looked only at his completely bare table.
>
> But Gabriel Dumont is blessed. His faith will not falter. He is strong by the grace of God; his hope and his confidence in God will be justified. He will emerge from the struggle, loaded with the spoils of his enemies. Jesus Christ and the Virgin Mary will give him back his joy.

Whatever the reason for Dumont's acceptance until the eleventh hour of Riel's ban on action, there is no doubt that this period of indecision isolated the Métis of Batoche and prevented the rebellion from extending beyond the Indian bands and the small groups of Métis outside Batoche who rose in rebellion during the first few days after the skirmish of Duck Lake.

But it might well have been otherwise. Sandford Fleming spoke with real insight when he said in his letter of warning: "Even a momentary check at the crisis would cause thousands of Indians who are at present quiet to rise." And one can sketch out a very plausible scenario of what might have happened even at this advanced stage of events if Dumont's wishes had been followed and Riel's protests had been ignored.

If there had been two or three successful derailments of trains with troops or goods destined for Qu'Appelle, and two or three ambushes that had shown the weakness of Middleton's tactics and captured some of his weapons and supplies, it is unlikely that the restive Chief Piapot would have remained inactive, and his adherence to the cause would have brought in all the Crees not yet involved, together with the Métis of Wood Mountain and Cypress Hills and those of the Sioux in Canada who had not already joined the rebellion. In such circumstances, it is unlikely that Crowfoot would have been able to restrain his warriors, which would have meant the entry of the whole Blackfoot Confederacy as well as the remaining Assiniboine and the Métis of Edmonton, St. Albert, and Lac Ste. Anne. In other words, the entire Indian and half-breed population would have been in revolt (for the English half-breeds would hardly have contrived to stay aloof), and Middleton's army would have been entirely inadequate — in numbers and training alike — even to contain such a movement. Macdonald would have been forced either to negotiate seriously or to face years of guerilla warfare for which the new Dominion was ill-equipped; the completion of the Canadian Pacific Railway would have been delayed indefinitely, and there would have been a rapidly growing danger of intervention by the strongly imperialist Americans of the 1880s, on the pretext that the Canadian West was ungovernable and therefore a danger to their own peace. There is no doubt at all that in such circumstances Macdonald's natural astuteness and his genuine patriotism would have surfaced, and he would have come to a quick agreement.

Dumont was in fact both militarily and politically a wiser man than the Riel he had called in to solve the problems of his people. But Dumont's advice was not heeded until Middleton began to move north from Clarke's Crossing in the direction of Batoche on the last lap of his campaign, and by that time the moment for a general uprising in the prairies had passed. Batoche must stand alone.

13. Fish Creek: A Battle Won

Middleton came with the spring. The hard winter of disappointment and mounting rage, the winter when the sound of hurrying horsemen beat on the hard ice and the blood of prairie war once again stained the snow between the birchwoods, gave way as the sallows burst into catkins and the prairie crocus thrust their hairy blue anemone heads between the brown draggled grass from which the snow had barely melted. On 23 April the Canadian army began to lurch forward from Clarke's Crossing on what Middleton thought must be the last thrust that would crush the rebellion.

Dumont's patience and that of his captains came to an end. He was restless to try his warrior's skill against Middleton's superior strength; he could not endure "letting him move around as he wanted", an emotion all the more understandable since this was the land Dumont had known since his childhood at Fort Pitt, the land where he had experienced — in the lost days of the buffalo hunt — a freedom and a sufficiency that even Riel did not know. Moved beyond endurance by this ultimate violation of a country where, as chief of the hunt and later of the St. Laurent commune, his word had once gone unchallenged, he shed his inclination to defer to Riel, that prophet whose usefulness — as events showed — seemed to lie only in his literacy.

"I told Riel that I could no longer accept his humanitarian advice, that I intended to go out and shoot at the invaders, and

194

that my men supported me." What Dumont did not say in his account of the rebellion — though he may well have mentioned it in his crucial confrontation with Riel — was that his force of reliable men was being gradually eroded, partly by the fear of facing an enemy who came, as their spies told them, armed with all the modern weapons of war, but partly also because many of them realized, as Dumont did, that each day of inaction made eventual resistance more difficult. When Riel argued for awaiting the enemy in Batoche, Gabriel replied that "those who show themselves weak and hesitant beforehand will be good for nothing when they hear the women and children crying!"

Riel, whose visions had recently been filled with menacing giants and "sons of evil", finally gave in to Dumont's urgent demands. "Very well! Do as you wish!" he said, and even agreed to accompany any sally against the Canadians Dumont might organize. At the same time he told "my uncle Gabriel" not only to "pay attention to his wound", but also "to fear his own boiling courage and his habit of recklessly exposing himself!"

That night, as Dumont's scouts informed him, Middleton's column camped at McIntosh's farm, six miles south of Fish Creek. Dumont immediately sent couriers to Poundmaker and Big Bear, telling them of the proximity of a decisive struggle, and asking them to lead their warriors to the defence of Batoche. Then he proposed to make a night attack on Middleton's camp, carried out like his exploits in Indian wars long ago, with sentries silently stabbed, the prairie set on fire, and two hundred Métis horsemen sweeping through the camp to kill, burn, and plunder, and then vanish into the dark. But that night Major Boulton's scouts were moving out from the army's camp to secure a store of forage that had been seen during the day; Dumont's scouts, observing their activity, concluded that the Canadians were on their guard, and the attack never took place. In fact, by now Middleton had been so lulled into a sense of security by the lack of activity among his enemies, that an assault after Boulton's men had returned from their expedition might easily have taken the General by surprise and resulted not only in casualties and the capture of arms much needed by the Métis, but also, in the tradition of prairie warfare, in the disruption of the Canadian transport and cavalry by stampeding and driving off their riding and pack animals.

Having lost the advantage of a night attack, Dumont now planned to ambush Middleton and his men by day, and his knowledge of the terrain suggested to him as the obvious place Tourond's Coulée, the ravine that twisted from Tourond's farm towards the South Saskatchewan, and down which Fish Creek ran to the main river. Into the coulée and up again on to the parkland south of Batoche, wound the most direct trail from Clarke's Crossing to Gabriel's Ferry, the trail which — as Jérome Henry informed Dumont — Middleton and his column intended to take. It was the kind of natural trap in which, if everything went well, a small army might be closed off and systematically potted until the survivors gave in. Marksmen carefully placed in the creekbed and on the slopes above could command the road all through the ravine, and, at the bridge which Middleton's men must cross, low thick woods came close down to the edge of the creek. There was perfect cover for the ambusher, and perfect exposure for the ambushed; it was a miniature Khyber Pass of the North, and after the battle was over General Middleton, whose past experience included the Indian Mutiny, would admit that, if it had not been for the excellence of his own scouts, his column might easily have been destroyed.

Riel and Dumont had set out the evening before at head of their own motley column of horsemen and footmen, including, according to Dumont's account, Cree, Sioux, and Salteaux Indians, as well as Métis and also "Canadians", by whom he presumably meant Québecois, though there is no other record of their being involved in the rebellion. It is significant of the shrinkage of the Métis ranks that he could leave only thirty men, under the command of his brother Edouard, to guard Batoche. After halting several times on the way, at Riel's insistence, to say the rosary, they stopped eight miles south at the farm of Roger Goulet, where Dumont had two cattle killed to provide supper for his men. It was midnight. "We had hardly finished eating," he recalled, "when two Métis, Noël Champagne and Moïse Carrière . . . came to warn us that the mounted police were coming by the Qu'Appelle road to surprise Batoche, and that Edouard wanted thirty men and either Riel or myself. I answered that I had set out to attack Middleton and I had no intention of turning back. [He did not in fact believe the report of a police advance.] Riel agreed to do as Edouard asked, and I let him have fifty men from my force." In fact, almost every man wanted to go with Riel, not from fear but because they were anxious for their families, but Dumont angrily lined them up and picked those he needed least.

This reduction of his minuscule army may have been an additional reason why Dumont changed his mind about attacking Middleton by night. He had less than a fifth of the Canadians' strength, and such a small force could be better used in an ambush than in an attack. He and his men rode south, and at about four in the morning, having given orders that no-one should use the road through Tourond's Coulée, he borrowed a fast horse belonging to Ignace Poitras and rode forward with Napoléon Nault to reconnoitre Middleton's camp. Then, having tried in vain to lure some of the enemy scouts into a wood where he could have dealt with them in a small preliminary ambush, he returned to Tourond's farm, where he found his men praying, and joined them briefly before he had a bull killed and its meat grilled on a fire of willow boughs so that they could breakfast before battle.

"About seven o'clock Gilbert Bréland, one of our scouts, warned us that a column of about eight hundred men was advancing towards us. I therefore placed a hundred and thirty of our men in a hollow on the left bank of Fish Creek, opposite Tourond's house, and hid their horses in the woods. I went on with twenty horsemen to take cover farther along the path which the troops would follow. I did not intend to charge them until the others thrust them back, and I gave my main force instructions not to attack them until they were all in the coulée." And Dumont added, with a touch of sardonic nostalgia: "I wanted to treat them as we would have treated buffalo." In plotting his tactics he still remembered the beasts milling and dying in the Indian pounds of his youth, and thought to destroy his enemies in the same way. He hoped not only to destroy Middleton's column, but also to seize its arms and equip his people militarily.

There is some disagreement as to how elaborately Dumont constructed his ambush. Middleton, who was never ungenerous in praising Dumont, perhaps because his enemy's abilities enhanced his own glory in being ultimately the victor, talked of

197

"cleverly-constructed rifle-pits", which were "so situated that their defenders were quite covered from our fire, both rifle and cannon." Dumont, however, scornfully remarked, when he heard Middleton's account, that the General had been mistaken in talking of rifle-pits, since he and his men utilized dips in the ground that were nothing more than footpaths hollowed out by the passage of animals in the woods." In fact, as we have seen, Dumont decided on the place of his ambush at the last moment, and improvised his arrangements; his men carried no trenching tools, such as spades or picks, and the most they did was to strengthen and disguise existing unevennesses in the ground with logs that happened to be lying in the copses.

Dumont was undoubtedly hoping to re-enact something like the battles of the past between the Métis and the Sioux, but those had taken place when his people were experienced in such warfare and aware, through the necessities of the buffalo hunt, of the need not only for vigilance and initiative, but also for a discipline that involved unquestioning obedience to the commands of a voluntarily chosen leader. Dumont's men, who had shown little eagerness to face the enemy when they had a chance to return to Batoche with Riel, were a less homogenous group than a band of Métis hunters might have been even a decade before. Almost imperceptibly, the inroads of civilization were affecting them. A few of the older men, like Dumont himself, were survivors of both Indian wars and the buffalo hunts, and he had with him such notable marksmen as Philippe Gariepy, James Short, and Gilbert Bréland, but many were youths not even old enough to have taken part as hunters in the last of the buffalo expeditions five years before, and, though Middleton's information told him that the Métis were well armed with repeating rifles, many of them in fact carried only shot guns or trading muskets, and Métis accounts say they had only three or four Winchesters. The Sioux, it is true, put on a more martial appearance, for they had painted their faces for battle, and they sang their war songs as they rode towards Fish Creek, while the Métis were more inclined to pray and tell their beads. But Indian warfare even at its most epic was not noted for discipline, and Indian war parties were inclined to disperse if the fighting lasted too long or the casualties ran too high.

Thus, contrary to the legend that at Fish Creek Dumont led

a small but experienced group of guerilla fighters who were all dead shots with a Winchester, he in fact had to rely on a mixed troop of largely untried and mostly ill-armed fighters, certainly little more experienced in warfare than Middleton's barely trained militiamen. For, if Middleton's men were scared of being ambushed, Dumont's men were to show themselves, at least on first acquaintance, terrified of artillery. In fact, Dumont's only possible advantages were position, surprise and his own resources of courage and tactical skill. His choice of terrain, and the way he posted his men, gave him all he needed in terms of the advantage of position, and his courage and resourcefulness served him well when he lost the third possible advantage, that of surprise.

For by the time Middleton's column reached Fish Creek, the Canadian general was already made alert to the possibility of attack. Dumont tells how some of the young Métis disobeyed his orders not to approach the trail running from Clarke's Crossing to Gabriel's Crossing, and galloped across it in the chase of cattle, so that the English half-breed scouts saw their tracks and warned their commander, Major Boulton. Middleton's account is somewhat different:

"Having been warned that we had a nasty ravine to cross on our way, I directed Boulton to push his advanced scouts further ahead, and to extend them more. . . . After riding about five miles we met a mounted man who had been sent to inform us that the scouts on the left of our trail had come across a camping place not long before vacated, the fires being still smouldering; that at least 180 or 200 mounted men had camped there."

Major Boulton sent his scouts to explore the ravine, and it was now that Dumont's own foolhardiness spoilt what remaining chance he might have to take his enemies by surprise. He tells how one of the scouts came riding towards him. Dumont's combative instinct rose up, and he forgot the need for concealment. "I had no wish to waste my cartridges on such a little matter. He saw us and made off; I chased him and was about to overtake him, when somebody fired at me. My people shouted to me that I was riding into a troop of forty men whom I had not seen, so intent was I on catching my prey. When I saw I had no time to club down the fugitive, I shot him, and at once I plunged into the coulée to rejoin my twenty horsemen, while the policemen dismounted." (The troop of forty were in fact Middleton's advance guard; Dumont consistently referred to any red-coated soldiers as policemen, evidently assuming there was no real distinction between the militia and a para-military police force.)

"It was now twenty past seven in the morning," Dumont's account continued. (Both Charles Trottier and Maxime Lépine give 9 a.m. as the time the fighting started, which seems more likely.) "They began firing at us, and some of my companions now left me, and ran away to join my group of a hundred and thirty, of whom a fair number had also run away. I tied up my horse and went down into the ravine on foot, so as to get nearer to the enemy. I found a young Indian there, and I began to shoot."

Clearly, with his men wavering, Dumont believed in setting an example, and he fired busily at any target that offered itself. One of these targets, according to the Canadian commander's own account, may have been General Middleton himself, who recorded in his account of the rebellion: "In passing some open ground we were fired at from the rifle pits in the centre of the enemy's line, one bullet passing through and seriously damaging my fur service cap, another grazing my horse Sam, to his great surprise and disgust, and another wounding Captain Wise's fresh horse, which fell, throwing his rider right under my horse's feet. Needless to say, we did not linger on that spot. This was not the first time I had been saluted from this same spot, and I was afterwards informed by Riel that I owed those delicate attentions to his Commander-in-Chief Gabriel Dumont, who had been good enough to swear he would shoot me." To which Dumont replied tersely, when he was told of the general's remarks, "He can congratulate himself that I didn't recognize him."

Dumont's carefully laid plans, of course, had gone completely astray. He had hoped that his troop of horsemen would close off the retreat of Middleton's column after it had entered the coulée, but he now found himself with a small and dwindling group of marksmen opposing the whole of Middleton's column. "When they saw I was making things too warm for them," the Canadians began to fire heavily into the copse where Dumont was concealed, keeping low, since the trees were still leafless. "I heard the branches breaking around me, and I decided that it was unwise to stay any longer. I do not know if I killed many of them, for as soon as I fired a shot I took cover, but I cannot have missed often."

He rejoined his troop of horsemen, and then encountered some of the Sioux, who told him that one of their tribesmen had been killed on the slope of the ravine. This was probably the man Middleton mentioned, an "Indian in full war paint" who "out of bravado, came dancing out and shouting his war cry and was immediately knocked over. . . ." Dumont scrambled down the slope to get the Indian's weapons. "I found the poor wounded devil, flat on his belly and singing away. I asked him if he was mortally wounded, but he said he was not. In the spot where he lay the bullets were whistling close, and I crawled back on all fours to my men so that I could get a better aim at the enemy, but we could not hang on there, for the police were occupying the nearby copses on both sides of the ravine, and we were too exposed."

With Napoléon Nault, one of the few men courageous enough to stay with him, Dumont went back to his horse and galloped off to join the party he had left higher up the ravine. He found the troop disintegrating from panic, and even when he had stopped fifteen men from deserting, only forty-seven of the original hundred and thirty were left. Fifteen of his own troop of horsemen remained, which meant that in all he had a little more than sixty men left to resist the four hundred riflemen — plus artillery — with whom Middleton was trying to shoot his way through the ravine.

But Dumont had no intention of giving way. He meant to expend in that single spring day all the energy and fury he had been storing up in the previous weeks of frustration. He was not in good shape; his head wound was painful and suppurating, and it grew more inflamed as the day went on, but he was inspired by a kind of excitement that made him almost unaware of his discomfort, and that enabled him to inspire the men who had chosen to stay with him.

"I said to the young fellows: 'Don't be scared of the bullets. They won't do you any harm,' and I showed them how to shoot so as to hit home. They began to shout with joy, while all the time the enemy cannon roared. We went down into a hollow in the prairie to get nearer the enemy lines, and when I saw an officer aiming at us, I shot him down, and when they heard him crying out like a child our young men laughed in mockery." It was, once again and for a few hours, the hard, merciless prairie world of Dumont's youth.

All that day until nightfall the Métis prevented the Canadian army from advancing, while the Canadian officers urged their men on, "en poussant des Goddams terribles." Dumont was left with the pick of his people, the old companions from the days of the hunt, and the best of the young men. They sustained their courage as they lay in the shallow depressions on the edge of the woodland by singing Pierre Falcon's song of the Battle of Seven Oaks and old songs from the Napoleonic wars. They lit their pipes "for relaxation and to mock our hunger." They also prayed, and many of them must have agreed with Maxime Lépine, who held a small crucifix in one hand throughout the battle, when he said, "I think prayer did more than bullets." But Dumont lived in the belief that God helps the man who helps himself, and all the accounts agree that, quite apart from directing the operations of his dwindled force, he himself fought with great tenacity: ". . . I kept firing away, and to make it quicker, the young men around me kept supplying me with cartridges, which disappeared at a great rate." This giving of ammunition was necessitated by the shortage of supplies, for most of the Métis had set out with a basic ration of only twenty cartridges.

When there were only seven cartridges left, Dumont decided on an old trick of plains warfare that he calculated would be unfamiliar to most of the Canadians. He set fire to the prairie grass, and the smoke blew in thick clouds towards Middleton's troops; under cover of it, while his men shouted and sang from their posts, Dumont crept forward, firing his last cartridges, so that the Canadians imagined it was a general advance and fell back. Dumont hoped to find arms and ammunition on the bodies of the dead enemy, but he was unsuccessful, and the grass fire did not have the effect of causing a general panic, as he had hoped, since the wind shifted and Middleton sent his teamsters to put out the flames.

Dumont returned to his own small group of fifteen men, who had remained close to him during this operation, and then decided to reconnoitre and see whether it might be possible to create a diversion by getting into the woods behind the enemy lines. He went first to try and establish contact with his larger group of forty-seven men, but found that the Canadians had cut him off from them. Returning to his horsemen, he discovered that the Sioux among them had slipped away, tired of fighting and of the worsening weather, for the rain was now turning to sleet; besides, twilight was coming on, and the Indians did not like to fight after dark.

With the seven men who remained with him, Dumont tried once again to reach the larger group, now surrounded in the coulée, but still fighting doggedly; the fire was so heavy that even Dumont did not try to make his way through it, for that would have meant "exposing myself to certain death." He therefore started with his little force to outflank the enemy so that he could mount a desperate diversionary attack, but at the end of the day he was saved by the arrival of reinforcements. All day he had hoped for help to come from Batoche, but Riel, who prayed for hours on end with his arms held up in the shape of a cross, and exhorted the women and children to do likewise, did not want to send any men, though the attack by Irvine and the Mounted Police did not materialize and the thunder of Middleton's guns could be heard quite distinctly in the village. Finally, Edouard Dumont's patience came to an end. "When my own people are in peril, I cannot remain here," he said, "My brothers are there and I cannot let them be killed without going to their aid." He was supported by an Indian named Yellow Blanket who added: "There is no need to wait until tomorrow to help one's friends." With Ambroise Champagne, they gathered eighty horsemen, and riding hard to Fish Creek, Edouard led his cavalry in a charge into the coulée that forced the Canadians back and made Middleton decide to withdraw and count the battle a draw. Edouard arrived none too soon; the Métis were running out of ammunition, and from noon onwards had been firing seldom but accurately. It was the sound of hunting rifles, different in tone from the military rifles and coming from the north that — young Elie Dumont remembered — gave them hope.

It was a victory for Dumont, since, with an effective force of less than sixty men (for, at the end, with the desertion of the

Sioux, their numbers dwindled to fifty-four) , he had held back a column several times as large, and in the process had severely mauled the enemy. The Canadian casualties consisted of ten dead and forty-five wounded, while of the Métis only four were killed (among them Gabriel's nephew, Pierre Parenteau) and three wounded, one of them mortally. In addition, fifty-five Métis horses, tethered in the woods, were killed, and this was a serious loss, particularly as it was not compensated by any great gain in ammunition, of which the Métis were in great need, though they picked up thirty-two Canadian carbines and a certain amount of baggage, including the medical officer's kit, which included "two bottles of brandy, in which we drank his health."

Wet through and chilled though he was, with his wound agonizingly throbbing, Dumont nevertheless wanted to pursue the retiring enemy. But most of his men were unwilling; indeed, it was as much as he could do to ensure that they take care of their dead and wounded. They went to Tourond's farm to get warm and have their first meal since breakfast, and then they were all anxious to hasten back to Batoche. Dumont believed that an undisciplined retreat might invite an attack by the enemy, yet he himself now began to feel so ill from his wound that he had to ride back as quickly as possible. With difficulty he persuaded his men to return in an orderly manner, many of them on foot since their horses had been killed, and at the first light of dawn he rode into Batoche, accompanied by Napoléon Nault and Charles Trottier. On the way Nault tore a piece of his saddle cloth to bind Gabriel's aching head. "I went straight to the Council House. I shook hands with those there and asked for tea. There was none. Then I went home." But before he did so Gabriel gave Riel an account of the battle, "in spite of my exhaustion and the pain that the wound in my head was now causing me." It is an example of Dumont's strange loyalty to Riel that almost four years later he could say, "I attribute our success to Riel's prayers," even though earlier in the same account he showed his displeasure at Riel's efforts to discourage his brother Edouard from relieving him.

But if Dumont was so gracious about transferring the praise for what must be regarded as a battle won, others, including many of his enemies, had no doubt who was responsible.

Middleton admitted in a wire to Caron, the Minister for the Militia: "Their plans well arranged beforehand and had my scouts not been well to the front should have been attacked in the ravine and probably wiped out." The correspondents accompanying Middleton were impressed, and the *Toronto Mail* appeared on the day after the battle with a report that "Gabriel Dumont commands the rebels, and does it with consummate skill." And Major Boulton, the commander of Middleton's scouts, who hastened to disclaim any wish "to disparage the bravery of the enemy," was so deceived by Dumont's tactical resourcefulness, that he believed the Métis must have had more than two hundred and eighty men in the field, which is roughly twice as many as Dumont had even before the desertions began. But, like Duck Lake, it was not a decisive victory; so far as the Canadians were concerned it was an annoying setback that would delay the eventual suppression of the rebellion, but it was not the kind of disastrous rout of the Canadian force that might influence Macdonald to change his policy and send the message for which Riel had allowed one telegraph line passing from Batoche to the outside world to remain uncut. It meant, for Middleton, the need for a pause to rest his men and re-organize his column; for Dumont and his followers it meant at most a respite in which, as they desperately hoped, their fellow Métis and their Indian allies might come to the rescue.

14. Batoche: A War Lost

After Fish Creek, it was evident to Middleton as much as to Dumont that the next encounter would be decisive. Both waited and both prepared. Middleton remained encamped at Fish Creek, and during the first few days after his setback he was depressed and pessimistic. Casualties had been heavy in proportion to the scope of the battle and the numbers of the Métis. As a regular officer, he was highly conscious of the poor training of his men and the poor direction offered by their officers. And he believed — perhaps because Dumont's agents had spread the rumour for his scouts to hear — that the Métis had established strongpoints all the way from Tourond's Coulée to Batoche at which, as he told the Minister of Militia and Defense, Adolphe Caron, "half a dozen men with lots of ammunition could kill a hundred or two without difficulty." It would, he said two days after Fish Creek, "take a force of five or six thousand men to turn them out."

The column which Lord Melgund had been leading up the west bank of the river was rather laboriously ferried over at Clarke's Crossing, but Middleton still awaited other reinforcements, which were coming down river from Qu'Appelle on the Hudson's Bay steamer, the *Northcote*, commandeered for the expedition. Owing to a variety of misunderstandings and misadventures, the boat did not leave Qu'Appelle until 23 April, and it took fourteen instead of four days to complete its "tedious journey, most of which seemed to have been made on

206

land," as Middleton remarked, going on to explain: "All the steamers on this river are stern-wheelers, and have four strong spars fastened, two on each side of the bow, by a sort of hinge. These spars are kept triced up until the vessel runs on a shoal or sand-bank — which are many and shifting — when they are lowered and the vessel is forced over the obstacle, made to walk over it as it were."

The *Northcote* brought reinforcements — about eighty men of the Midland Batallion — and, which pleased Middleton even more in his present state of discontent with the amateurish militia officers, a professional soldier, Lieutenant-Colonel van Straubenzie, who "had served in the Crimea with the Old Buffs". Of much more moment in fact, though Middleton did not immediately recognize it, was the arrival of Arthur L. Howard, a lieutenant in the Connecticut National Guard who happened to be in Canada as an armaments salesman to demonstrate the military advantages of that primitive automatic weapon, the Gatling gun, one of which accompanied him: a strange-looking wheeled contraption with a revolving bundle of barrels, turned by a hand crank, which ejected a continuous stream of bullets.

On the same day, Middleton heard that Colonel Otter and his expedition sent to relieve Battleford had been defeated at Cut Knife Hill on 2 May by Poundmaker's Indians and their Métis companions, using traditional prairie warfare tactics not unlike those adopted by Dumont at Fish Creek. This led Middleton, who had personally taken part in reconnaissances into the surrounding countryside, to decide that he would march up the riverside trail only as far as Gabriel's Crossing, since on this part of the river there were no places that could be used for effective ambushes; then he would strike inland over the open parkland, and advance on Batoche from the east, over the stretch of grassland which the Métis called La Belle Prairie.

Though Dumont's scouts, who patrolled the whole environs of Batoche on both sides of the river, were well aware of Middleton's movements, they were so alert that he rarely found signs of them. "In these reconnaissances only once did we come across any of the enemy. A party of them were in a house near the river some five miles from our camp. Their outlying scout caught sight of us and gave the alarm. They rushed out and galloped off with such a start that it was useless our following. Their dinner, consisting of chunks of underdone beef, which they had evidently just begun, served to allay the appetites of some of our Scouts who were hungry and not too particular."

As for the local inhabitants, most of them had left their farms and retreated to Batoche or to St. Laurent across the river, and in this no man's land Middleton's men as well as Dumont's regarded the edible property they had left behind them as legitimate booty. With the rather naive straightforwardness that would make him astonished when he was later accused of looting rebel property, Middleton told how, though they saw few of the Métis, he and his companions "often saw their cattle, horses, ponies and sometimes fowl, and always brought some of them back with us; and we must, on these occasions, have looked like 'moss-troopers' of old, returning from a raid. The cattle were converted into rations for the men, the horses and ponies handed over to the mounted corps, and the fowls sent to the hospitals for the wounded." Where they could, the Métis paid the Canadians back in their own coin, for Elie Dumont, coming back from Fort à la Corne just before the Fish Creek battle, in which he fought beside Gabriel, encountered an Indian who was tending twenty-two cattle that belonged to the government; he appropriated the herd and drove it before him into Batoche.

By the time the *Northcote* and the reinforcements it carried had reached Fish Creek, Middleton had recovered his confidence, and had decided, as part of his tactical plan, to combine naval with military operations, placing thirty soldiers with two officers on the *Northcote*, with instructions to create a diversion on the west side of Batoche by sailing downriver and making a landing below the village while the major attack was made from the east. On 7 May the Canadian column was in motion again, consisting now of 850 men with four cannon and Howard's Gatling gun. With its long baggage train of 150 wagons, whose beasts ate through half the freight they carried, it had some of the unwieldiness of the vast, straggling armies of pre-Mutiny India that Middleton had known in his youth, and it would have been difficult to prevent severe losses and setbacks through surprise attacks from Métis and Indian horsemen, had Dumont been able to mount them.

But in Batoche, once again, there was disagreement between the two leaders as to the appropriate action to counter the invaders. Dumont proposed to harrass the enemy in their camps and ambush them in the wooded areas through which, by any route, they would have to pass. Riel maintained that through his visions God had informed him of the need to fight in Batoche. And a simple hunter and leader of hunters like Dumont could hardly presume to argue on that level with Riel the prophet, who had five days after Fish Creek defied the priests themselves when they threatened with excommunication those who proclaimed — as the Exovedate, Gabriel among them, had done under Riel's influence — such heresies as the transitoriness of Hellfire and the celebration of Sabbath on the seventh day, as decreed in Genesis. On 4 May, four days before Middleton began his final advance, when any other leader of a community threatened with military extinction would have been considering matters of defence, Riel was debating with Father Fourmond about the divine nature of his own mission, denouncing the clergy as traitors because they claimed it was "a crime to take up arms against a tyrant in defence of one's rights," and declaiming to his followers: "Listen to this priest who dares to tell you that it is a crime you are committing under my direction, in the fulfilment of my sacred mission, who dares to call rebellion your taking up arms in a sacred cause, a cause ordained and directed by God, the cause of your native land which lies bleeding and prostrate at the feet of tyrants, a sacred cause involving the rights, liberties and lives of your women and children for all time to come!"

Dumont agreed with Riel about the priests, and to the end of his life he would hold them largely responsible for the defeat of the Métis cause. Yet at the same time the Riel who spoke so eloquently for the freedom he longed to preserve for himself and for his children was advocating a strategy which Gabriel and the other old hunters who shared his tactical experience recognized to be suicidal. Riel's plan was for the Métis to close themselves into the miniature city of God that Batoche had become in his mind, with no way of escape, so that the only alternatives would be defeat (probable) or victory (a miracle). But the Métis were not fitted for siege warfare, even if they had possessed the necessary arms and ammunition, which they did not. They could throw up a laager to hold off an Indian raid. But in the face of even a Victorian colonial army, the positional warfare that Riel envisaged was almost certainly doomed to early defeat, whereas if they were to use the space of the prairies, which they knew as they knew the palms of their hands, the Métis, under leaders like Dumont and his brothers, might still keep Middleton and his men at work and and in constant tension for months and perhaps for years.

Dumont knew this, and his best captains knew it also, yet when Riel would not be moved by their arguments, they set to and built their lines of defences, consisting of carefully spaced rifle pits and trenches, disguised by loopholed logs and parapets of turf, that would make the defenders of Batoche invisible and invincible so long as their ammunition lasted. The riflepits, which were about eighteen inches deep with a foot-high parapet, held two or three men each, the trenches six or seven, and they were spaced out about fifty feet from each other, in staggered lines over the prairie to the south and east of Batoche, with the present church and rectory lying outside them, in what the event of battle turned into a no man's land.

Later on, Captain Young, who acted as Riel's escort after the latter's surrender following the fall of Batoche, would assert at the trial in Regina that even on this point — from what Riel had told him — there was disagreement between the two leaders: "Gabriel's opinion was that the rebel right was the key of the position and should be defended. The prisoner's opinion was that the whole line should be especially defended. The matter was decided in council in favour of his view." There is in fact no record of an Exovedate decision against Gabriel on this matter, but if Dumont did argue for heavy fortifications on the right, he was, once again, the better tactician, for the main Canadian thrust did come, not on the eastern side where, as Middleton remarked, the Métis defences were "a veritable Sebastopol", but from the right, in the direction of the church, where they were less elaborately built and therefore more difficult to hold. It seems likely that everywhere Gabriel was responsible for the excellent construction of the pits, but that Riel had a hand in their less than perfect disposition.

On this matter we shall probably never know the final answer, and more important in hindsight, and perhaps even to the people of Batoche while they waited to see what Middleton would do (and to see how far their own leader's prophesies would be fulfilled), was a desperateness in their situation that even a Vauban could not have remedied with the most efficient of fortifications. They were from the beginning lacking in arms and ammunition. Gabriel and a few others who were relatively prosperous in the past had their Winchesters and modest supplies of cartridges, and others, like Edouard Dumont, had been able to capture army carbines with adequate ammunition. But many had still only the most primitive of firearms or none at all, and a Sioux Indian who was something of a gunsmith spent his time putting old muskets into good enough order to serve for a few days, while others occupied themselves melting the lead from tea chests into bullets and cutting scrap metal into slugs to be used in shotguns when the buckshot gave out.

Manpower was almost as scarce as lead. Against Middleton's 850 men, Dumont had less than three hundred. Sixty men, under Albert Monkman and Patrice Fleury, were guarding the west bank. A few men under Alex Fisher looked after Batoche's ferry. Round about two hundred were left to man the riflepits and in general to defend the cluster of shacks and a few large houses that constituted the Métis capital. It is hard to say how high morale actually stood. There were to be suicidal acts of individual heroism, especially among the older men who felt they were putting up the last fight for a free way of the life whose passing they had no great wish to survive. But, though the outcome of the Fish Creek fight had shamed some of the deserters on that occasion into returning, many may well have been lukewarm in their desire to fight to the death against what were obviously superior forces. Louis Schmidt who stayed in the safety of Prince Albert throughout the rebellion, estimated that only between a third and a fourth of the people of Batoche were really committed to resistance, and there may be some evidence to support him in the fact that after the capture of the village Canadian officers reported that the Métis talked bitterly of Riel and Dumont and claimed they had been forced into compliance. But such behaviour often occurs among the defeated, and it seems likely that at the time of Middleton's advance many of the people were actually inspired by Riel's enthusiasm and Dumont's courage and then, after it was all over and Riel was a prisoner and Dumont a fugitive, they felt deserted and resentful.

Yet Batoche was no place for men of faint heart or peaceful thoughts, as Nolin had early realized, and even those who remained most faithful to their leaders must have been depressed by a growing sense of isolation, for after White Cap's Indians arrived in mid-April, the only additions to the defence force were a few Sioux stragglers from the Cypress Hills. On the day after his victory at Cut Knife Hill, Poundmaker received the urgent message from Dumont asking for help, but though the Cree decided to go to the support of the Métis in Batoche, they did not start on their way until it had already fallen. A column of sixty well-armed Métis from the Battleford region, men who had fought beside Poundmaker and now pushed on ahead of the Indian army, only arrived in time to see the white flags flying over the houses along the South Saskatchewan and to withdraw hastily. And according to the surveyor William Pearce, who was in the region at this time, a hundred Métis from St. Albert, perhaps led by relatives of Dumont, formed a mounted column as soon as the news of Fish Creek reached them and set off to join Gabriel at Batoche, turning back only when they met messengers bringing news of the total collapse of the Métis cause. These reports — if they have any basis in fact — suggest that if Dumont had taken decisive action in defiance of Riel immediately after the battle of Duck Lake, support would have come to him, and come in time to have some effect on events. But by the time of Fish Creek it was already too late, and Gabriel's men, with their few Indian allies, were doomed to fight and be beaten alone.

Undoubtedly this realization affected them in different ways, stirring defiance in the hearts of the Dumonts and their kind, but inducing in others — even though they might at first have been enthusiastic — an inclination to calculate the chances and to wonder whether they might not make some kind of personal accommodation with the enemy. Certainly both Dumont and Riel suspected some of their associates of treason to the cause, and this suspicion came to the surface in the affair of Albert Monkman. The Monkmans were a family of half-breeds in whose veins ran both French and English as well as Cree blood, and their alliances during the Métis rebellions were somewhat varied. Joseph Monkman had opposed Riel on the Red River in 1869-70; Henry Monkman had played an early part in the agitation on the Saskatchewan, but had dropped out before the rebellion; Albert Monkman was elected a member of the Exovedate and seemed committed to the rebel cause, though at times he was outspokenly critical of Riel, whose religious pretensions he does not seem to have accepted. During the interlude between the battles of Fish Creek and Batoche, however, doubts began to arise — or to be manufactured — regarding his loyalty.

One day [said Dumont in his account] Riel went off to the other side of the river, in the direction of Duck Lake, to carry out a reconnaissance with a party of fifty men commanded by Gilbert [sic] Monkman. On his return, he said to the Council: "The man in command on the other side is going to betray us, for he has approached someone else to desert with him." He asked me to go over to this commandant and warn him that he knew of his intent to play him false. So I went across, assembled the men, and asked if anyone had advised them to desert. No-one would answer me directly. When I reported this to him, Riel crossed over with me, meaning to get at the truth. We called the men together in the Baker house. Riel addressed them in this way. "Friends, I know there is one of you who has been making suggestions of desertion. You have refused to admit this to Monsieur Dumont. But you can rest assured that I shall find out the truth, even it it means ordering the shooting of the man I suspect." Then Patrice Fleury said: "It is true. Monkman suggested I desert." Garçon Abraham Bélanger the younger said the same thing.

We then went back to Batoche to call a council, and it was decided to put Monkman under arrest. I brought Monkman in, with Patrice Fleury and Garçon Abraham Bélanger as witnesses. And before the Council I called on Monkman to answer the accusation brought against him. "It is true," he answered, "but I had no intention of deserting; it was simply to find out if Riel has second sight. I now believe that Riel has indeed had a revelation." I told Monkman that for acting like this I was going to imprison him.

"You will be doing me an injustice," he said. "Whether you like it or not," I said, "you are my prisoner, for you must have had in your heart to do what you proposed." And I had him tied up.

Monkman was put with the English-speaking prisoners in the cellar of Batoche's great house. He was released after the rebellion, but only to become a prisoner of the Canadians, who do not appear to have taken seriously the talk of his inciting other men to desert, since they sentenced him to seven years in prison, while Patrice Fleury, his accuser, was let free. It is an incident that none of the historians of the rebellion or of the biographers of Riel has chosen to discuss, perhaps because it leaves one uneasy with its unexplained factors, the ambiguities that lodge in one's mind. Did Riel really have some kind of psychic insight, or was he merely trying to frame an annoying critic? Was Patrice Fleury a dupe or an *agent provocateur*? Why did Monkman present such an extraordinary defence? As for Dumont, one is first impressed by his credulity, his unquestioning ruthlessness, and then becomes aware of the sinister psychological acuteness of his final remark to Monkman, an acuteness bred of the man of action's habitual identification of thought with deed. And even when one has considered all the individual motivations, the incident stays in one's mind as a bizarre emanation of the tensions and suspicions that were boiling to the surface in the embattled community of Batoche on the eve of its last and most desperate fight for survival.

On 7 May, Middleton marched only to Gabriel's Crossing, about eight miles north of Fish Creek, proceeding by the riverside trail, and encountering none of the Métis scouts who watched his progress and reported it to Dumont. For the Canadian soldiers, it was their first sight of the way in which the Métis actually lived. The houses, as Major Boulton recollected, "were all open, and the interiors showed evident signs of comfort and prosperity. In almost every other house was seen a fiddle on the walls, to help in whiling away the long winter evenings. . . ." For men who had imagined their opponents to be thoughtless savages, the experience was often salutary; it bred among many militiamen a feeling, as one of the newspaper correspondents put it, "that the half-breeds have been wronged. . . ." For obviously these were the houses of men who had too much to lose for them to embark lightly on rebellion.

"The sight of these comfortable homes and the coupled knowledge that the men who reared them, suffered the rigours of frontier life and fostered a love for the very soil itself, cannot get sufficient title to raise $10 by mortgage on one thousand acres, bring home to every man the reality of the residents' grievance."

There is of course the possibility of bias in such reports, at least in their attempt to project the feelings of Middleton's troops, since the rebellion seemed to all opposition journalists a golden chance to discredit Macdonald and his policies. Some militiamen quite obviously had no such feelings of compunction, as is evidenced by the enthusiastic destruction of Gabriel's habitation and the looting of his property when the Canadian column camped that day on his land. Boulton's scouts made their way through his house and store, picking up what they fancied as souvenirs. Then his stables were pulled down at Middleton's orders and their timbers, together with his sacks of grain, were used to fortify the upper deck of the *Northcote*. Finally, but only after Gabriel's billiard table and Madeleine's washing machine had been put on board the steamer, his house and the other buildings were burnt down; even Madeleine's simple wardrobe, it is said, was looted. Gabriel appears to have resented the taking of the billiard table more even than the destruction of his stables and his house, for log buildings were easier to replace than expensive imports, and the reverberations of this particular theft long plagued official correspondence. Months afterwards Middleton was writing to Caron in self-justification: "I find that a Billiard Table was taken out of Gabriel Dumont's house before it was burnt, and one was taken at Batoche. They are both at Prince Albert, and certainly no women's clothes were taken." Lamely and wearily, perhaps thinking of the row that was building up over his own appropriation of fine furs captured during the campaign, Middleton went on to remark that it was a question of "the property of undeniable rebels who had just been shooting down our men and according to the usage of war might fairly be taken by the soldiers."

Gabriel's men watched the looting and burning of his farm, saw the timber and the sacks from his stable being taken on board the *Northcote,* and heard the hammering that went on afterwards. When they carried their report to Batoche, Gabriel wasted no time lamenting the loss of his property, but immediately understood that the *Northcote* was being fortified to play a part in the forthcoming battle. It was the one reasonably definite indication he had of the enemy's intentions, and to an extent he fell into the trap that Middleton had devised by concentrating his attention, if not his forces, on this attempt to attack Batoche from the river.

On 8 May, Middleton and his men marched east and then north from Gabriel's Crossing, until they reached the trail from Batoche to Humboldt, and there, beside one of the large alkali lakes that are features of the region, they camped for the night. The arrangement was that the land party and the *Northcote* should approach Batoche more or less simultaneously, at 9 o'clock in the morning of 9 May, and Middleton's column was already on the move in the pre-dawn light before five o'clock. But it proceeded so cautiously, with Boulton's scouts fanned out as a screen before it, and the wagon train screaming slowly in the rear, that it took more than four hours to cover the nine miles between the night's campsite and the Métis village. The *Northcote* sailed from Gabriel's Crossing at 7 o'clock, and for once there were no impeding sandbanks to be walked over in the manner of a gigantic crab, so that, for all the caution with which the captain navigated the channel, the ship swung round the great bend below the church of St. Antoine de Padoue at eight o'clock in the morning.

Dumont was ready for it. Patrice Fleury and his men, from riflepits on the west bank, and another group of thirty men placed below the church on the eastern shore, were to fire on it in the hope of disabling the helmsman, while the cable of Batoche's ferry would be lowered to trap the boat so that its crew might be forced into surrender and added to the stock of hostages whom Riel dreamed of using to bargain with Middleton and ultimately with Macdonald.

Thus it was on the river that the battle of Batoche first began, and Middleton heard the clatter of musketry and the agonized shrilling of the *Northcote*'s whistle while he was still too far away to help or to profit by the incident. The Métis sent a wild fusillade into the ship from both sides of the river. (It was, in fact, the only incident in the defence of Batoche in which Fleury and his west-bank contingent took any part.) Though unwounded, the helmsman threw himself to the floor of the wheelhouse, and the ship drifted, first onto a sandbank, and then, uncontrolled, into the main stream. "I dashed on horseback along the bank," Dumont remembered, "to give the signal to lower the cable." But his men were too slow, and the cable merely tore off the *Northcote*'s smokestacks, starting a fire which was quickly put out, and slipped off the stern of the boat, which continued on its drifting course until it was out of rifleshot and effectively out of the battle, since the captain resolutely refused all the demands of Major Smith, the officer in charge of the troops on board, to return upstream into the thick of the fighting.

The first honours of the battle went thus to Dumont, but his personal involvement in the attack on the *Northcote* had made him less cautious than he might otherwise have been, and it was not until the ship was out of range that he thought of the second stage of his plan for the day, and sent Isidore Dumas with some other men to set a fire on La Belle Prairie that would diminish visibility for the Canadians and enable the Métis sharpshooters to harrass them even before they came within range of the riflepits. Isidore Dumas, however, found Middleton's advanced scouts too near for this to be possible, and so the Métis decided to wait in their trenches and riflepits while Middleton, instead of attacking from the east as Riel had expected, swung round towards the south, and established his headquarters, protected by a quickly dug earthwork, at Jean Caron's farm, overlooking the river and about half a mile from Batoche. "He pushed forward," as Dumont related, "on the ridge near Batoche, roughly half a mile from the new Catholic church, at the spot where the road looks out over the river bank before turning and descending to the village." The soldiers advanced in skirmishing order, the cannon were established on a knoll about a mile from the village, and the battle began, almost ritually, with bugle calls and with Lieutenant Howard firing from his Gatling a burst or two which went over the heads of the Métis, ensconced in their riflepits on the slope of the hill so that they could fire, as they did with often deadly accuracy, on the Canadian riflemen who appeared above them on the skyline.

Dumont, who settled himself "forward on the prairie, seated on one of my heels, with a knee on the ground", where he could quickly give orders that were shouted from pit to pit, both directed the battle and played an active part in it, so that his men never felt that he was asking them to do anything he was not willing himself to do. Even his enemies, in their admiring reports to Ottawa, talked of him "fighting like a tiger all day long", and at the end of the battle the Métis prisoners reported that he had barely slept day or night for a whole week. His rifle, Le Petit, was rarely silent as he orchestrated the Métis operations, their rushes to outflank the enemy, their feints to give the impression of numbers, and their melting withdrawals into screens of bush or lines of invisible gunpits, so that their casualties were once again slight compared with those of the Canadian militiamen; indeed, Dumont afterwards claimed that in the first three days of the battle not a single Métis was killed and that all that the Canadians hit were "dummies which we displayed for their benefit and on which they wasted their shots." The Canadian cannon pounded away, knocking down and setting on fire buildings in Batoche and on the far side of the river, but did little harm to the simple Métis fortifications, and the Gatling gun was effective only when Dumont tried to advance and it kept his men tight in their trenches.

The fighting on the first day was completely indecisive, and Middleton retreated to the zareba he had made at Caron's farm, where his men were kept awake by shots and Indian warcries from Dumont's scouts who hovered around the camp. Though the casualties in such attacks were mainly horses, the nightlong sniping had its effect on the nerves of the assailants.

The next two days passed in much the same way, with Middleton's men marching out like the soldiers of the brave old Duke of York and advancing on to the hillside where Métis fire held their attacks all day long until the bugles sounded and Middleton marched them back again. If Riel, tramping around armed only by his cross as he encouraged his men to fight on, felt that the divinely ordained apocalyptic hour was near; if Dumont realistically calculated that his men's ammunition was almost ended, with slugs of metal and nails and even stones taking the place of bullets, Middleton was in no less anxious a state of mind. His information services were far worse than Dumont's, the quick manoeuverability of the Métis had convinced him they were more numerous than he had expected, and he feared that half-breed or Indian reinforcements might arrive and make his position untenable; in fact, on the third day, when his men had advanced no farther than on the first day of the battle, he wired to Ottawa: "Am in rather ticklish position. Force can succeed holding but no more — want more troops."

Yet on the fourth day, 12 May, Middleton's expectations were far exceeded, Riel's visions were dashed away, and Dumont's fears were justified in a total and sudden defeat for the Métis cause. If one wishes a simple explanation for the conclusion of the battle, when a few companies of militia disobeyed orders and rushed the Métis defences, it is easy to give; the Métis were so lacking in ammunition, so exhausted by their days of unrelieved fighting, and in many cases so unfitted by age for physical combat, that they were incapable of resisting.

But there were other aspects of the situation that weighed heavily in Dumont's memory, and he believed to the day of his death that the Métis were betrayed by the priests. Early on the first day of the battle, contact was established between the priests and the Canadian officers, when Father Moulin emerged from the rectory in no man's land, waving a white flag, and Middleton went to meet him. Later in the day, some of the Canadian wounded were temporarily given shelter in the rectory, and that night, after the Canadians had retreated, Dumont went down to demand the surrender of the wounded men. They had been taken away already by stretcher bearers, but Dumont nevertheless upbraided the priests with a breach of the neutral stand they had chosen to take in the conflict. There is no doubt that on that evening and on the later evenings, other Métis — and especially some of the women — went to the rectory to see the priests and the Grey Nuns who were living there, and there is also no doubt that contact between the priests and the Canadians continued. In his account of the rebellion, Dumont does not directly accuse the priests, but the implications of his statements are quite clear:

> Middleton . . . despaired of defeating us, when certain
> traitors, whom I have no wish to name, made it known to

him that we had no more ammunition and that, with a few exceptions, all the Métis were in a state of discouragement. Also, if the besiegers did not hurry matters, help would soon be arriving to reinforce the defenders. These traitors were continually in communication with the enemy, and with our people, whom they urged to lay down their arms by offering them safe-conducts. What contributed greatly to the discouragement of our soldiers was that all religious succour was refused to them, their wives and their children.

Yet, while it is possible that the priests may have let fall some enlightening scraps of information, Middleton's obvious feeling of frustrated indecision on 11 May, and the actual course of events on the 12th make one regard with some caution the theory of the Métis defeat as the result of a priestly conspiracy.

It was during the afternoon of 12 May, while Middleton was attempting one of those slow and cautious diversionary manoeuvres which always failed because the Métis had time to anticipate them, that the patience of the militia broke, and led by a number of disaffected officers, they rushed forward in a wild charge down the hillside where they had held back on previous days, and flushed the Métis out of the riflepits, so that there was no real resistance until the defenders made a stand among the houses of the village. It was in this last resistance that most of the Métis deaths took place, including those of valiant patriarchs like Joseph Ouelette, aged ninety-three, Joseph Vandal, Dumont's neighbour, aged seventy-five, Donald Ross, and Isidore Boyer. Damase Carrière, one of Dumont's closest associates, was — according to a Métis account that had never been effectively disproved — wounded in the leg, and then dragged by the neck with a rope tied to a horse's tail and thus strangled to death.

During these final hours of Batoche, Dumont was at his most active, and he left a much more vivid account of their concentrated peril than of the three relatively eventless early days of the battle.

When the troops entered Batoche . . . our men first withdrew half a mile. I myself stayed on the higher ground with six of my brave comrades. I held up the enemy's progress there for a whole hour. What kept me there, I should say, was the courage of old Ouelette. Several times I said to him: "Come on, Father, we must pull back!" And the good old man always replied: "Just a minute! I want to kill another Englishman!" Then I said to him, "Very well, let us die here." When he was hit, I thanked him for his courage, but I could not stay any longer, and I drew back to my other companions, who told me that they had left a barrel of powder behind in young Tourond's tent.

I went to look for it with Charles Tourond, who gave it to one of our men. Then I went down to the riverside, where I ran into seven or eight men who, like plenty of others, were in flight. I asked them to come with me so that we could ambush the enemy. When they refused, I threatened to kill the first man who made off. They then came with me, and we kept the English at bay for another half-hour.

Then we went back along the river bank where I met the man to whom Charles Tourond had given the powder. He replied that he had left it in a house he pointed out to me about seven arpents* from the enemy. I asked him to go and get it, but he looked frightened, so I asked a nephew of mine, Honoré Smith, if he was also afraid. "Look after my gun and my shoes," he said, "and I'll make a dash for it." And, indeed, he brought me the barrel.

By now the Métis — those not already killed or taken prisoner — had been pushed out of the village, and it was in a wood on the outskirts that Dumont came upon Riel for the last time. Having so often restrained willing fighters, he was now urging unwilling men to continue a lost battle.

"What are we going to do?" he said as soon as he saw me: "We are defeated." I said to him: "We shall perish. But you must have known, when we took up arms, that we would be beaten. So, they will destroy us!"

I then told Riel that I must go to our camp to find some blankets. He said I was exposing myself too much, and I answered that the enemy would not be able to kill me. At that moment I felt afraid of nothing.

* Assuming that Dumont meant, when he used it as a measure of length, the side of a square arpent, this would mean about 500 yards, within range of the rifles the Canadians were using.

15. Six Dry Cakes for
the Hunted

The siege of Batoche was ended, the Canadians — having lost all the previous battles — had won the war, and the Métis cause as it existed on the prairies since the early days of the century had come to an actual as well as a symbolic end with that last meeting of Dumont and Riel. Both of them had ceased to be leaders, since there were no followers left to be led and the illusion of a Métis nation could no longer be sustained. They went on to their separate fates, Dumont to be a fugitive who would eventually return to his native valley to live out his days in peace, and Riel to become a prisoner, a martyr, and a symbol of passionate divisions within the Canadian national consciousness that extended into Laurentian rivalries rooted far more broadly in time and place than the Saskatchewan Valley of 1884-5.

The history of Riel's last days, which touch Dumont only indirectly, has by now often been told, and we are concerned with it here only in so far as it affected Dumont, distantly yet still profoundly. For Gabriel never lost the traces of his encounter with the leader whom he disagreed with and yet revered, and the days he spent after the defeat as a fugitive in the woods around Batoche were divided between providing for the comfort and safety of his wife Madeleine and trying to arrange for Riel's escape to the Montana from which, on that spring day less than a year ago, he had come riding into Batoche.

Ever since the day of Fish Creek, when the Métis first met

the Canadian troops in battle, Madeleine Dumont, with old Madame Batoche, had been tending the rebel wounded. Now, with the wives of other men who had been actively fighting in defence of the village, she moved into the woods, about six hundred yards from the Métis camp to the north of Batoche's ferry, where Dumont found her after he left Riel. He wanted to get the blankets he had mentioned to Riel, for her and for Riel's wife and children.

The tent where the bedding had been left was about fifty yards from a house where red-coated soldiers whom Dumont called "mounted policemen" were on guard, and he described starkly how he dealt with this perilous situation.

I saw a policeman standing in the doorway, and I weeded him out. Another of them came out to look at the body, and I killed him too. I took two blankets and two counterpanes which I carried to my wife. . . . I asked her to give them to Madame Riel so that she might have covering for herself and her children during the night, but Riel would only accept the blankets. I then returned to our camp to get some dried meat and flour, and this time I saw no-one; I asked my wife to divide the food among women with children. I saw that the others wanted to find safety by moving farther away, but I asked my wife to stay where she was, saying to her: "If the enemy take you prisoner, and blame you for what I have done, tell them that if the government cannot make me behave, it is not easy for you to do so."

He went off again, looking for horses, but saw some army patrols and returned to lead Madeleine into another patch of woodland. He went back, encountering other fugitives and eventually acquiring a mare and a sack of flour. "I put my wife and the sack of flour on the mare, and led it to another clump of trees where we camped. I had nothing over my shirt, and the night was not warm. The next day I hid my wife farther off, and I went back to the river to see if I could find Riel."

While Gabriel was trying to find Riel (for he "could not bring myself to leave until I knew where my unlucky friend might be"), the police were trying to find him, and the army reports and telegrams for the first days after the fall of Batoche are full of accounts of his having been sighted in various places within a wide radius around Batoche. Father André, who felt a reviving sympathy for his recalcitrant parishioners once they were defeated, remarked to the searchers: "You are looking for Gabriel? You are wasting your time. There isn't a blade of grass in the whole prairie that he doesn't know." And the tough old Breton priest was right, for Dumont watched his pursuers more carefully than they watched him. "Two hundred horsemen were looking for me in every direction, while I was always behind them. I hid in the woods at night, and I watched them from the hills during the day, ready to pick off any man who detached himself." During all the days he remained around Batoche, Dumont did not go farther away than Belleville, which is about nine miles off, for he knew intimately from his hunting days all the possible hiding places of the region, and whenever he was seen he would melt like a ghost into the woods which the advancing spring was endowing with convenient curtains of young leaves.

He described how, on the second day, going out on his search for Riel, he saw the white flags flying from the roofs of all the houses in Batoche, and learnt that even the men on the right bank, led by the once militant Napoléon Nault, had surrendered. There were still a few men who refused to give in (notably his brothers), and he found Elie Dumont looking after a group consisting mainly of women and children, with a few men. "Elie had killed a cow to give them something to eat, and had cut some hay to give them protection from the cold. I found it painful to see these poor people lying in the hay like beasts, and when I saw the bare feet of the children, I made them something resembling shoes out of raw hide. The women were very brave and even laughed at their situation."

On the third day, when he realized that he could not continue indefinitely in the environs of Batoche, Dumont sent Madeleine to stay with his father, old Isidore Dumont, who lived some miles north of Batoche and because of his declining health had taken no part in the uprising. Keeping within cover, he followed her to make sure that no harm befell her on the way, and then returned to the search for Riel, at the same time visiting the site of the battle, where he picked up cartridges that had been dropped there by the Canadian soldiers. After dark, he went to his father's house, and told old Isidore that he meant to stay in the region and to spend the summer harrying the police with the help of any Métis or Indians who would join him in guerilla warfare. Isidore urged him to abandon the plan. "I am proud," he told his son, "that you have not given up, but if you follow this idea of staying here just to kill people, you will merely be thought an idiot." Isidore advised him to cross the border, and Madeleine added her pleas, asking him to go at once, since she feared he would soon be caught. Gabriel answered that he had always found Isidore's advice worth taking, and he wanted to take it again, but first he wanted to find out what was happening to Riel. Isidore then told him that he had better go and see his brother-in-law, Moïse Ouelette, who was transmitting a letter from Middleton to Riel.

Gabriel went to find Ouelette, who told him that the letter indeed existed and had been read to him; it promised both Riel and Dumont that they would receive justice. (In fact Middleton's letter to Riel did not mention Dumont, and said merely: "I am ready to receive you and your council and protect you until your case has been decided on by the Dominion Government.") Ouelette appears to have urged Dumont to accept, for Gabriel flared up and shouted: "Go to the devil! The government has sheared you like sheep, and now it has disarmed you, you are marching to its tune." Ouelette answered that he and the others had given in for love of their children. Gabriel swept aside his protestations with contempt. "You can tell Middleton that I am in the woods, and that I have ninety cartridges to spend on his men!"

On the fourth day, 15 May, Gabriel saw Ouelette again, and Moïse told him that he had given Middleton's letter to Riel, who had gone "to see the English general". Dumont wanted to catch his friend before he actually gave himself up, "but Ouelette gave me to understand that he had already surrendered, which was not true." In fact, Riel did surrender on the 15th, and since Dumont gives no time for his meeting with Ouelette, it is impossible to tell whether his brother-in-law really deceived him on this point. Even if he did, Ouelette may have been trying to prevent Dumont from running into pointless danger. "The good Lord," said Dumont sadly in recollection, "did not want me to see my poor Riel again. I wanted to tell him not to give himself up, but he might very easily have converted me to his point of view."

Since there was nothing more he could do for Riel or for

any of the other Métis, Dumont decided to start off the next morning, 16 May, on his journey into exile. He spent that night encamped in a wood with Jean Dumont and young Alexis, his favourite "nephew", and with a few young men who had remained free and who very soon would follow Gabriel on the road to the border. Since the way to his father's house was now being watched, it was unsafe for Dumont to go there himself, so, thinking that a boy would not be suspect, he sent young Alexis, with a message to Madeleine that at last he was leaving, and a request to his father to send him some food for the journey. There was not much left in Batoche during those days after the battle, and all old Isidore could send were six galettes, the Métis bannock, each of them weighing about three quarters of a pound.

Gabriel had by now been able to get his own horse, "which was the best courser in Batoche," and he saddled it and walked with his companions to the edge of the wood. He still had his famous rifle, Le Petit, with its ninety cartridges, and he also had a revolver with forty rounds which he had taken from Albert Monkman when he arrested him. It was enough, he felt, to scare off most likely enemies, and at worst he intended to shoot it out to the death with any patrols who intercepted him, rather than to surrender. He said goodbye to his companions, but he had hardly ridden a hundred yards when he heard a voice calling his name. He turned with his rifle ready at his hip, but it was Michel Dumas, who had been with him when he had brought Riel from Montana. "Are you armed?" Dumont asked him. Dumas had lost his gun in the scramble from the pits when the militia charged on the last day of fighting. "Le Petit will do for us both," Dumont replied, "but have you any food?" "Only a few galettes!" Laughing, they turned their horses towards the south.

"We set out by the Grace of God!" said Dumont, and with those words he ended his account of the rebellion.

Dumont and Dumas travelled for eleven days before they reached safety at the American border. The first part of the journey was over land which Dumont had known since childhood; the latter part he had traversed twice on his journey to bring Riel to the Saskatchewan, which was enough for such an experienced traveller.

Not only were the fugitives uncaptured, but they were not even threatened, though the prairie trails were infested with military and police patrols and the news of the escape had been sent everywhere in the region by the telegraph lines that had come there almost as the first attribute of the new civilization. But there was probably more than luck and skilful track-finding to the success of the escape. Many of the men patrolling the prairies were not anxious to encounter Dumont, partly because admiration of his courage was now widespread even among his enemies, but mainly because it was well known by the time he left Batoche that he was well-armed and had every intention of using his celebrated marksmanship on any policeman or soldier foolish enough to approach within shooting distance.

The route which the two men followed was a long and devious one. By the most direct trails they need have ridden less than three hundred miles to the border, but because they preferred rough terrain, with friends on the way, they actually rode a total of six hundred miles. They struck south past Gabriel's holding, where he paused to look sadly down on the charred timbers tumbling into the empty cellar holes which symbolized the complete impoverishment that the rebellion had brought him, and then, to deceive possible pursuers, struck east over the prairie towards Vermilion Lake, and then south in a curve that avoided the village of Saskatoon. They crossed the elbow of the South Saskatchewan where Diefenbaker Lake now spreads and made their way over the deserted northern spur of the Missouri Coteau, coming down again into the South Saskatchewan Valley and fording the river to disappear among the smooth folds and dark wooded groins of the Great Sand Hills west of Swift Current. They emerged near the present site of Maple Creek, and entered the traditional prairie sanctuary of the Cypress Hills, following its intricate buffalo paths in such a way as to avoid the Mounted Police post at Fort Walsh, and reaching the valley of Battle Creek, down which they rode over the border to the Milk River.

All this, of course, was not done on a couple of satchels of dry bannocks. The way the fugitives took was chosen not merely for its broken terrain and its remoteness from widely used trails, but also because these were the regions where they were most likely to find encampments of Indians and Métis who, even if they had taken no part in the rebellion, were sympathetic to its motives and not likely to turn away or betray such a famous and formidable chieftain of the prairies as Gabriel Dumont, with his family's prestige among the Métis and his own links with the Indian peoples of the prairies. In such camps, or in well-concealed ravines or wooded coulées, the fugitives hid by day, travelling mainly at night and especially in the dusk and dawn hours. The Indians and the Métis not only gave them directions on their way and sometimes guided them over terrain difficult to cross in the darkness, but they also provided them with food, for in the plains of 1885, almost denuded of wild animals, it would have been impossible for men travelling an average of fifty miles a day to kill enough game to keep alive. Sometimes they were hungry; often they were cold, for a touch of the bitter winter of the rebellion still lingered in the May nights of that year. Yet, despite Dumont's anger against the priests, his peasant-like piety continued to sustain him. "I felt that I was protected," he later told Adolphe Ouimet. "And I never failed to say to the Holy Virgin: 'You are my mother! Guide me!' " And when they were safely across the border, he and Dumas dismounted, and knelt to say the rosary in thankfulness.

Shortly afterwards, the two Métis were arrested by a military patrol of the American army under Sergeant Prévost, and were taken to Fort Assiniboine, where the commander, Lieutenant-Colonel Coppinger, recognizing that a political rather than a military decision was involved at this point, decided to keep them in custody while he wired his immediate superior, General Terry at St. Paul. Terry moved the matter on to his superior, General Schofield, officer commanding the Division of the Missouri in Chicago, who in turn telegraphed on 27 May to General Drume, Adjutant-General of the United States. At this point the whole embarrassing affair was switched from military into political channels. The Secretary of War consulted the Secretary of State, and the Secretary of State consulted President Grover Cleveland, with the final result that the two men were set free on 29 May, after a very comfortable confinement telling their tales of war and consuming American victuals, under a ruling that "the military forces have no authority to arrest or detain them. They must therefore be released from military arrest." The formula seems significant, since it obviously leaves open the possibility of civil arrest; Cleveland and his Secretary of State were postponing the question of what might be done if the British Ambassador in Washington were to submit a request on behalf of the Canadian government for the extradition of the two fugutives. But no request was made; Macdonald and his ministers were already disturbed by the political waves rising around the fate of Louis Riel, and they did not want to have another political martyr on their hands. So, on 29 May, when Dumont and Dumas were allowed to ride away from Fort Assiniboine, they were free to stay as long as they wished and to travel as far as they wanted in the United States.

From Fort Assiniboine, Dumont went to Spring Creek, near Lewiston, then one of the leading Métis centres in Montana, where his brother-in-law David Wilkie was living, and later to Fort Benton, a centre of American trading into Canada, where his presence was reported on 10 June in the local newspaper, to whose reporter he talked of his role in the rebellion, maintaining that the uprising "was principally his own doing. Riel, he asserted, was for peace." He was possibly inspired by a thought of assisting Riel, who now faced a trial for treason; one of the principal directions taken by Riel's counsel would in fact be to stress the part played by Dumont in turning a movement of peaceful agitation into ways of violence. When the trial in Regina began in July, Riel's lawyers wished to bring Dumont as a witness from Helena, where he was then staying. But the Canadian authorities refused to promise him immunity from arrest, and he remained south of the border, seeking other ways of helping his leader and his friend.

In Montana Dumont encountered a good deal of initial sympathy, not only from his fellow Métis, many of whom were related to him by blood or by marriage, but also among the other inhabitants, for Riel was warmly remembered by many people there, and the merchants of Fort Benton still resented the way in which the arrival of the North West Mounted Police had ruined their profitable and not always very honourable trade with the Indians north of the border. A local cattle dealer named Singley, who was married to a Métis woman and gave employment to refugees from Canada, had some success in raising money to support Dumont and his schemes, though his efforts were in the end frustrated by the behaviour of Michel Dumas, who spent a great deal of the funds that were collected on drinking heavily in public, and whom Dumont found an increasingly embarrassing companion as he himself tried to convince people of the reasonableness of the Métis cause.

As the summer went on, other refugees followed Dumont over the devious paths of the prairies to exile in Montana. They included Edouard and Jean Dumont, and also Baptiste Parenteau, and they soon began to discuss with Gabriel and the Montana Métis how they might set about reviving the fortunes of the Métis nation. There was some wild talk of invading the Northwest Territories, but it was obvious that the Métis did not have the resources in either men, money, or arms for such a venture; moreover, now that Poundmaker was defeated, Sitting Bull a spent force, and Big Bear on the run in the northern forests, they could expect no help from the Indians.

Dumont and his friends therefore turned their attention to a more modest and also a more congenial scheme, the rescue of Riel, who had been condemned to death on 1 August, from his Regina prison. The evidence of what was actually plotted is tenuous, as is inevitable in a conspiratorial venture carried on mainly by men who, since most of them could not write, had no urge to commit their plans to paper. Yet it was common knowledge in the West, even at the time of Riel's trial, that Dumont had a rescue in mind. Fearing a Métis attempt, the Mounted Police took special precautions even in July when Riel was brought to trial. "And Gabriel Dumont on the other side of the line," said Riel himself in his final rambling speech from the dock, "is that Gabriel Dumont inactive? I believe not. He is trying to save me from this box." And on 3 August the *Globe* of Toronto speculated on the possibility of a rescue attempt by Dumont, encouraged by Sir John A. Macdonald as a way out of a politically embarrassing situation. "Then there would be the chance for the veteran histrionic to wring his hands and elevate his eyes to heaven as he measured out the time-honoured words, 'Would to God I could catch him.'"

Joseph Howard, whose *Strange Empire* is perhaps the best

book on Louis Riel, lived for thirty years in Great Falls, Montana, and through talking to local Métis survivors of the 1880s, he was in no doubt that the restless journeys which Dumont made throughout the summer and early autumn of 1885 — to Sun River and Lewiston and Spring Creek and Fort Benton and Great Falls and Helena and, under pretence of hunting, into the Indian country on the Canadian border — were directed towards the establishment of a series of relay stations where mounts and escorts and provisions could be placed to speed Riel to safety when Gabriel and his marksmen made the raid on Regina that would set their leader free. There were legends that Dumont even penetrated into Canada; a Regina paper reported his presence in that city, and there is even a tradition that he ventured back to Batoche, though one can hardly see how so foolhardy an act might assist a plan to spirit Louis Riel southward into the United States. Nevertheless, it is significant that in August, when Major John Burke, representing Colonel W. F. Cody, came to Lewiston in the hope of recruiting Métis rebels to embellish the Buffalo Bill show, Dumas agreed, but Dumont — despite the attractive remuneration he was offered — merely expressed interest and postponed his decision, as if he had more pressing matters on his mind, as indeed he had.

The rescue attempt never took place, for the simple reason that the Mounted Police took elaborate precautions to prevent it. Until after Riel's execution, three troops of police — a total of three hundred men — were kept at Regina under the pretence of a reconstruction of the force. The cordons of guards were tightly drawn, especially at night, and on the day of the execution, as Corporal John Donkin (who was there) recorded in *Trooper and Redskin,* the whole force was on duty from three-thirty in the morning. "When the sun had risen, we could see the polished arms of the sentries — a perfect ring — around the barracks. Scouts were out in every direction, trotting off in the distance. Bugle-calls rang out in the clear air. An inner cordon of fifty men was posted around the guard-room at seven, and at the same hour a party of forty men, mounted, drew up at the end of the bridge opposite to us." No-one, however impeccably White-Anglo-Saxon-Protestant, was allowed to enter the jail without showing a pass, and certainly nothing short of a major assault by a large and well-armed body of men could have rescued Riel. The fact that no attempt was made to break this elaborate defence system suggests that, as always, Dumont's intelligence network was efficient.

Gabriel is said to have suspected that his plot was betrayed by Charles Nolin, but — as we have seen — the possibility of a rescue attempt had been in people's minds ever since Riel's trial, and it may have been merely an intensification of these rumours that prompted the Mounted Police to take precautions that in their extremity were a tribute to Dumont's reputation for courage and resourcefulness.

While Dumont was involved in the plot to rescue Riel, he was joined by Madeleine. She had grown restive without him, and had persuaded Patrice Fleury, who was her sister's husband, to escort her down to Lewiston, where Gabriel was staying. She brought with her the news that his father Isidore had died, from old age, but perhaps also from grief at seeing his son Isidore killed and the rest of his family dispersed into exile.

All through this period, both before and after Riel's hanging, Dumont was being watched not only by agents of the Mounted Police, but also by spies who reported directly to Edward Dewdney, Governor of the Northwest Territories. One was the Scottish half-breed, James Anderson, who had so little knowledge of Montana when he went there in search of Dumont that his first report was sent from Billings on the Yellowstone River, in the far south of the Territory. There he discovered that the Canadian Métis were in fact gathered in the centre of Montana, around Lewiston, which he reached four days later. He reported from Lewiston that, while many of the Canadian refugees had gone to Sun River, to settle where Riel had once lived, the members of the Dumont clan, Gabriel, Edouard and Jean, and Baptiste Parenteau, with their families, had remained in the Lewiston area. Gabriel, with Madeleine and Annie, was still living in the house of David Wilkie.

"The others are building small houses for the winter," Anderson continued. "They arrived here with 20 horses and very little money. I had a long conversation with Dumont and find from him that they all intend settling in the Turtle Mountains, and will leave for there, as soon as spring opens out, as they cannot get any land in the district worth having."

The Turtle Mountains, of course, were a long way east of Montana, in the area of Dakota where Gabriel had hunted with his father and his uncles long ago in boyhood. Dumont in fact, like his friends who solemnly assured Anderson that the recent rebellion had been a mistake, seems to have been cheerfully pulling wool over the dull eyes of this spy who felt "confident that Dumont has no intention of giving any further trouble." After attending a Métis dance, where he "had the pleasure of dancing the Red River Jig with some of the young ladies," Anderson departed, having "arranged through an Englishman, a schoolmaster, to keep me posted as to Dumont's movements."

The final record of this early Canadian experience in international intelligence is provided by a letter, dated 4 December, from H. G. Webb, Anderson's English schoolmaster, who appears to have at least suspected that Canadian spying methods might be somewhat transparent.

"Gabriel Dumont, together with one or two of our own Breeds, is now out hunting, so shall not be able to see him for some time; if possible I will go up the Creek Sat. or Sun., and see what he is doing. He may have been scared, but don't know yet; he is somewhere between the Judiths and the Missouri. Will write you again, as soon as I find out anything worth communicating. Winter with a vengeance. Hands too cold to write."

As far as information about Dumont was concerned, Webb's hands, and Anderson's, remained cold. There was nothing more about him that seemed worth reporting. And indeed, after his efforts to organize Riel's rescue had been frustrated, Dumont was faced with the urgent problem, now that he had lost everything he had accumulated in Canada, of finding some new way to survive. He went hunting, as of old, but Montana was no different from the Canadian West; the game had been decimated several times over, and there was no reliable living to be gained from it. He had no longer the capital to become a freighter or a trader, or the knowledge of the local terrain that would enable him to work as a guide, and when he talked of acquiring land it was with the inbred indifference of the hunter.

The offer that Major Burke had made on Cody's behalf — an offer repeated more than once during the winter of 1885-6 — began to tempt him as it had never done while he still hoped there was a chance of rescuing Riel and starting the great venture over again. To perform before the American people might not only be a means of escaping the exile's everlasting circle of poverty; it might even be a means of bringing home to the world beyond Canada the grievances of his people — his nation — whose plight he knew had grown even worse since the defeat of the rebellion.

He had been held back from accepting Cody's offer, even after the failure of his plan to rescue Riel, by two considerations: his own health and Madeleine's. His head wound continued to trouble him long after he crossed the border. He experienced unpredictable blackouts when he would fall to the ground for a few seconds and then recover. Once he was in a hardware store when he lost consciousness and fell with his face in a pile of sharp metal objects which slashed and disfigured it. The doctors whom he was now able to consult told him that an artery had been cut by the bullet wound and — later — that it had reknitted, and if today this sounds like the mumbojumbo of frontier quacks, the fact is that Gabriel survived and steadily recovered so that he could once again contemplate performing the feats of riding and marksmanship that had once made him the acknowledged leader of the Saskatchewan buffalo hunt, the feats that Cody wished him to repeat for money and for acclamation.

There was no commensurate reblossoming for Madeleine. Ever since she rejoined him at Lewiston, Gabriel had been aware of her unaccustomed lack of energy, of her drawn features, of the strange alternations of depression and elation in her behaviour. In the spring of 1886 she was thrown from a buggy. No bones seemed to be broken, yet she never recovered, and when she died shortly afterwards some said it was from her injuries and others from the sickness of consumption that only a few weeks before had claimed Riel's young wife.

Now there seemed no longer any reason for Gabriel to remain in Montana. It could not help the Métis cause. It could not reverse the procession into death of those he had liked and loved; of his brother and his father who shared the name of Isidore; of his wife Madeleine; of his friends, Riel and Damase Carrière; of the old men who long ago had helped to teach him the ways of the prairies and now had died the unexpected death of heroes in the last hours of Batoche; of the Indians who had come to fight beside him because he was their friend by treaty and had departed with the warpaint on their faces and the deathsongs fading from their lips. It could not bring back the men he had killed without hatred because he believed his cause was just, but who also haunted his memory.

He accepted Cody's offer, and early in June he set out on the journey that would take him into the heart of the world that had destroyed his own.

Too much can be made of Dumont's connection with that consummate showman, William F. Cody. He was a star of Buffalo Bill's Wild West show for no more than three months. He was chosen, like most of Cody's stars, partly for his personal notoriety and partly because he represented, like Sitting Bull and Curly "the Crow Scout, the only survivor of the Custer Massacre" and John Matthews the "Deadwood Stage Driver", the dying past of the frontier, a world and a life that, in the United States as well as in Canada, had already been rendered obsolete by the advance of settlement. Buffalo Bill's Wild West was in fact one of the first shows that successfully exploited the nostalgia which urban North Americans were beginning to feel for the anarchic past of the frontier that had retreated ever westward until now, in the shadow of the Rockies, it had lain down to die.

Travelling for the first time on the railway that had done so much to destroy his hopes of an autonomous Métis world, Gabriel arrived in Philadelphia, where he joined the Wild West show, on 7 July 1886. Afterwards he accompanied the show to Staten Island, where Buffalo Bill put on his New York exhibitions and from which the show toured to other towns of the eastern seaboard. At first Gabriel's duties were slight. He rode in the parades (once along Fifth Avenue), looking defiant, with Le Petit crooked in his arm; he posed for visitors with his saddle and his gun and answered their questions through an interpreter. Most of the newspaper reporters were content to accept the releases put out by Cody's partner and publicity director, Nate Salsbury, and there is a depressing sameness to the accounts they give of Gabriel's bravery as Riel's general. Only occasionally would one of them trouble to question Gabriel himself, and then to comment inanely on the sturdy independence with which he defended his rebellion.

One has the feeling that then, as now, Canada seemed, to the average eastern American, stellar distances away. And indeed, when Gabriel's mere presence had shown itself less than a nine days' wonder, and an act had to be devised for him, there was no incident of his career that seemed likely to interest Philadelphians or New Yorkers; instead of re-enacting memories of Duck Lake or Fish Creek or Batoche, Gabriel became merely another among the crack shots of the show, competing with Miss Annie Oakley ("The Celebrated Girl Wing Shot") and Miss Lillian Smith ("The California Huntress") and Johnny Baker ("The Cowboy Kid"), as he raced his horse across the arena at the Gentleman's Driving Park in Philadelphia and the Staten Island Amusement Park, shooting down blue glass balls which a cowboy threw into the air. It was not a performance individual enough to attract attention, and one shrewd reporter, on the occasion of an open visitor's day to the Wild West show's camp on Staten Island, remarked that "Gabriel Dumont, Riel's half-breed lieutenant, who boasts of being the only political exile in America, studied the big crowds more than they studied him."

Within the show, it was another matter. Here Gabriel was among people who knew his world, and many of whom had been shaped by the free nomadic life of the old West that knew no frontiers; to them his past had meaning. He was especially popular among the Sioux Indians, who feasted him and with whom he loved to exchange reminiscences of lost but glorious battles with the white man. But he was also pleased when some of his white enemies emerged from the past, attracted by his name on the posters, like Major Crozier, who had left the Mounted Police, and Lieutenant Howard who claimed that he had always been careful at Batoche to aim his Gatling gun above Gabriel's head. Gabriel greeted them gladly, regarding it as an act of chivalrous comradeship when they came to see him, for it was not in his nature to bear resentment, and, enemies or not, they reminded him of the great empty land of the West, so far from the noisy, teeming streets of eastern cities.

Less than two months after Gabriel joined the Wild West show, towards the end of July 1886, the news arrived that the Canadian government had issued a general amnesty to those who had taken part in the Northwest Rebellion. Buffalo Bill gave a feast in celebration, and, not without calculation, offered to release Gabriel from his contract if he wanted to return to his country and his people. But there were no pressing personal reasons to go back, now that Madeleine and old Isidore were dead and his friends and brothers were still in Montana. And in any case he did not trust the Canadian government, and wanted assurances more convincing than a newspaper report before he would risk his freedom and perhaps his life returning over the border. So he told Cody that he would stand by his contract, and remained with the Wild West show until, as the weeks went on, he began to realise that the news of the amnesty had deprived him of interest to the American public. He was no longer a fugitive, nor was he a true inhabitant of the American frontier, and his act with blue glass balls did not endure a great deal of repetition. In September he withdrew from the show, and though he returned for periods in 1887 and 1888 to earn a little money, he was not engaged as a star, but as one of the supernumeraries, a good man to play a minor role in holding up a stage coach or resisting an Indian raid on a wagon train.

Yet, for the time being at least, Gabriel did not return permanently to the West. He had learnt that — even if the American public was indifferent to what he had been and done — there were people of French descent in these eastern states, sympathetic to the Métis cause. Not long after he arrived on Staten Island, he received, through Nate Salsbury, an invitation to address an audience of Americanized French Canadians at Holyoke, Massachusetts. He had never before spoken except among his Métis people in Saskatchewan, but he travelled to Holyoke on 27 July, and gave a simple description of the background of the rebellion and the course of the fighting to an audience of five hundred people. In August, he addressed another audience of five hundred people at Woodcrest, and they presented him with a gold watch and chain that are still treasured by a member of his family at Duck Lake. In September, yet another French-speaking audience in New York City presented him with a large silver medal. He refused to address English-speaking audiences even through an interpreter; even if they were American, he did not trust them.

One of the most influential of the French-speaking Americans he encountered at this time was Major Edmund Mallet, a

237

former Inspector of Indian Agencies under the U.S. Government, who was well acquainted with conditions in the West, and had befriended Riel during his period of exile in the eastern United States a decade earlier. Through Mallet, Gabriel was allowed to participate early in 1887 in one of President Grover Cleveland's public audiences. The President was interested in seeing this famous prairie rebel, but no more, and when Gabriel presumed on their meeting to send a petition asking for rations to be granted to impoverished Canadian Métis in Montana, the request was politely rejected. The American government, which might have been willing to fish in the troubled waters of a universal prairie uprising, became cautious about interfering in Canadian affairs as soon as the revolt was suppressed and the completion of the Canadian Pacific made the dominion from sea unto sea a strategic as well as a political reality.

16. Direction Homeward

It was now obvious to Gabriel, if it had not been before, that the most his people could expect from the Americans, for all their talk of freedom, was a place of exile. The Métis cause rang its responding bells only in ears attuned to the French language, and during 1887, when he spent six and a half months visiting border communities in Montana and Dakota and the rest of the year in New York, he began to understand how the consequences of the rebellion, and especially of Riel's death, had become woven into the political map of Canada, so that Québecois politicians and even churchmen, who had raised no finger of assistance when the people of Batoche were fighting for their lives and their rights in the land, had now made a martyr-hero of Riel and were all at once interested in Dumont, the man who had been closest to him during the fatal insurrection.

The records of the links which Gabriel somewhat tenuously forged during the winter of 1887-8 with French Canadian ecclesiastics and politicians are preserved in a bundle of papers which the Assistant Commissioner of the Mounted Police, William Herschmer, received in May 1888 from Maxime Lépine, Gabriel's old comrade in the rebellion, and which the Police Comptroller, Frederick White, passed on to Lieutenant-Governor Dewdney. Lépine had demanded Herschmer's "word of honor that they should not be published", and one understands why when one reads the opening letter which Dumont begins by saying to his old friend: "I address myself to you in preference to all others deeming you always honest as I have always known you to be."

The letter, dated 19 February 1888, and the enclosures, are written from Staten Island, on the letter heading of a cork merchant named E. Riboulet, presumably of French Canadian extraction, who must have prepared them from Gabriel's dictation and who perhaps had a hand in framing them, since on at least one occasion he adds his signature to Gabriel's. The letter to Lépine mentions that Gabriel had recently been meeting Honoré Mercier, the Quebec nationalist leader who in 1887 had gained power in his province by exciting public opinion over the execution of Louis Riel, and, as a further evidence of Gabriel's inability to bear resentments, it sends his good wishes to Charles Nolin. More important, it encloses a letter "To Our Friends the Half Breeds and Indians of the Canadian Northwest" whose contents Gabriel asks Lépine to make known at a meeting of the Métis and the Indians.

In this second letter Dumont writes as one who believes he has the ear of powerful people, including even "an exalted person" in France "who is interesting himself in, and sympathizes with our cause." Regarding as a beginning the Amnesty Proclamation (which he now trusts, having received a copy of the document in December 1887, from the Québec federal MP, R. Préfontaine, a vice-president of the Riel Defence Committee), he proposes that the Métis should now demand, first, an indemnity for the financial losses they experienced during and after the rebellion ("an indemnity such as has been accorded to those who had not the courage to take part in the rising") and also the land scrip for which they had been petitioning long before the rebellion began. A degree of self-interest entered into both these proposals, for Gabriel had received no scrip or document recognizing his Métis rights, and he could not help remembering the loss of his property, in a cause he thought just, when he heard that old Batoche, who stayed out of harm's way during the agony of the village that bore his name, was given $19,900 compensation for the damage to his house and store. He threatened, if nothing were done, to give lectures in Canada and afterwards in France exposing the injustices endured by the Métis, evidently assuming that his words would seem as fearful as his famous gun.

More interesting are the accounts the letter gives of Dumont's encounters with the notable Canadian ecclesiastics who visited New York. When Cardinal Taschereau, Archbishop of Québec, arrived, Gabriel called on him and received his blessing. Since Taschereau had been in no way connected with the differences between priests and rebels in the Northwest, and evidently tactfully refrained from discussing them, Dumont trusted him, and in November he wrote to the Archbishop confiding his aim of "writing a history of my life from infancy to the present time. I shall recount the mode of life and the customs of Indians and Half-Breeds and also the truth of the Rebellion in the Northwest in 1885, the truth about my friend and chief Louis David Riel, also my life since that time." He remarked that in this way he hoped to "render a service to the Half-breeds and do homage to truth, at the same time realizing a profit of which I am in great need, having lost everything in the defence of my rights." He asked the Archbishop's advice, and Taschereau replied with tactful discouragement, pointing out the difficulties of autobiography and of writing impartially of events in which one has taken a part and a side.

With the two other ecclesiastics who came to New York and who were his old acquaintances and in some degree his old opponents, Gabriel's encounters were much less cordial. He had seen Bishop Grandin of St. Albert (within whose diocese Batoche lay) in the autumn of 1887, and then the Bishop had tried to persuade him to "cross the line and return to Batoche." And in January, when Grandin came again, and Gabriel visited him in the company of Father Lacombe, the missionary to the Blackfoot, the Bishop told him that, despite the Amnesty Proclamation, there would be danger in his going to Quebec as he planned; doubtless Grandin feared that Dumont would be led in his speeches into some indiscretion that would involve him in trouble with the authorities. Father Lacombe also tried to persuade him to go back to the Saskatchewan, and Gabriel decided that both of the priests, and all the others who urged him to return to Batoche, were "interested in my not telling the truth in Canada," where he intended not only to lecture but also to enlist the support of MP's. "I should also tell you that Father Lacombe asked me my plans. I answered him that if it entirely depended on myself I would again take up arms, for today I have very much more power than in 1885, but in the interests of the Half-Breeds and the Indians we believe it would be better to try and employ pacific means."

Just what Dumont meant by having more power than in 1885 it is hard to say, but he was probably talking in political terms, since he was in correspondence not only with Honoré Mercier and R. Préfontaine, but also with such powerful Quebec nationalists as Laurent Olivier David, editor of *Le Bien Public,* member of the Québec Legislative Assembly, and president and real activator of the Riel Defence Committee, and these were the people who were urging him to visit eastern Canada and lecture there. Undoubtedly, whether he conceived the idea or was led into it by Riboulet and the nationalists, Dumont saw himself at this moment as a successor of Riel, abandoning the role of man of action for that of orator and propagandist. And though he yearned to see Batoche again and wrote with a touching warmth to his fellow Métis, disclaiming all enmity and begging their forgiveness for any offences he might have committed against them, he was convinced that he could be of most use in Canada, by which he meant Quebec with Ottawa as its appendage. "Riel is dead and I am anxious to speak for him in the name of those for whom he laid down his life," he wrote to David, "and no matter if I should have to die after delivering simply one lecture that would not debar me from going among you."

In his more ambitious moments in New York, Gabriel Dumont even thought of going to France, for in December 1887, he and Riboulet wrote a joint letter to George Demanche, editor of *La Revue Française et de l'Exploration* in Paris, in which they suggested organizing a Wild West Exhibition like Buffalo Bill's, but adapted to the French taste and manned by Canadian Métis and Indians. "Our Indians, principally our Chiefs, would be happy to visit France and know the French." Demanche, who had himself visited the Canadian Northwest and had written articles in *Le Figaro* sympathizing with the Métis and Indian rebels, replied in a friendly manner but offered no practical advice, and nothing came of the plan. This was partly because Buffalo Bill took his own show to Paris, with Ambroise Lépine, Riel's former Adjutant-General during the Red River Provisional Government, as one of his stars, and with Michel Dumas masquerading as the celebrated Gabriel Dumont until he was finally dismissed from the show for persistent drunkenness.*

Dumont claimed in later years that he himself went to France, but like much relating to his life after he left New York in the spring of 1888 the whole matter remains very obscure, and I have found only the scantiest evidence that corroborates his own assertions, which are uncharacteristically laconic and self-contradictory. However, since it is impossible that he could have made his visit between February 1888, when he was concocting letters with Riboulet on Staten Island, and April in the same year when he finally crossed the border back into Canada, I shall leave the question of the French trip for the point where, if it ever took place, it seems to fit best into the course of his life.

There is no doubt that when Gabriel Dumont returned to Canada from New York, going first to Montreal, he was not merely returning home, for the largest city of Canada was as alien to his accustomed way of life as New York had been. We should see him rather as a man with a mission of justice in his heart, traelling to the place from which his French grandfather Jean-Baptiste had set out for the far west. It was a city whose people, speaking one of the languages of the Métis, must surely support them. He had no regrets over his act of rebellion, except that it had achieved nothing, and it was this lack of achievement that he hoped to remedy. As the letters from Batoche told him, not only had many Métis not received the land grants which the government had promised, but after their defeat many of them were so poor that they had neither the means nor the heart to cultivate any land they might be graciously given. However he might boast, Gabriel knew that the days of armed rebellion were ended. The police were stronger and more watchful, and the Métis, like the Indians, were be-

* Dumas seems to have made something of a habit of this kind of impersonation, for in January 1886, the Scottish half-breed James McKay visited the Métis in the Turtle Mountains, and found that "Michel Dumah" — as he reported to Dewdney — had been there, boasting that "he had all the *Sioux* to join him", having given them to understand that he was "Gabriel Dummont."

coming a minority in the land that had once been their own. But from the new nationalist leaders of Quebec who had recently been wooing him, from Mercier and David with their lavish promises, he expected a great deal, particularly as he was invited to travel in Quebec under more or less political auspices, with a nationalist member of Parliament, M. A. J. Voyer, as his cicerone. Mercier was consolidating his forces in 1888, and the goodwill of French-speakers in the prairies was important to him; Dumont — he calculated — could be presented as an impressively defiant victim of English tyranny.

However, it quickly appeared that Gabriel was not the man for the hour — or at least for Mercier's hour. To the Montrealers — francophone to a man — who heard him in the strangely incongruous setting of the Académie de Musique, he looked rustic and ponderous, with the city clothes hanging uncomfortably on his great shoulders. He spoke slowly and simply and roughly. He had none of the charismatic exaltation that Riel occasionally projected, and the special quality that made him an inimitable leader in the extreme situations offered by buffalo hunts and guerilla warfare were not evident to these urban men who watched him with a curiosity that might have been more intense if the Riel drama had still been at its height (but this was 1888, not 1885), and a sympathy that did not always outlast his oration.

For Gabriel's tale of the causes and course of the rebellion was already familiar to his listeners, and his interpretation of the Métis defeat — which was his own — was unwelcome to many of them, since what he stressed most of all was the treason of the priests. "When we had taken up arms," he told an audience on 24 April, "the priests ranged themselves against us. They did not want to hear our confessions — neither those of men nor of women nor of children. That was hard for the poor Métis. It discouraged us. Before that time, we were unenlightened, and the word of the priests was the word of truth; but since then we have seen a little more clearly, and we understand that they may very well be telling us falsehoods."

Not only did Dumont thin out his audiences with such statements; he was subjected to attacks by clerically dominated newspapers, while Mercier, who was trying to reach an understanding with the church on the question of the Jesuit estates, was embarrassed by this Métis hunter with his frankness and his grievances about what had happened far away from the valley of the St. Lawrence. The nationalist politicians withdrew their patronage (as Quebec nationalists in recent years withdrew their support from beleaguered francophones outside their own province), and Dumont went back to Montana in the summer of 1888. There he found himself less acceptable than in 1885, for heroism soon loses its lustre and the local Métis had their own problems. He wandered into Dakota searching out the Canadian Métis who had not yet gone home under the amnesty, and up to St. Vital on the Red River to stay with Louis Riel's brother Joseph. By the end of the year he was in Quebec City again, where he was now taken up by the group of amateur journalists and their friends which gathered around Adolphe Ouimet and Benjamin de Montigny. These men were dominated less by hard political nationalism of Mercier's kind than by a rather sentimental cult of the primitive innocent — Québec habitant or Métis hunter — and it was in this manner that, in the volume they published in 1889, *La Vérité sur la Question Métisse,* they presented the rebellion and Dumont as its daemon; the volume included Dumont's earlier narrative of the rebellion, which he dictated to Montigny in December 1888, and which was approved by him in January 1889, when it was read back to him before witnesses.

It is not certain where Dumont went when he left Quebec City in the spring of 1889, but — on the basis of what evidence exists and a good measure of conjecture — I suggest that in this blank drawer of the card index we may with some plausibility insert his visit to France.

His own first statement about this visit appears in 1893, in an application he made in Winnipeg for land scrip to which he was entitled as a Métis who had not benefited under the Manitoba settlement of 1870. (I shall return to that application in another context.) Then, making no explicit reference to the rebellion, he said that he "left" Batoche in 1885 for "Montana, New York, France & Canada & Dakota", and in a covering recommendation — the only piece of external evidence — Roger Goulet of the Winnipeg Land Office states that after his flight to Montana, Dumont "went to many cities in the United States, to France & Lower Canada." In another document, also signed in 1893 and relating to the retention of his homestead, Dumont stated that since 1885 "I have been travelling in America & Europe," and elsewhere in the same statement he answered a question regarding his place of residence since 1885 with the words "in the United States and in France." To complicate the question, in 1903 Dumont told an acquaintance that he did not go to France until 1895, when he spent almost a year there, entirely in Paris. This, however, is impossible in view of his statements two years before, in 1893, and in any case we know that in 1895 Dumont was living in modest circumstances in Batoche. The order of countries given in 1893 by both Dumont and Goulet suggests that Gabriel went to France early in 1888 after leaving New York and before going to Quebec, but, as we have seen, there was just not enough time for any such trip.

In 1889, however, Dumont was well placed for a trip to France, and may also have been well disposed towards such a venture. He was in Quebec City, from which he could take a ship in the spring as soon as the St. Lawrence became free of ice. The men with whom he was associated had interests and links abroad; Montigny had been a papal zouave and held a title granted by the Vatican. These friends could have provided him with contacts in Paris, and they probably paid him generously for dictating his memoirs of the rebellion to them. All in all, this seems the only time when Dumont had — all at once — the time, the port of departure, the introductions, and the money that would have made a trip to France possible. He may also have been in the mood for such a change of setting, since neither Quebec nor New York nor Montana had provided a place where this restless man might feel at home. But one is still faced with the strange fact that, though he claimed on at least three occasions to have lived in France, there is no instance on record when Gabriel Dumont, a man not much given to reticence, explained what his mission in France had been or told a single anecdote of what happened to him there. We are left with two possibilities; either he never went there and was lying, or he was unhappy in the City of Light, which can be a place of remarkable darkness for those who are lonely and poor and unsophisticated.

It may indeed have been in a totally alien setting like the French metropolis that — perhaps in 1889 — Dumont realized how deeply his roots were set in the region where he had lived most of his life and to which his brothers and his friends were returning. In 1890 he finally went back to the Saskatchewan for the first time since the rebellion, but found it so greatly changed that he could not immediately settle down there. He wandered back to Dakota, living in Métis hunting camps, and it was there that, one night in 1891, he was attacked as he lay in his tent by a would-be assassin. Stabbed in the head and body, his hand cut to the bone through seizing his assailant's knife, Gabriel still managed to hold his attacker until people arrived from the other tents, and then, characteristically, he let him go, and the man fled into the night. No-one recognized this would-be assassin, and Gabriel always believed he was paid by the Canadian government, but it was probably no more than an attempt at murder and robbery or perhaps even the act of a madman.

In 1892 Dumont was again in Quebec, trying to raise money for Métis who were still impoverished as a result of the rebellion, and he returned to Batoche by way of Winnipeg, where once again he visited Joseph Riel, this time to find out what had happened to relief funds that appeared to have gone astray. It was only in 1893 that he finally decided to return permanently to the Saskatchewan, and then — none too soon — he set about mending the fences of his life that in the past eight years had notably decayed.

Most of the writers on Dumont have asserted that when he went back to Batoche he sold his land and became a landless hunter once again. The records show that this is not true, and that there was a confusion in the minds of such writers between the land Gabriel held under the homestead regulations, and the land scrip to which he was entitled as a Métis who had not received it under the Manitoba settlement. Both matters came up in 1893, and Gabriel spent several months in Winnipeg regularizing his position as a political exile who had decided, after all, to accept his status as a British subject, and this may have added to the confusion.

The land on which Gabriel had built the house and outbuildings that Middleton burnt in 1885 was, as we have seen, a quarter-section acquired by him under the homestead regu-

247

lations, and, as the official papers make clear, he never surrendered or sold this land at Gabriel's Crossing. In March 1893, he received a notice from the Ministry of the Interior, calling on him to show cause why his entry for the quarter-section should not be cancelled. It was then that he travelled to Winnipeg and, with the assistance of Roger Goulet, filled out the required forms, describing himself as "Voyageur now, Farmer before", and giving his address as Batoche. This was in July, and in August, now describing himself as "Farmer", he applied for a patent to the land. For some unknown reason — perhaps the fact that he had not lived on his holding for so long — the patent was not issued at that time, and in 1901 the file was resurrected, statements were obtained from Gabriel's neighbours, it was proved that Gabriel had not "assigned or transferred" the property, and on 31 January 1902, he finally received title to the land he had first occupied in 1872, a prime example of what the Métis had to suffer from the Canadian version of the "insolence of office". That he did not sell the land even then is shown by the fact that in April 1908, almost two years after his death, the Department of the Interior in Ottawa and the Dominion Lands Agent in Humboldt engaged in a correspondence in which it was established that Gabriel Dumont, even if he was no longer alive, held title not only to his original lot, but also to another lot for which he evidently entered some time in the early days of the present century, and which was not patented until February 1907, when he was beyond enjoying its possession.

Thus, Gabriel Dumont not only retained his homestead; he added to it, by pre-emption, presumably paying for the second lot. What he may have sold was his land scrip to the value of $160, for which he applied in August 1893 by a "Claim to participate in any grant to Half-Breeds living in the North-west Territories," and which was allocated to him in October 1893. A few years later he certainly sold for a fraction of its value some land scrip he inherited from a female relative; when reproached with his improvidence, he characteristically answered: "You are right, but I did not want to run from door to door. That would be making myself too small."

Yet, though Gabriel kept his land, for which after all he had risen in armed rebellion, he allowed his relatives to till and graze it, for he had no inclination to rebuild and live alone in the house he had once inhabited with Madeleine. Nor did he, like his father, ever think of marrying again, and as he grew older he became more isolated and self-contained. There was no longer a cause for him to lead, or even a community. Of the men who followed him in the rebellion, many had retreated northward, as the Métis have tended to do ever since, into the marginal lands that so-called civilization pushes before it, and there they sustained a pathetic semblance of the old free hunting life. The rest had remained on their land beside the South Branch of the Saskatchewan and by default rather than design had become unwilling farmers. After the débâcle, they had no more faith in rebellion or in political agitation, and distrust of the priests had sapped their religious faith. If it had been possible up to 1885 to think of the Métis as a new nation, this was so no longer; at most they showed an obstinate and unreasoning resistance to assimilation. But if they remained a separate people, their existence was unnoticed by others, for they did not even have the negative dignity of recognition as a separate people that the treaties had granted to the Indians. They had become a people without standing in the new world of the future, and without rights in the old world of the past, and the best they could hope to retain was the individual dignity that Gabriel Dumont never lost.

He retained it at the cost of becoming a solitary old widower. Some of his former comrades tried to draw him out of his loneness. Charles Nolin, with whom he had become reconciled, even asked him to share his house. But Gabriel preferred to build with his own hands a little log cabin on the land of young Alexis Dumont, who had now become a farmer at Bellevue, about ten miles from Batoche, and to occupy himself with fishing and hunting, which often took him for weeks at a time into the forest country north of Battleford or eastward into the Touchwood Hills. He remained remarkably vigorous, as good a marksman and rider as ever, and in his late sixties he could still outwalk most of the younger men in Batoche. Sometimes he would go to Duck Lake and St. Laurent to see his old comrades from the rebellion and the buffalo hunt, and often he would call at the rectory of St. Antoine de Padoue to talk over the past with Father Moulin, who was still curé of Batoche, for though Gabriel retained his antagonism towards the priests as a species, it was not in his nature to hold lasting resentments towards a man he had known as flesh-and-blood. At intervals that grew longer with the years, he would get on his horse and ride south of the border to visit the friends he had made in Montana and Dakota during his exile, and rather less often he would be seen in the streets of Winnipeg.

He liked to talk spiritedly and at length about the past, but it was not the intermediate past of his exile, for he had little to say of the perplexing world he had encountered in New York and Montreal and Paris and had never fully understood. It was of the old days of the unspoilt plains that he talked, of the free and abundant life, of the great buffalo hunts and the skirmishes that counted as battles in the Indian wars, and always of the rebellion itself and of that strange Riel, the only man Gabriel had — and even then against his better judgment — ever called his chief. "When he speaks with animation, when he talks of his feats of arms," said one nameless man who saw Gabriel not long before his death, "there emerges, out of his mouth which opens with a strange contraction of the lower jaw, a voice that echoes like a rolling barrel, a voice that would carry to thousands of men gathered on plains as vast as his courage. Everything in this man is large, the sentiments and the heart as much as the physical solidity and the alert intelligence."

Yet if Gabriel liked to declaim for visitors, it was with the children of his nephews and his cousins, and with their friends, that he was most at home, sitting at his cabin door and expounding like some patriarchal teacher the lore of the old West. One of these children, who had grown old in St. Laurent, told me how he remembered the very feel of the scar on Gabriel's head as the old hunter took his hand and put it there, saying, "You see, my skull was too thick for the English to kill me!"

The years passed, and now they were uneventful, for Gabriel was no longer a man to whom his fellows called for leadership, though sometimes they asked his advice, nor did he wish to lead them. He withdrew into the rhythms of the hunting years, doing a little trading, catching his own meat and fish, and always pleased when he had a few skins to sell at one of the stores in Batoche or Duck Lake. On feast days he would put on a suit, and wear, as insignia of a heroic past, the gold watch from Massachusetts and the silver medal from New York. He thought of that past without guilt and without rancour, glory-ing in his own deeds as Homer's heroes must have done, yet sad always for that vanished primitive world to which he had been so superbly adapted.

He never experienced sickness or felt the grip of decay. Just before his death, he went on a hunting trip to Basin Lake, in the hills a few miles east of Batoche. It was mid-May, the hunt was successful, and he enjoyed the bright spring weather, the opening flowers, the flights of migrant birds. When he came back, he complained to Alexis of pains in his chest and arms, but as he seemed otherwise in perfect health they decided he had merely strained his muscles. For the next few days he went about in his usual way, doing a little fishing and a little walk-ing, and talking to the friends he met by the roadside. On Satur-day, 19 May 1906, he went again for a walk. When he returned, he went into Alexis's house and asked for a bowl of soup. He sat down, ate a few mouthfuls, and then, without speaking, he walked across to a bed in the room and crumpled onto it. His death was like the flash of his gun, sudden, accurate and — since one must die — merciful.

When Gabriel Dumont died, the world did not think of him because the world did not know. He and the cause he fought for, and the way of life he personified, had so faded out of memory that only the little local newspapers in Battleford and Prince Albert noticed his death and his funeral. The papers of Toronto and Winnipeg and Montreal, that once had spoken of him with the kind of fearful admiration Milton reserved for Satan, did not even remark his passing. But when he was buried in the cemetery on the top of the hill at Batoche, where the dead men of the rebellion were already lying under the great stark cross, the Métis from all the settlements around came riding in, and the Cree tramped from Beardy's and One Arrow's reserves to crowd into the little wooden church, scarred with the bullet marks of Lieutenant Howard's Gatling, where Father Moulin, his white beard hanging almost to his waist, conducted the service; then the young men of the Dumont clan carried Gabriel to his grave, on the crest overlooking the point on the river where, twenty-one years ago to within a few days, the *Northcote* came whistling round the bend to open the battle of Batoche that marked the death of the Métis nation.

Bibliographical Notes
and Acknowledgements

Like most historians, I am indebted to the help and the work of many people, and I am conscious that in these acknowledgments I have not been able to include the name of every person to whom I owe gratitude. To those who helped me and are not named here, I collectively repeat the thanks I expressed orally at the time.

First among those who must be thanked publicly are the prime encouragers of the work that has gone into this book — Robert Fulford, editor of *Saturday Night*, who commissioned the article from which it originated, Robert Weaver of the CBC who encouraged me to write a radio documentary on Dumont and his times, and Mel Hurtig who suggested and commissioned the present book. Among other individuals I would specifically thank Mrs. M. A. Simpson and her staff at the Battleford Historic Park and the Batoche National Historic Site, Mr. D. F. Robertson and his staff at the Special Collections Library in the University of Saskatchewan, Mr. Allan R. Turner of the Saskatchewan Archives Board, Mr. John A. Bovey and M. Gilbert-Louis Comeault of the Manitoba Public Archives, Mr. Brian Cockhill of the Montana Historical Society, Ms. Ruby M. Shields of the Minnesota Historical Society, Ms. Sheilagh S. Jameson and Ms. Sally Herbison of the Glenbow-Alberta Institute, Ms. Mabel Ledgard of the Saskatchewan Photographic and Art Division, Ms. Eleanor M. Gehres of the Denver Public Library, and in a more general way the staffs of the Public Archives of Canada and of the University of British Columbia Library, all of whom helped me with information, with books, and in many cases, to be acknowledged separately, with valuable primary material. I must especially thank my wife, who drove me on a summer expedition to northern Saskatchewan to visit the sites of the events of 1885 and who assisted notably with the research there.

In the field of primary material, I am indebted to the Public

Archives of Canada for the account of the Laws of St. Laurent in 1873, for papers relating to Gabriel Dumont's application for scrip in 1893, and for information about land claims of the Dumont family; to the Saskatchewan Archives Board for papers relating to Dumont's ferry and homestead at Gabriel's Crossing; to the U.S. National Archives and Records Division for documents relating to Dumont's detention at Fort Assiniboine and to his petition to President Grover Cleveland; to the Public Archives of Manitoba for material from the Alexander Morris papers and the Louis Riel Collection, and especially for a copy of the manuscript notes taken down in 1903 from the dictation of Gabriel Dumont and other participants in the events of 1885, preserved in the archives of L'Union Nationale Métisse de Saint-Joseph and said to have been transcribed by A. H. de Trémaudan; to the Glenbow-Alberta Foundation for access to the Edward Dewdney papers and to copies of CPR telegrams relating to the 1885 rebellion; to the Special Collections Library of the University of Saskatchewan for access to the A. S. Morton papers and to W. B. Cameron's interviews with the survivors of the Duck Lake battle; to the library of the Battleford Historic Park for manuscript notes relating to the Dumont family, and for access to files of the *Saskatchewan Herald* and to the typescript of Frank W. Anderson's unpublished "Louis Riel — Patriot and Rebel"; to the Denver Public Library for references in the Salsbury Scrapbook to Gabriel Dumont's involvement in the Buffalo Bill Wild West show; to Mr. George Shepherd of the Western Development Museum and to the University of British Columbia Library for a variety of information.

With regard to published material, that relating specifically to Gabriel Dumont is slight. Frank W. Anderson contributed a somewhat imaginative serial biography to the *Western Producer Magazine*; entitled "Captain of the Plains", it ran from February to June 1958. He also contributed a brief article, "Gabriel Dumont", to the *Alberta Historical Review*, while his "Captain of the Plains" was condensed into a popular booklet, *Gabriel Dumont, Indian Fighter* (1973). John Andrew Kerr's "Gabriel Dumont: A Personal Memoir" appeared in the *Dalhousie Review* in 1935. The latter part of *La Vérité sur La Question Métisse au Nord-Ouest* (1889) contains the "Récit de Gabriel Dumont sur les Evénements de 1885," which was transcribed by B. A. T. de Montigny, and later translated by G. F. G. Stanley and published with an introduction under the title of "Gabriel Dumont's Account of the North-west Rebellion 1885" (*Canadian Historical Review,* 1949). Stanley also wrote an article on Dumont's participation in the St. Laurent commune of 1873, entitled "The Half-Breed Rising of 1873" (*Canadian Historical Review,* 1936).

Moving out from Dumont into the wider description of the events in which he was involved, undoubtedly the most relevant general books are George F. G. Stanley's *The Birth of Western Canada* (1936) and Joseph Howard's *Strange Empire: Louis Riel and the Métis People* (1952). Dumont of course plays his part in all the books on

254

Louis Riel, of which I have found the following most relevant: *Louis Riel* by G. F. G. Stanley (1963), *The Man Who Had to Hang: Louis Riel* by E. B. Osler (1961) and Hartwell Bowsfield's two books, *Louis Riel: The Rebel and the Hero* (1971) and *Louis Riel: Rebel of the Western Frontier or Victim of Politics?* (1969).

Of the Métis culture which Dumont so strikingly represented, the definitive work is undoubtedly Marcel Giraud's *Le Métis Canadian* (1945); less reliable is A-H. de Trémaudan's *Histoire de la Nation Métisse dans l'Ouest Canadian.* (1935). Mason Wade's *The French Canadians 1760-1967* discusses the Métis in the general context of "the French fact" in Canada, and *Cuthbert Grant of Grantown*, by Margaret MacLeod and W. L. Morton (1963) gives a useful insight into the early days of the Métis "nation". Useful also is Father A-G. Morice's *Dictionnaire historique des Canadiens et des Métis français de l'ouest* (1912).

Accounts of the rebellion of 1885 include a number of official reports, of which the most important are the Department of Militia's *Report Upon the Suppression of the Rebellion in the Northwest Territories* (1886), *North West Rebellion 1885* (published by the Department of Justice in 1886), and the report of Riel's trial, *The Queen vs. Louis Riel,* first published in 1896 and recently re-issued (1974) with an excellent introduction by Desmond Morton.

Desmond Morton is also the author of a good military history of the 1885 rebellion, *The Last War Drum* (1972), and with Reginald H. Roy he edited and admirably introduced the invaluable Champlain Society edition of *Telegrams of the North-West Campaign, 1885* (1972). Contemporary accounts of the campaign, mainly by participants, include Major C. A. Boulton's *Reminiscences of the North-West Rebellions* (1885), General F. D. Middleton's *Suppression of the Rebellion in the North-West Territories of Canada, 1885* (edited and with an Introduction by G. H. Needler, 1948), *Trooper and Redskin in the North* by John G. Donkin (1889) and Charles Pelham Mulvaney's *The History of the North-West Rebellion* (1885). Most of the English accounts are those of conscious victors and I have left out as virtually useless many works on the rebellion which contribute no useful facts and are mainly polemical or sensational. The same, on the opposite side, applies to many of the French accounts, but there is a great deal of valuable information in Jules Le Chevallier's *Batoche: Les Missionaries du Nord-Ouest pendant les troubles de 1885* (1941) and Donatien Frémont's *Les Secrétaires de Riel* (1953). The *Mémoires* which Louis Riel's friend, Louis Schmidt, published in 1912 are also interesting. R. E. Lamb's *Thunder in the North* (1957) is a sound study of the repercussions in eastern Canada of the two Métis rebellions.

Among works that have helped to give a feel of the historical setting, it is pointless to mention the numerous general histories of Canada in the nineteenth century that have given useful facts and helpful insights, but moving closer into the time and place, I found the Official Reports of the Commissioners of the North West Mounted Police from 1874 to 1885 valuable if sometimes surprisingly scanty. My feel for the setting was largely kept awake during writing by two books of combined geography and history, Edward McCourt's *Saskatchewan* (1968) and Majorie Wilkins Campbell's *The Saskatchewan* (1950) and among prairie histories I found R. G. MacBeth's *The Making of the Canadian West* (1898) and Norman Fergus Black's *Saskatchewan and the Old North-West* (1913) especially useful in their evocation of a period to which they were relatively close. Among later works, Arthur S. Morton's *A History of the Canadian West to 1870-71* (1939) was invaluable and Douglas Hill's *The Opening of the Canadian West* helpful for its focussing of issues. Three more local histories contributed interesting facts: *The Battlefords: A History* by Alean McPherson (1967), *Prince Albert: The First Century* by Gary Adams (1966), and that very pleasant little book, *The Carlton Trail* by Ralph C. Russell (1971).

The contributions of the Indians to the 1885 rebellion is well-told in Norma Sluman's *Poundmaker* (1967), but this is limited to a single chief and his part, and the general situation among the Indians at the time (which appears in Ms. Sluman's book in the shady background) still awaits a definitive work.

Finally, among the books that in their own ways contributed to this book, I cannot neglect the various accounts of the prairies by nineteenth century travellers, traders, and even policemen which have helped to fill out the background to Dumont's youth. These include Paul Kane's *The Wanderings of an Artist*, Alexander Ross's *The Red River Settlement* with its splendid accounts of the great buffalo hunts, William Francis Butler's two flamboyant travel tales, *The Wild North Land* and *The Great Lone Land*, George M. Grant's narrative of his journey with Sandford Fleming, *Ocean to Ocean*, the aristocratic adventures of the Earl of Southesk (*Saskatchewan and the Rocky Mountains*) and Milton and Cheadle (*The North-West Passage by Land*), Isaac Cowie's fur trader's memoirs (*The Company of Adventurers*), Sam Steele's *Forty Years in Canada*, and Henry Youle Hind's accounts of his explorations in the 1850s (*Narrative of the Canadian Red River Exploring Expedition*, etc.), to which I would add two invaluable recent background books, Irene M. Spry's *The Palliser Expedition* (1963) and Arthur J. Roy's *The Indians in the Fur Trade* (1974).

Last of all, I found much useful information in the files of the *Saskatchewan Herald*, published in Battleford, and of the *Prince Albert Times*, whose writers saw the events from a short distance and were by no means always unsympathetic to the Métis cause. A useful compilation of facsimile newspaper reports and editorial comments on the uprising, gathered mainly from the Ontario and Winnipeg press, is N. and H. Mika's *The Riel Rebellion, 1885* (1972).